P9-CAL-013

WITHDRAWN

918.1   Ridgway, John
R544a   Amazon journey
cop.1

PUBLIC LIBRARY
DANVILLE, ILLINOIS

AMAZON JOURNEY

John Ridgway

AMAZON
JOURNEY

DOUBLEDAY & COMPANY, INC.
GARDEN CITY, NEW YORK
1979

ISBN: 0-385-07152-3
Library of Congress Catalog Card Number 72-84939

Copyright © 1972 by John Ridgway
ALL RIGHTS RESERVED
PRINTED IN THE UNITED STATES OF AMERICA
FIRST EDITION IN THE UNITED STATES OF AMERICA

Contents

918.1
R544a
cap.1

Saukleday 9/19/79 8.95 (5.37)

PUBLIC LIBRARY
DANVILLE, ILLINOIS

1

The Idea

The first time I ever discussed the idea of canoeing down the Amazon was in 1966, with Chay Blyth. We were several hundred miles off the Eastern seaboard of North America, rowing a twenty-foot dory to Ireland. The sun shone warm on our backs, and we were glad to be free of the cold, foggy waters of the Labrador Current, for at last we were riding the warm, indigo tide of the Gulf Stream, which moves slowly across the North Atlantic towards Europe. The unaccustomed warmth encouraged conversation about the future.

"We could pack a folding canoe and all our food and equipment on a couple of mules in Lima," I suggested. "That's on the Pacific coast in Peru; then we'd make our way up over the Andes and so down the river."

"Better make it two canoes; then we can take Marie Christine and Maureen." Chay didn't think our wives would put up with any further separation—after our three-month rowing trip in the dory.

We talked of the idea for several hours. After all, when you are alone with someone for ninety-two days in a small, open boat, there is plenty of time to discuss things at length. In the short term, however, the immense task of rowing across the Atlantic pushed all other plans aside.

Two years later, I was fifty days alone in a thirty-foot yacht, the first of nine men to set out in a race to be the first person to sail around the world single-handed and nonstop. Although my attempt failed at the outset—as the result of a collision with a trawler carrying a television crew—I managed to think out a working plan for my future life, well before the voyage ended at Recife on the eastern coast of Brazil. At thirty years of age, I felt I should spend six months of the year working at our remote croft (farm) on the northwest coast of Scotland, where the mountains sweep down to meet the empty Atlantic. We would build a School of Adventure in which people could experience—genuinely, but within the limits imposed by their physical condition and working circumstances—the same direct confrontation with the "real" world that I find so stimulating and satisfying. During the six months of winter each year, I planned to make a "journey"—either mentally or physically. I hoped this would broaden my experience of life and help me to enjoy myself at the same time. I hoped that if I followed the plan, I would be able to make a contribution to society and yet avoid becoming stale and set in any particular way of life.

Needless to say, the building and establishment of the School of Adventure took longer than seemed likely at first; however, with the invaluable help of Rod Liddon, things were running well by the end of 1969. And so, during the early months of 1970, while running cross-country to keep fit (in the wild hills around the croft) I started to work on plans for the winter of 1970–71. I've always found that cross-country running stimulates mental activity. Perhaps it's simply a matter of getting my mind off the painful boredom of the running itself. Surely the journey would be warmer in the Southern Hemisphere, for at least it would be summer there during the Scottish winter; also it would be interesting if I could make the journey with someone unknown to me—someone with completely divergent interests—from whom I could learn something of another kind of life.

South America had intrigued me during my brief visit at the end of my lone sailing voyage to Brazil, but then perhaps any place containing people would have seemed interesting after fifty days alone. Somehow, however, South America appeared full of potential, in much the same way North America must have appeared to European immigrants in the early years of this century. Weeks of running and writing, and a few visits to London during the early months of 1970, produced three names as potential fellow "journeymen": Paul McCartney, Herman Kahn, and Eduardo Paulozzi.

Paul McCartney was my idea. He had taken to living at a remote place in the west Highlands, as I had, and we would have that in common. More or less my own age, he had, however, lived his life in a musical world unknown to me, though now he seemed to be tiring of the Beatles. Maybe the dramatic change I had in mind would be just what he needed, and maybe he would find the journey stimulating for his musical talent. (I can't read a note of music; it is a pity to be missing something in which others find so much wonder.)

A prominent American advertising executive in London was completely against the McCartney idea, but it was he who suggested the noted Herman Kahn of "Think Tank" fame, the theorist of nuclear warfare.

John McConnell, a brilliant young designer of my own age, came up to Ardmore from London. He wanted to look at the place before designing a new brochure for the School of Adventure. Although he stayed only a few days, and much of his time was spent heaving concrete blocks for the foundations of Rod Liddon's new house, John did come up with plenty of ideas. "Eduardo Paulozzi—now there's a man with an entirely different way of life from yours. I'll see if I can arrange a meeting so you can discuss the idea." Dressed in his ragged, rabbit coat, ready to start the long journey back to London, John's eyes glinted with amusement at the idea of the eccentric sculptor arguing with the philistine.

My contact with Paul McCartney was through an ex-journalist who had a friend in another well-known pop group; this friend was in turn a friend of McCartney. Sad to say, that line of communication failed when the police arrested the journalist's friend at a Brixton party. It seems he had threatened the law with a carving knife and was subsequently "otherwise engaged" for a while. If Paul McCartney ever did get to hear of the idea, he can't have liked it, because he never got in touch with me. . . . It seems a pity really.

It was altogether too overwhelming an idea even to try to contact Herman Kahn in America; physically he looked rather unfit, and I felt sure the proposal wouldn't interest him.

On 20 April, I was in London, and John McConnell took me out to dinner in Chelsea, with Tony Evans, the photographer, and his wife Caroline. Since they all knew Paulozzi, after the meal we called at the sculptor's studio, which was just off King's Road. It was nearly midnight, but John assured me that this presented no difficulty, as the great man always worked late. I felt ill at ease in the car as John went off to seek an audience. "It's O.K. He's still working; let's go on in," John reported, bending through the open car door. Inwardly quaking, I dragged myself after his retreating figure.

The studio, a long high-ceilinged room, only sparsely furnished, seemed to me as if it might once have been a small gymnasium—but then, of course, I knew nothing about art studios. Eduardo Paulozzi is an impressive-looking man, rather like a "Goldfinger" figure from a James Bond movie. Powerfully built, even squat, he has an air of a judo black belt about him. A great deal of black hair and large, expressive, square hands with blunt fingers lend weight to an atmosphere of eccentric ego. I felt as if I were looking at the extreme limit of the human mental and physical form. For a few minutes, John, Tony, and Eduardo discussed the latest manoeuvres in the art world; then Eduardo outlined a new project he had been planning with his friend Arturo before we had come in. I stood quietly on the outside of the group understanding nothing and trying to imagine some way in which Paulozzi and I could get along together in the jungle—or anywhere. "Well, what is this idea you have come to see me about?" he turned sharply and asked me. "Let's all sit down." He dropped into a big armchair and waited for me to start. The others seemed to be sitting on the floor at his feet.

I stood with my feet apart, hands behind my back, looking at a big clock high up on the wall at the far end of the room, and feeling acutely embarrassed. "This is one of those moments in a lifetime when one feels in a totally wrong situation; I shall not forget this," I said. Then I gave an awkward outline of the idea, knowing all the while that Paulozzi was preparing to make a mockery of everything I was saying.

There was a brief pause when I finished. Then he started. "I can't think of anything more ridiculous, or of anything I am less likely to do," he said. Then, for some ten minutes, he held court at my expense, before concluding: "I'm going to bed now. Arturo, see you lock up when these people have gone."

We all trooped out saying nothing until, within the safety of the car, John turned and said, "Perhaps he's not feeling too well." Next day I felt that Paulozzi and I were so different that we really should go together. I almost wrote and suggested that he rethink his refusal—almost.

By this time, the end of April, we had already held our first course of the new season for forty preparatory school boys, and early in May, we began six one-week courses for twenty men of thirty to sixty years of age. I was preoccupied with the School of Adventure, and Paulozzi had more or less persuaded me to give up the whole idea. Even Michael Sissons, my literary agent, who had given up football and thirsted for an adventurous substitute, could find no real enthusiasm for the idea. My five daily three-minute rounds on the punch ball failed to give me any inspiration: it seemed that the winter of 1970-71 would be wasted. But, as often happens, something came up—out of the blue.

On 17 June, I got a letter from John Cowrie. Although I had not really got to know John, he had served with me in the 3rd Battalion, Parachute Regiment, in 1964. Now married, with a family, he had been farming for three years in Dorset since leaving the Regiment. An enthusiastic amateur photographer, John was keen to become a professional photo-journalist and he was looking to the Amazon and the winter of 1970-71 to make himself a reputation.

John's letter said: "[The Amazon] has been described as probably the last of the world's great river navigations. No one has ever succeeded in following its entire length of over 4,000 miles from its source high up in the Andes to the mouth at Pará Belem. A lot of people have been killed trying to navigate parts of the rapids and whirlpool-infested stretch, where it is known as the Apurímac and plunges through 5,000 foot gorges between densely forested mountains. Outline note: Fly to Lima. Native bus and on foot to the source 60 miles west of Lake Titicaca. Follow River several hundred miles on foot until navigable. Balsa logs can be obtained en route to make rafts to short

rapids. Canoes can be obtained en route from Indians. . . ." I
was interested.

Early in July, I had to be in London to discuss the syllabus
for a two-week course we were going to run at Ardmore in September for junior management executives from Shell-Mex,
IBM, and other firms. This meeting provided an opportunity to
call on John Cowrie; he was staying with Alistair, an architect
friend, in a typical Edwardian terraced street in Kennington,
near the Oval Cricket Ground. London was in the middle of a
heat wave, and I flew down from Inverness during the afternoon. In the early evening, I found John and Alistair stripped
to the waist, working on extensive improvements to the house;
in fact, the place was practically gutted.

As we sat in the bedroom, which was the only room relatively untouched by the turmoil, John outlined the idea. Three
years working with livestock on the Dorset farm had left him
lean and hard. His hair was much longer—almost to his
shoulders—but his hooded eyes, so reminiscent of Prime Minister Macmillan's, still gleamed with the cool determination I
had come to expect from all Parachute Regiment officers. "You
shall lead the expedition, John, because I will need twenty-four
hours a day if I am to do my job as photographer properly,"
said Cowrie.

"O.K.," I replied. "But I feel it should be a two-man expedition; we don't really know what the country will be like, so there
will have to be a great deal of flexibility."

"Right. I'll find out all I can from Sebastian Snow; he knows
that part of the world and went down the Marañón a few years
back on a raft in pretty hair-raising fashion." Cowrie was
clearly determined to go ahead.

Late into the night we talked out the various immediate
problems. The aim was to follow the whole course of the Amazon River from its furthest source high in the Andes near Lake
Titicaca, down the Apurímac, Ene, Tambo, and Ucayali tributaries, and down the Amazon itself, over four thousand miles to
its mouth in the Atlantic Ocean in eastern Brazil. We would
leave for Lima, capital of Peru, by air, in just under three
months, in the early days of October. I would have to be back
in Scotland at the latest during February 1971 to prepare for

the new season at the School of Adventure. Financially, we hoped the expedition would at least pay for itself; it would be my job to attract sponsorship. John Cowrie would determine, by research, whether or not the journey was climatically feasible during October–February. This is what we *intended* to do.

As I sat in the back of the taxi on the way back to my mother-in-law's mews house just off Gloucester Road, I had a pretty good idea the expedition would be on. There was the familiar feeling of elation connected with any act of positive living, and the usual sinking feeling in the pit of my stomach: once again I would know fear in anticipation and experience that calm one feels out on the edge of life, where a single mistake means death. The frustrations of preparation and travel would all be worthwhile for just one brush with the reality of life and death.

I now knew more about John Cowrie and I felt confident that he had the drive to get things moving while I was completely involved in Scotland. Born in 1938 in Aldershot (his father was an officer in the Dorset Regiment), John took up farming in Dorset, as I have said, and had several children. He was educated at All Hallows School in Devon and had four years farming experience in Kenya—much of it as the sole white manager of a remote farm in the White Highlands. At that time, white families were being butchered by treacherous Kikuyu farm workers during the Mau Mau troubles, and John's only contact with the outside world was by daily radio transmission to the handful of other white managers in the surrounding area. In answer to one of these calls, he learnt that his nearest neighbour had been bound in a chair and forced to watch his wife and child being chopped to death with razor edged pongas. The poor man was then left for dead, after suffering similar treatment, but he managed to crawl to the radio-telephone and summon help.

The years alone on the farm had started John in his interest in photography, for he found that the farm owner had left a small library of technical books on the subject. John read every word of these books in the long, lonely evenings—with a loaded pistol always by his side.

In 1964, at the end of his contract in Kenya, John decided

to return to London from Dar es Salaam, travelling overland
alone and third-class on the railway that follows a large part of
the course of the Nile. During this journey, he caught malaria
and smallpox, thus becoming dangerously ill, alone in a foreign
land with little money. Luckily, he was found just in time by
some nuns who nursed him back to health. This kind of experience strengthens a man to be alone, and I realised that I would
have to appreciate John's individual view of life while on the
expedition.

When he got home to England, he enlisted in the Parachute
Regiment, and after nine months in the ranks, he was awarded
a three-year Short Service Commission. While with the 3rd Battalion of the Regiment, he served in the United Kingdom, the
Middle East, and British Guiana; during his time in the Persian Gulf, he was seconded to the Sultan of Muscat's Armed
Forces in the Oman for four months. At the end of his Army
service, John met and married Louise, an attractive, dark-haired
girl. They moved to the backwoods of Dorset to farm and live
happily ever after, adding to their family along the way. The
drama and excitement of his early days in Africa, combined
with an increasing interest in photography, urged him out of
the comfortable, hard, farming life in search of a living in the
tough world of the photo-journalist. On the Amazon expedition, I was to lead and do the writing, while he devoted his
time to assembling a set of first-class photographs that would
help him to secure future assignments.

By the time the taxi arrived at Gloucester Road, I had convinced myself that the idea was a good one. A two-man expedition travelling light and living off the country would not be
hard to organise: the clothing and equipment could, in the
main, be provided by the School of Adventure. Only two
points had to be settled. First, John Cowrie would have to be
sure the weather in Peru and Brazil would not make the river
impassable from October to February. Second, and only when
the first was assured, I would have to raise enough sponsorship
to cover at least the cost of the expedition, which we would
have worked out well in advance.

On my return to Scotland, I spent what little spare time I
had in preparing detailed kit lists to cover the full range of

climatic conditions from subarctic, at the source of the river around fifteen thousand feet up in the Andes, to tropical, in the Amazon basin itself. Care and thought at this stage would eliminate frustration and danger later on. In the past, on both the rowing and sailing projects, I had found that it is better to buy equipment, rather than try to get it free, for even relatively small items seem to require a board meeting before they can be given away for expedition purposes. It is always best to buy at the earliest possible date, better in fact to purchase unnecessarily, rather than be hamstrung at the last minute by the late delivery of one vital item.

Lists of clothing, equipment, emergency rations, and medical necessities are all tabulated in the Appendix to this book. It is upon these fundamentals that the success of an expedition is based. Hours spent in checking and rechecking are not wasted.

By the second half of July, John Cowrie had finished his research and reported that it was virtually certain that the mountains and the river would be passable in October. By the time Christmas came, we assumed we should be past the most dangerous part of the journey, as far as mule treks and raft work were concerned, but the dangers of ill health would be present throughout the journey. This report was based on the helpful information John received from the explorer Sebastian Snow and the Peruvian Embassy in London. From Father Ambrose Lambert of Worth Abbey in Sussex, John managed to get first-hand information resulting from Father Lambert's eighteen months work at the Benedictine mission on the upper reaches of the Apurímac River, at Sivia (near San Francisco) where the river passes through the foothills of the Andes, in what is called "The Eyebrow of the Jungle."

Once we had John's assurance about the weather, Michael Sissons of A. D. Peters & Co., the literary agents, set about establishing a financial foundation to cover the heavy cost of return air fares to South America, cameras and film, clothing and equipment, and the rather easier cost of food and travel within South America itself, to sustain two people for up to five months. On Thursday, 30 July, with two months remaining before we were due to fly to Peru, John Cowrie, Michael Sissons, his assistant Pat Kavanagh, and I had lunch with Bob Edwards,

editor of the *People* (a newspaper) to discuss *Amazon Journey:*
and for the third time, the *People* agreed to run a series on one
of my adventures. Without this kind of support from newspapers, practically every one of the big adventures on land and
sea within recent years would never have got off the ground.

With this foundation, we approached the other media.
Hodder and Stoughton responded immediately with a generous
advance. An afternoon with Brian Branston of BBC TV persuaded us that the time remaining was too short to mount an
expensive documentary film exercise; in the end, ITN supplied
us with a Bell and Howell 16 mm movie camera, film stock,
and a portable tape recorder for news coverage. The uncer-
tainty of the terrain on the upper reaches of the river made
filming rather uncertain—and on a raft, cameras would not
come before lives.

John Newton, a friend of Michael Sissons, agreed to take on
the difficult task of drumming up support from industry. The
weakness here was largely one of too-short notice: several companies showed interest, but little could be done in the time
available, since advertising budgets are usually mapped out far
in advance. We were content with four Smith's watches of the
same kind I had used without difficulty on both the rowing and
sailing projects. We were also grateful for the detailed assistance and facilities provided by the banks of London and South
America and for the donations they made towards the cost of
the expedition. Mr. Faulkner was always ready to spare some of
his valuable time; he made the complicated problem of arranging credit facilities right across the South American continent
seem the mere work of a moment.

The *Daily Telegraph Colour Magazine* showed interest but
felt they could not commit themselves until they had the actual photographs before them—and this meant no payment
until after the expedition. Although an American publisher also
seemed interested, it would be some time before anything was
finalised.

Having the contracts with the *People* and Hodder and
Stoughton, John Cowrie and I were able to proceed with our
preparations in Britain.

2

Preparations in the U.K.

With two months, August and September, available for our preparations before flying to Peru, John Cowrie and I set to work to cover a lot of ground in a short time. John enrolled at the Berlitz Language School in London for a crash course in Spanish, and this took up all of each morning. In the afternoons, he raced around visiting embassies, museums, libraries, hospitals, photographic shops, newspaper offices, airline offices, sports shops, explorers, and all manner of other people and places connected with minimising the risk and the cost of expedition. On top of all this, he took an evening job at a theatre as an assistant for stage lighting—"something entirely unconnected with the Amazon, to help me relax," as he put it.

I flew back to Scotland after the lunch with Bob Edwards, carrying an armful of books on the Amazon that I had bought in great haste at Hatchards in Piccadilly, on my way to the West London Air Terminal. There was much to learn, and my responsibilities were twofold: first, to ensure the safety of the expedition under my leadership; second, to maintain communications with the newspaper, whilst taking the expedition right across the South American continent through the most appalling country, from around 17,000 feet up in the Andes, down over two miles in altitude, into and across the steaming equatorial jungles that form 2.3 million square miles of the Amazon basin.

Books on the Amazon must surely provide the most hair-raising tales of horror of all adventure stories. Here are some of the

facts I read in preparation for the expedition: The Amazon is
the world's largest and longest river, if the mouth is taken to be
at Pará Belem—a total distance of well over 4,000 miles. If the
north bank of the river were in London, then the south bank
would be in Paris. The waters flow out of the mouth at the rate
of 7½ million cubic feet per second. This discharge is more
than 25 times as great as that from the mouth of the Nile, the
Amazon's nearest rival in length. Of the 1,100 major tributaries, ten are longer than the Rhine, which is the longest
river in Europe. If all the rivers of the world were one vast
stream, then the Amazon would provide one fifth of the water.
In the first 600 tumbling miles, the river drops 16,000 feet; yet
in the remaining distance of over 3,500 miles to the mouth, it
drops only 700 feet. The waters for the Amazon are drawn from
every stream within an area only slightly smaller than the continental United States. This area comprises six countries: Vene-
zuela, Colombia, Ecuador, Peru, Bolivia, and Brazil. With
50,000 miles of navigable waterways, ships from Liverpool and
New York travel to Iquitos, 2,500 miles up the Amazon.

In the high Andes, there is desperate cold and the deadly
soroche, the altitude sickness. The mountains are the lonely
haunt of the mountain lion, the llama, and the mighty condor,
with its ten-foot wingspread. Electrical storms are so appalling
and the rainfall so severe that the name Apurímac, which is the
furthest source river, means in English translation "Great
Speaker," because of the roar of its rapids. In 1953, the French
explorer Michel Perrin pointed out that the Apurímac is the
longest tributary of the Amazon. He also believed the Amazon
to be considerably longer than had been credited and attempted to prove this by travelling from the source region of
the Apurímac to the mouth. His expedition ended with the
tragic death of his companion, when their canoe overturned in
the rapids of the "Great Speaker."

Further down the river, where the green tentacles of the jungle grope high into the foothills, known as the Eyebrow of the
Jungle, it seemed we would have to shoot the rapids on a
homemade raft made of balsa logs lashed together with bark or
vines. The waters teem with electric eels, and sting rays litter
shallow sandbars in wait for the unwary traveller trying to push

out his raft. On the banks at night, the awesome jaguar prowls, and Campa Indians, with poison arrows from their bows, or deadly darts from silent blowpipes, shoot in the back those who trespass on their sacred paths. In the air, the black vampire bats circle and swoop on the exposed head or foot of the sleeping explorer, sucking blood and leaving behind the fatal rabies, from which no human being has ever recovered.

In the jungle, the abundance of flora and fauna swamp the imagination. There are 2,000 species of fish, compared with only 250 in the Mississippi; porpoises, 3,000 miles inland, and sharks, also thousands of miles from the sea; the crazed, little man-eating piranhas make stagnant backwaters boil in their frenzy. There are turtles, tortoises, and alligators. It is the home of the world's largest snake, the giant anaconda, which stretches as much as 38 feet, and is associated with legends of hypnotism, luminous eyes, and fetid breath. There is the deadly, poisonous, 12-foot bushmasters with fangs an inch long, and there are countless other species of serpent. The Amazon also features the world's largest beetle (more than six inches) and the world's largest rodent, the Copylara (four feet); butterflies of incredible variety, colour, and size; sprays of vivid parakeets exploding from foliage that itself reaches far over a hundred feet above the jungle floor in its ceaseless search for sunlight; Indian cannibals, human heads shrunk to the size of an orange, white Indians, tales of Amazon women-warriors, and of El Dorado—legend and fact mixed inextricably. And the stories of man's inhumanity to man are nowhere as varied as in the Amazon.

There are, in addition, millions of square miles of palm trees, laurels, rubber trees, rosewoods, mahoganies, 120 species of cedar, chocolate trees, cashews, and balsa trees—to name just a few of the different kinds of trees to be found. Creepers and vines abound; the dead trees are thus unable to fall and so lean against the living. Six-foot sprays of orchids are born, live, and die tens of feet above the ground. The undergrowth is so thick that any movement without a machete is almost impossible. So dense is the growth that little animal or bird life can be seen, but the vibrant noise of insect life dominates everything. Above all, the Amazon basin is the land of the ant, which comes in all sizes, shapes, and colours up to 1.4 inches. No matter where one is in the jungle, ants are moving silently within just a few feet. At night there is the constant drone of malarial mosquitoes, which at dawn are found blackening the mosquito nets in their effort to get in and devour the sleeping traveller.

From this background reading, I worked out a plan of action, methods of transport, scales of equipment, and rations. John Cowrie kept in touch by telephone and two or three times each week added new facts and rumours to those I gleaned from the books. If we did what we set out to do, quite clearly, there were people all along the Amazon, some of whom might be hostile. Since we should be able to get food as we went along, we would carry only an emergency ration. We had the advantage that other people had been to the various places to describe conditions; thus, it should not be impossible to link the whole series of different regions in one journey, with a lightly equipped and highly flexible expedition.

While I believed that common sense and patience would see us over the natural obstacles of terrain, I did not feel nearly so confident about the medical aspect of the journey. Then, in the middle of one rainy morning in late August, the phone rang in the croft. It was John Cowrie. "I'm speaking from the Royal Army Medical College. Came here to see if they want any kit tested. Looks as if they may send a Medical Corps sergeant with us on full pay. What do you think?" John sounded excited, I felt the same, it seemed a heaven-sent chance to deal with my greatest fear—disease.

"What's he like?" I asked cautiously.

"Name's Macdermott, thirty-three, says he was in the Paras —with you—3rd Para, I think."

"There was a Macdermott in the swimming team," I murmured slowly.

"That's him, swam for the Army," interrupted John.

"Is he fit enough?" I asked, knowing the answer would be yes.

"Well, he looks pretty seedy right now; he smokes about forty a day, I'd say, but he's pretty wiry, and if he was in the Paras . . ."

"What do you think?" I asked.

"Well, I reckon it's a good idea, even if we have to pay his air fares. It's an investment, really, and at least he will have all the right kit with him."

"O.K., that's great; see what you can do," I answered.

With the medical problem well on the way to being solved, I felt much easier in my mind. When we woke up in our little croft on Sunday mornings, Marie Christine would snuggle up to me and say, "Only a few Sundays left and then you will be gone." It felt a little better, somehow, to know that as far as sickness and injury were concerned, we stood a good chance of expert attention.

While the wheels of the Ministry of Defence slowly ground away, deciding Sergeant Macdermott's fate with the expedition, John made another important discovery at the Berlitz Language School. The staff knew he was going out to Peru, and one of the instructors mentioned this during the course of conversation with one of the advanced pupils at the school, who in return immediately showed interest in the expedition and asked to be introduced to John. Certainly John was pleasantly surprised to find this person, who was fluent in Spanish, to be an attractive, slim, long-limbed, and fair-haired girl of twenty-nine. The quiet determination in her grey eyes was certainly borne out when John learnt she was the third-fastest downhill skier of all time.

Anna Ashenhov wanted to join the expedition. What's more, she had some convincing reasons that made her inclusion seem distinctly worthwhile, although on the phone to me in Scotland once again, John found me none too keen—with Marie Christine fuming at the open door of the kitchen. "She speaks Spanish much better than I will ever be able to in this short time," said John.

"Oh, blimey, John! I've got a mutiny here. Marie Christine is going to throw something at me," I answered nervously.

"The *People* will think it's a great idea," murmured John.

"Oh yeah! Of course they will," I shouted sarcastically. "They won't have just a simple triangle; it'll be a trapezium!"

"There is one other thing on her side," said John. "Her brother is editor of the *Peruvian Times* in Lima; he has done an expedition for the *National Geographic* himself, and Anna says he would be most helpful in getting our copy and film back to London."

"Oh! John—look, let me think about it for a couple of days," I asked Cowrie.

Suddenly, the whole idea seemed worth the hours of patient talk that would be needed to calm my raging wife and respond to her main line of attack: "What do you think people are going to say?" If I could not make the journey with McCartney, Kahn, or Paulozzi, I now had a most interesting problem to deal with. I had reached the conclusion that I could hope to lead a small expedition of three men in normal health, backed with expert medical assistance. This physical challenge had seemed interesting enough in itself. Now there was the opportunity to live out the plot of a novel: Three married men and an unmarried girl find themselves together in the high Andes and the steaming jungles of the Amazon—all four complete strangers to each other. . . . Follow next week's gripping episode! How would those four people, who didn't know each other, get on? I was suddenly interested to watch and learn.

Early in September, it was agreed that Anna should come with us, although I still had some misgivings about it. Armed with the kit list, Anna made for Pindisports in Holborn, which supplies the School of Adventure with kit and equipment. She was on home ground there because Pindisports also supplies the British Olympic Ski Team; so Anna knew the manager well. If the weight of the kit worried her, she certainly never said anything to John or Mac. Later we were to find this typical —no matter what the conditions, Anna never complained. But then, perhaps, that was because she couldn't get a word in edgewise, for all the complaints I would be making.

All too quickly, the days passed in September. John encountered and overcame problem after problem. At one time it really looked as if the military government of Brazil would not grant visas for the expedition on the grounds that three of the members had military backgrounds—indeed one was a Regular Army sergeant. We agreed to make the arrangements for Mac, even though the Ministry of Defence had not yet finally decided whether he would come with us. After a lot of coaxing, John persuaded the Brazilian Embassy that we would not stray from the main river while we were in Brazil, and they said they would forward the visas to Iquitos; they would be ready for collection when we arrived there sometime in December.

Another obstacle was the weight limit set by the airlines and the likelihood of X-ray screening of our kit, in the wake of the recent skyjacking troubles. John found that one go with an X-ray machine, while we were not looking, might neutralise the three hundred rolls of film he planned to take on the expedition. Also, accurate maps of the Amazon were unobtainable in London. Even the Royal Geographic Society's most recent map was made in 1931, and this showed insufficient detail, so John and Anna agreed that the best chance to get one was in Peru. Anna was flying out to Lima, the Peruvian capital on the Pacific coast, a week ahead of Cowrie, Macdermott, and myself, which would give her time to enlist the help of her brother Nick and smooth the way for the arrival of the main party on 4 October.

Although this meant I would not meet Anna until we arrived in Lima (and I had not yet met Mac—and in fact I had only met John Cowrie on three occasions) I was quite satisfied with the progress of the planning and preparations phase under the circumstances. The less the four of us knew of each other in advance, the more interesting would be the expedition itself, since four strangers would have to rely entirely on one another.

At Ardmore, the last of the main summer courses came to a close on 12 September, and this was followed by the most testing fourteen-day course we had ever run. The students were five high-grade management executives, aged twenty-one to twenty-eight, from each of six international companies, and each under the watchful eye of a training officer from each company. They carried out an exacting mental and physical programme, the syllabus for which had been devised by the companies themselves. To back this up, there was my own staff of eight instructors and a signals network provided by a detachment of fifteen soldiers from 14 Light Regiment, Royal Artillery, under the command of Lieutenant Charles Nisbet, R.A. Despite the great help of Peter Mitchell with the organising of the course, I found little time to think of, let alone read about, the Amazon.

The days slipped by. The next thing I knew, Anna had flown

out to Peru, and the Army had agreed to Mac's coming with us on full pay. When the industrial course ended on 27 September, Marie Christine and I stayed only a few more days at Ardmore to tidy up. The season was over. Lance and Ada Bell kindly agreed to stay on and finish the preparations for winter, while Dick Shuff, the chief instructor, packed his kit for a winter on a kibbutz in Israel. Gus Tocher was due to start his first term at a college of higher education in a few days time. David Johnson had to report to Southampton to start his new job as an accountant with Union Carbide, which had resulted from one of the directors of Union Carbide having spent a week at Ardmore on a businessman's course in June. Gavin Young went back to Magdalen College, Oxford, to continue his reading for a degree in medicine. Robin Bryant prepared to return, at the end of his leave, to his job as manager of a rubber estate in Malaysia, and, finally, Peter Mitchell returned to London to continue reading for the degree in estate management, which he had started after ten years in the Army.

On 29 September, Marie Christine and I drove south with our small daughter Rebecca and Gavin Young. Our sadness at saying goodbye to the good friends we had made during the summer was tempered by the feeling of surprise that, within a week, I should be in Peru. Our drive to the Motor Rail Terminal in Perth was eased considerably by another enormous lunch at the home of Donald and Bunty Davidson in Inverness. Just as they had done throughout the building of the School of Adventure, the Davidsons did their best to help now.

With only four days in London before the flight to Peru, the time passed in a whirl. As always, my mother-in-law's house became the base for frantic last-minute activity, and Lady D'Albiac herself put up with the considerable inconvenience with what looked like an amused smile. Final items of equipment were bought, arrangements were made with Peruvian Airlines about our overweight baggage, we called at ITN for the 16 mm movie camera, the tape recorder and film, and we collected all the film for the still cameras from Kodak in Kingsway. Then we staggered across to the Customs and Excise Offices to get all this cleared for export and so freed from a certain amount of tax. As far as we could tell, all the documents were in order for entry into Peru and Brazil. For me, the four days were all rather impaired by swollen arms and headaches resulting from injections against cholera, smallpox, yellow fever, typhoid, paratyphoid, tetanus—and oral drops against polio for good measure. A definite feeling of being run down, and the beginning of a cold, added up to a condition I had had before rowing across the Atlantic. On that occasion, I was admitted to the Chelsea Naval Hospital in Boston with severe blood poisoning resulting from an injured foot.

Fortunately, John Cowrie had managed very well on his own with the preparations in London. We had a medic, a Spanish interpreter, a photographer, and sickly me. One outstanding problem was the sheer bulk of the medical equipment that Mac was planning to take. John Cowrie had not got very far in persuading him to cut it down, so we both decided to visit the Royal Army Medical College at Milbank and beard Mac in his den.

It was raining softly at the end of a long, hot summer in London, but still the reddening leaves showed no sign of falling from the trees lining the road which, running behind the Tate Gallery parallel with the Embankment, passes the front of the college. I got a nod of assent from the dark-blue-uniformed security man at the guardroom door and walked across the empty quadrangle and into the cold, grey, college building. After wandering along dark corridors, which smelt of musty formalin, and up and down bare, stone stairways, I found myself knocking at a door. Through a big, glass panel in the door I could see a thin, narrow-faced man with sandy hair and an unhealthy pallor. He was wearing a long, white laboratory coat over his khaki uniform. As he crossed the room, I couldn't help thinking he looked too thin and unfit.

"Hello. I'm John Ridgway," I said, as the door opened, and I looked into a pair of steady green eyes.

"Good morning. I'm Sergeant Macdermott—most people just call me Mac." We shook hands and I said I thought John Cowrie would be along soon. "Would you like to see some of the things we can expect to meet?" Mac waved a hand at the rows and rows of shelves, each carrying hundreds of bottles of insects or snakes. Again I noticed the smell of formalin, this time mixed with the sweetness of methyl. "I'm a laboratory technician here, very keen on insects and butterflies. I hope to collect a lot while we're in South America—it's the best place in the world for them, you know."

"Yes, from what I've read, it looks as if there will be an awful lot of bites ahead for us. . . . Look—if you like, I'll just wander around here looking at these shelves and wait for John Cowrie; that is, if you've something you want to be getting on with." I did not want to get in the way.

"O.K. I've still to collect the rest of the medical gear together in another room upstairs, if you will be all right." Mac didn't look the sort of person to be long content with nothing to do. He went out, closing the door behind him, and I was left with thousands of our future problems—from the deadly to the mildly irritating. It was going to be different from the northwest Highlands of Scotland, I thought to myself.

Sean Macdermott was born in Durban in 1937. His father was a South African and had been a jeweller in the little Gold Rush town of Barberton in the Transvaal near Swaziland. While there, he met Mac's mother, a Swiss missionary language teacher, in Portuguese East Africa. Together they moved to Durban, where they first had a daughter and then Mac. After his schooling in Swaziland until the age of fourteen, the family moved to East London, and Mac went on to Selbourne College until he was eighteen; while there, he swam in five successive years for the Border Province. I was especially pleased to learn this because I knew only too well the tremendous stamina Chay Blyth had gained from hard swimming training during his adolescent years—stamina that helped to keep us alive while we were rowing across the Atlantic. Although he had passed the composite university entrance exam, Mac decided that in view of his father's increasing ill health, he would have to earn some money to support the family, rather than go on to the university. He became a student laboratory technician at Umtata in the Transkei and completed four years of the five-year course. At the end of this period, he gave up the demanding swimming training, since by this time he was convinced he would not make international class; he then took up cycling in its place and concentrated on club racing.

Towards the end of 1959, at the age of twenty-two, Mac decided the time had come to see the world, but just before leaving South Africa, he was challenged to cycle three thousand miles around the whole country inside twenty-eight days. In a typically "Mac" fashion, he accepted, made the distance, and won—five shillings. Years of gruelling swimming training and that unforgettable ride had given the disarmingly slight figure a lot of bite.

He arrived in London in November 1959 and first took a job dishwashing in various hotels. He followed this with three months work as an assistant laboratory technician at the Middlesex Hospital and thus came close to qualifying. However, in search of greater excitement, he joined the Parachute Regiment in 1960 as a private soldier for six years, the shortest engagement possible at that time. During the six-month period of his basic training, he contemplated desertion because he was not allowed to keep his racing bike in the sports store! When he was posted to the 3rd Battalion, a great friend of mine, Alec Larkman, noticed Mac swimming in an intercompany water polo match; soon the reluctant private was swimming both breast stroke and butterfly for the Army—reluctant because he could not and would not buckle down to the rigid nonsmoking training regime of the Army team. To this day, he still insists that his best swimming for the Army was actually done when he was able to sneak away for a quick drag just before the event.

After three years service with the 3rd Battalion, Parachute Regiment, in both the Middle East and the U.K., Mac transferred to the Royal Army Medical Corps and belatedly qualified as a laboratory technician. While studying, he met Jenny, a very pretty, fair-haired registered nurse serving with the Queen Alexandra's Royal Army Nursing Corps. When they married, Jenny left the Nursing Corps because Army Regulations prohibit a husband and wife from serving, and hence living, at the same unit. Now specialised in tropical medicine, parasitology, entomology, and bacteriology—and also father of a small son and a daughter—Mac gained a special interest in the jungle while working on a research project with a unit of Special Air Service in Malaysia. It was there that he extended an interest in collecting insects (dating back to his childhood in the South African bush) into a near obsession with collecting butterflies. In a novel, I feel, Mac would have a separate chapter devoted entirely to him; it would be entitled "The Man Who Loved Insects." In addition to his collection, Mac also has beautiful, large-scale drawings of insects, which he does for lectures at the college. While he could surely make a living from drawing, he derisively points out that the best insect drawings in the world only earn fifteen hundred pounds a year.

There was a knock on the glass-panelled door, and there was John Cowrie, fresh from another tussle at the airline office. "Hello. Mac's upstairs doing the medical kit," I said.

"I know where the room is. Let's go up and see if we can persuade him to cut it down a bit," said John.

In a small side room, we found Mac with large piles of every conceivable variety of medicament for the explorer, the whole lot heat-sealed in small individual polythene packets. "John's got a lot of it at home all ready." Mac looked pleased with it all.

"It's good to see it packed up so well; that way it'll escape the humidity." I was really impressed by the neatness.

"I think I've covered most things. It's just a pity there has to be so much of it. . . ."

"Yes, Mac, that's just the point," I interrupted. "I honestly believe we will have to cut it down a bit."

"I know. Let's go down and see Colonel Adam; he will have some ideas on this." Mac smiled, perhaps seeing the battle to come.

We all three trooped downstairs to the Colonel's office. I knew Colonel Adam, a burly man with a great practical experience of the effects of both the elements and straightforward endurance, well known for his bluntness. He's not a man to suffer fools lightly. If everyone carried a copy of his five-shilling paperback, *A Traveller's Guide to Health*, hospitals would be saved a deal of work. I was pretty sure the Colonel would side with Mac, and so I was more than pleased, as we went into his laboratory-like office, to see the smiling face of Dr. Ewen Thomas, who was there with him. Ewen had been the Medical Officer with the 22nd Special Air Service Regiment during the short time I had been with it, and he had personally handmade the strong, wooden medical box, complete with A *Traveller's Guide to Health*, that I had carried aboard my yacht *English Rose IV* on my attempt to sail around the world. I had a good idea Ewen would side with me. One man in every four of a long-range four-man patrol in the Special Air Service is a trained medic, but even so, he is severely restricted in what he carries, simply to retain flexibility. Ewen would understand what I meant by a "lightly equipped, highly flexible expedition."

"Good morning, Colonel. We've got a bit of a problem with all this medical kit. I wonder, could you spare a few minutes to give us a bit of help?" I got right down to it. "My own feeling is that we don't know what the country is really like; although the climate will range from severe cold to tropical heat, we can't be certain of porters and therefore we should be prepared to manpack all our gear ourselves."

"I am sure we'll be able to hire mules and guides," John Cowrie chipped in.

"It's all right with the Army," said Mac. "You know, there is always a medical backup in case of sickness or injury. Out there, we will be all on our own; if anything goes wrong with us, I shall have to treat the case myself, with no hope of doctors or hospitals. I must have the kit."

I could see from Colonel Adam's amused smile that he recognised three strong individuals in the team. No doubt he also wondered what Anna would be like. It was clear to me that we all three thought we were right, and there was not going to be much compromise.

"If you're on your own, there's a limit to what you can carry, and then you just have to make do with what you've got. That's all there is to it," said Ewen.

And so the talk went on. One minute we would be frozen ice-blue in the snow-capped Andes, suffering from oxygen starvation, and the next minute we would be crying out for paraffin gauze, after being badly burnt by a petrol-cooker explosion in the heart of the steaming jungle. We really weren't getting very far. The Colonel wasn't saying much, and I could see he felt we should take as much medical kit as we could. If we found we couldn't carry it all at some point, then we would just have to leave it with the Indians, and that would be good for what the Army calls "hearts and minds."

I bought a thin, three-inch rod of some kind of magnesium from Ewen for ten shillings, as an emergency fire maker. He showed me how to use it: all that's needed is some dry cotton wool, a pen knife, and the magnesium rod; grate a few particles of the rod onto the cotton wool with the knife; then, holding the rod close to the wool, rapidly scrape the blade down the rod, keeping the blade at ninety degrees to the rod. The sparks will ignite the magnesium particles, which in turn light the cotton wool.

Somehow, I was not convinced we would have a ready supply of dry cotton wool in the jungle. Yet it seemed worth a try if the matches got wet, the lighter ran out of fuel, the flints got lost for a patent flint striker I had in my emergency belt equipment, or if I broke the magnifying glass. In the Special Air Service, I had learnt how to make fire by rubbing two sticks together, but, of course, it was not just any two sticks—and the assortment of hard woods, soft woods, nylon cord, bow stick, and metal cap seemed as bulky as the medical kit, so we didn't take it.

After about an hour, it was agreed to take all the medical kit with us, and keep it with us for as long as we could. I left the Colonel's office with some misgivings about the resulting overweight luggage. The cold in my head and the injection pains in my arms didn't help.

Next evening, we all met at Mac's Army quarters to do the final packing for the flight out to Peru. John and Louise Cowrie were already at the smart Putney flat when Marie Christine and I arrived, laden with packs, kit bags, grips, and boxes. Jenny and Mac had cleared their sitting room floor to make a sort of "packing arena." Muted sounds of the Modern Jazz Quartet came from the record player, and Jenny dispersed homemade pâté and cream crackers, while Mac handed around glasses and bottles of Schlitz, a gift from an American Army friend.

The girls sat on the floor with John, Mac, and myself; they called out the kit lists while we tried to compress more than was really possible into the big, green, Lodestar rucksacks. I was glad Ada Bell had double-stitched all the seams of my pack before we left Ardmore. Looking around the little group, I wondered how Jenny and Louise were feeling at the thought of Mac and John leaving in only two days time; so much depended on the wives because, in some ways, the waiting is worse than the worst experience. If Jenny and Louise were unhappy at the idea of the expedition, then this would surely reflect in Mac and John in the coming months. As far as I could tell, there was no dissent.

The doorbell rang and Jenny left the room. She returned a few moments later with Terry Schofield, another R.A.M.C. sergeant who had brought two R.A.F. survival rations in flat, oblong, aluminium tins about eight or nine inches in length. Chay and I have great faith in these rations because we had used them during the rowing trip when food began to run low. "I wish I was coming," said Terry, stepping carefully over a pile of discarded kit that all but blocked the doorway from the passage outside.

We had just about crammed everything into our rucksacks and the emergency belts, with their four large pouches, which we were going to wear in case (after a mishap) we found ourselves separated from each other—and from our kit. There was really no room for anything more. It was John who would have to carry a heavy aluminium camera case in his hand—for the tripod and all the various lenses and cameras he needed to take black and white for the *People*, colour for books, magazine articles, and his own collection, and specialist photographs of insects and flowers. Mac had agreed to take a separate grip with extra medical kit in it for sorting out in Peru.

"Now, here is my secret weapon!" said Louise, holding up four bulky rolls she produced from a kit bag behind her. "Your mosquito nets, complete with zips you can do up when you are in your hammocks at night, and special holes with sewn-in drawstrings to tighten around the four lines leading from the hammock to the trees at either end. On the top here you will see the tapes for tying to branches above, to keep the net from touching you." These modifications may have seemed unnecessary when we were all sitting comfortably in a London flat listening to soft music, but I well remembered nights in the Malaysian jungle when the mosquito net had been as important as breathing. Without complaint, each of us rolled a net into his high-altitude, lightweight sleeping bag and then wrapped the whole bundle in an Australian Army waterproof poncho before strapping it under the overweight rucksack. Mac stuffed Anna's net into the grip with the medical kit.

By two o'clock in the morning, the job was just about done. The Macdermotts' bathroom scales measured tens of pounds of overweight luggage, but John Cowrie was confident that the Peruvian Airlines would not let us down on this account. We waved goodbye to Jenny and Mac as they stood under their front door light, in the early hours of Saturday, 3 October; there were now only twenty-nine hours left before the Inca Imperial DC-8 would jet up and out of winter's closing grasp, to carry us to the warmth of Peruvian early summer. The die was cast: either we had the right kit or we didn't. Now there was nothing for it but to get out and get on with the job of dealing with all those fearful things I had read about the Amazon during the summer in Scotland.

Everything at the airport went well; no trouble with the X-ray machine and no trouble with the weight. But all this did nothing to lessen the sadness I felt waving goodbye to Marie Christine, Rebecca, and Lady D'Albiac.

On the plane, we found the jovial Irishman Bill Cashan, who, as the airline freight manager, had done so much to help us with the baggage problems; he was, like any good Irish horse fancier, going over to Paris for the day to watch the Arc de Triomphe race meeting at Lonchamps. By lunch time, we were in Madrid, and it was summer again. After the plane filled up with passengers, we chased the setting sun across the Atlantic to Port of Spain in Trinidad, and on to Caracas and Bogotá. During the flight, seven miles above the lonely sea, I read Chay and Maureen Blyth's new book *Innocent Abroad*; I was surprised to find in it a plan Chay had made with Chick Gough, while he was in South Africa at the end of his attempt to sail around the world alone, to make the very same journey down the Amazon. Now, instead, Chay was making final preparations at Portsmouth for a second attempt to circumnavigate the globe, alone and nonstop, this time against the prevailing winds, in the superb fifty-nine-foot Bermudian ketch *British Steel*. My thoughts would be with him. When the chips are down, Chay is the boy to be with.

3

Preparations in Lima

We finally touched down at Jorge Chavez airfield in Lima at two o'clock in the morning, local time. There was a slight sea mist in the air that quickly dampened our clothing once we left the airport. Since it was too late to telephone Anna, we decided to lie down in the open until dawn. We couldn't carry all the gear very far; we were glad, then, to find what in the darkness appeared to be a ruined storeshed, standing forlornly beside the main road that leads into Lima.

"This looks all right," said John, heaving a sigh of relief.

"Looks more like a public lavatory for dogs to me," said Mac, flashing his torch around the inside of the building. "Look! There's a rat over there in the corner!"

"Well, we could sleep outside in the shelter of the wall." I thought we were hardly starting the expedition by walking down a red carpet. "Be good to get used to the old hard ground, anyway," I mumbled halfheartedly.

We unpacked the bed rolls we had so carefully strapped to the bottom of our rucksacks just a few hours ago in the warmth of the Putney flat. "I wouldn't sleep too close to the wall if I were you, John; there may be an odd dog's mess," Mac warned Cowrie.

Wrapped in my poncho waiting for sleep, I stared up into the sky. The mist seemed to be clinging in only a shallow layer along the ground; straight above me were the same stars I had watched two years before, as I nursed my crippled yacht towards Recife on the other side of South America. Here we go again, I thought.

When the first light of the new day came at six o'clock, it found us cramped stiff beneath our dripping-wet ground-sheets; across the road a huge billboard said that "First National City was the Right Bank in the Right Place," or something to that effect. Chevrolet trucks were already beginning to rumble down the road, and we all felt a great need for a wash and shave and some hot coffee.

I noticed John sniffing. "I told you!" Mac said, pointing at the brown smear on the corner of John's poncho. "Dogs!"

The large, modern, airport building was well equipped for washing and shaving. There were one or two odd glances at the three of us in our semi-military garb, while we dried our faces with the "nappies" we were to use as towels on the expedition. John Cowrie soon found the restaurant, one floor up from the main hall and overlooking the runway and the park of brightly coloured international aircraft. When I found him, he was already deep in conversation at the counter with a sparky-looking young man wearing the monk's habit of the Franciscan Order. "This is Father Mario. He is just about to fly out to his mission at Sivia; it's close to the Benedictine mission of Father Ambrose, who gave us all our information on the Apurímac," said John, pushing a cup of coffee towards me.

"Well, most people just call me Bill." The short, fair hair and calm, blue eyes combined with the soft American accent seemed to belie his monk's habit, but his curiously open, young face, uncluttered with lines of material care, more than counteracted that first impression. I have always envied the expression of serenity usually found on the faces of those in holy orders; perhaps some of them have found peace of mind.

"Father Bill has offered to take some of our film with him today, and he'll hand it to the Benedictines to await our collection in November. But the call has already gone out for his plane. I'll go down to the gate with him—it's number five. Can you get hold of some of the film and join us there?" said John, getting up and pushing some money across the counter towards the waiter.

I gulped down my coffee and dashed down the stairs to where Mac was lounging in a black leather armchair, surrounded by all our gear. He too was deep in conversation with

PUBLIC LIBRARY
DANVILLE, ILLINOIS

someone, but I just grabbed some packs of film and ran off towards gate five, arriving only just in time, as the passengers were called forward to the waiting Faucett plane. As we walked back down the hall, John suggested I should try to reach Anna on the phone, and after some alarums and excursions we finally got through to her brother Nick's home; Anna said they would be at the airport within half an hour to pick us up.

We found Mac earnestly conversing, as only Mac can, with a Canadian monk who had spent some time in Chile before coming to Peru. "You better be sure and take firearms with you," he said, and then retold the story which had so engrossed Mac. It appears that one of the Indian tribes on the other side of the Andes had been waylaying trespassers in their area, killing them off and then boiling the fat down to make ultra-fine precision oil which, a newspaper reported, was then bought by a firm in Lima for lubricating precision instruments. There had been a long court case, running right up to a month before our arrival.

By the time we had all had our say on this little saga, the Canadian also had to leave us to catch his plane, and Mac was anxious to get some breakfast. Just as he was about to go up to the restaurant, he caught sight of Anna. She was coming through the crowd with a slim, fair-haired man in his early thirties who looked quite clearly to be her brother Nick. With them was a little boy with very black hair who was introduced as Nick's eldest son, Igor.

"I'll get some breakfast while you collect the parachute flare and machete from the airline office," said Mac, already well on the way towards the restaurant.

"We need someone who speaks Spanish now, Anna. Because of the hijacking scene, we had to hand in a few things in London for the pilot to bring out for us, and last night we couldn't get them back," I said.

"O.K. Let's go and get them now. Igor and Nick can stay with John Cowrie and look after the luggage." Anna looked pretty efficient as she headed down the hall to the office, and she certainly had no trouble persuading the staff to have the flare and machete delivered to Nick's newspaper office in the middle of Lima as soon as the servicing crew brought the stuff in from the plane. The fashionable, giant, bicycle-wheel glasses and thinned-out, layered hair style, may have been straight from London, but the utility beige slacks and sneakers were made for walking.

Anna was born in 1941 in London, Ontario, in Canada. Nick was a couple of years older, but there were to be two younger sisters. Their parents were both doctors; their father, a White Russian bacteriologist, was a contemporary of the fictional Dr. Zhivago, and their mother is an English pathologist. Anna went to school in Canada until she was eight years old, but then her parents were divorced, and the children moved to England with their mother, while their father remained behind. At Malvern Girls' College, Anna preferred swimming, lacrosse, and winter skiing holidays to the schoolroom desk. In 1951, aged ten, she went, for the first time, on a skiing holiday at Engelberg in Switzerland; thanks to the sheer hard work of her mother, she was able to repeat this holiday for five successive years, all the while steadily increasing her ability along with all the other children. But there was something different about Anna's skiing, and this didn't escape the notice of Mrs. Raynsford, daughter of the skiing and rugby enthusiast, Lord Wakefield. She, in turn, recommended Anna to Mrs. Hepworth in Wengen, where, at the age of sixteen, Anna spent the whole winter.

Mrs. Hepworth's careful management groomed Anna for stardom, as Nick put it.

"It's funny, really; she's so quiet and never seems particularly interested in things. We used to ski together, and we were about the same standard. Then I missed one year, and next time she was streets ahead—you wouldn't really expect a girl to have such nerve, but then ninety miles an hour is a hell of a speed."

Anna was in the British team from 1960 to 1964, skiing the Slalom, Giant Slalom, and Downhill—but preferring the sheer speed of the Downhill. She skied in the Chamonix World Championships and the Innsbruck Olympic Games. In 1963, Anna was British Champion, but her greatest achievement was to come in 1964, at the end of her competition career, at the Flying Kilometre Race at Cervinia in Italy. It was there she covered the distance at an average speed of eighty-nine m.p.h., becoming the third-fastest woman skier of all time. The two ahead of her were only fractions of a second faster, and the race was considered to be so dangerous that it was discontinued for women thereafter.

Retiring at twenty-three, Anna suffered three shoulder dislocations, among a multiplicity of other injuries. Luckily, none of them left any mark or effect, except, perhaps, remarkable determination.

From 1960 to 1968, Anna toured the Mediterranean countries as part of an international waterskiing show, which was made up of ten men and women and organised by a French World Champion trick waterskier. During this time, her sister Tania was seriously ill for long periods. Both Tania and her mother believe that it was Anna's inspiration and dogged persistence that kept her sister alive and helped speed her recovery. Between skiing shows, Anna chose to make a good living for herself by following her own imaginative flair and working in London as a freelance designer and manufacturer of belts, bracelets, hair clips, and other accessories for high fashion.

Already fluent in French and German, Anna soon absorbed Spanish during stays with Nick in Peru, and with typical determination took an advanced Spanish course at the London Berlitz Language School. There she met John Cowrie and leapt at the chance to see and photograph both the High Sierra and the jungle.

As we all drove into Lima in Nick's big American car, he gave us a good briefing on "the city of contrasts," as Lima is usually called—"contrasts," because the bustling city of over three million people contains both the grand old buildings of Spanish colonial days and modern office blocks and flats; both palatial town houses and appalling slums, or *barriadas*, as they are called; both families with fine-sounding names and huge Swiss bank accounts and many many more families with nothing. The present stark division of wealth stems from the Spanish system of enormous estates, which were awarded to faithful aristocratic employees of the Crown. Peru grew into an oligarchy, with a handful of noble families controlling around 90 per cent of the country's wealth. With a population of only twelve and a half million, the government encourages both

Roman Catholicism, which was brought in by the Spaniards and an inevitably high birth rate.

The military revolutionary government is popular with the majority—the poor; with its intent to ensure human dignity for the *campesino*, or peasant, the junta has achieved much, but always at the expense of the rich families and foreign investment in Peru. Petro-Peru, the American-owned fuel oil company, has been taken over by the government, and foreign mining concerns also have felt the bite of nationalism. The rich have found it much harder to take their money out of Peru, with the result that there is a flourishing black market money exchange system. The greatest single measure introduced has been the Agrarian Reform, which outlaws the holding of land, beyond comparatively small acreages; this is going ahead well, despite desperate opposition by the big landowners. The small peasant farmers are finding themselves suddenly released from bondage. This, of course, is tremendously popular in the short term, but its long-term effects have yet to be felt.

None of these nationalistic moves is particularly new to South America. At least in Peru, however, the government appears stable and popular with the majority. North Americans are the most unpopular foreigners, in spite of the large quantities of aid the United States dispenses. And all the time, the *barriadas*, consisting of shantytown shelters, continue to grow at an alarming rate on the outskirts of Lima.

Nick very kindly offered to put us up while we made final preparations in Lima, and we were very pleased to accept his hospitality, after our night out by the ruin near the airport. When the car drew up outside a comfortable house in the pleasant suburb of Miraflores, the front door burst open, and two children came running down the path to meet their father; they were followed a few steps behind by their pretty Peruvian mother, Consuela, with the fourth young Ashenhov in her arms. Soon, we had parked our gear in various bedrooms and, after a cup of coffee, we split up to go our various ways, Anna to follow up a lead she had been given for maps, Mac to arrange the homeward transmission of the insects he expected to collect, John to photograph the *barriadas*.

Nick and I returned to his office in the middle of town to set

up a rapid and practical means of getting film and copy from
the Sierra and jungle back to London with the BOAC airline
pilots. "I'm trying my best to arrange for me to come up with
you to the source," said Nick, while we were still in the car. "I
could cover some interesting mining stories further south after
I leave you. The problem is the revolution they are having in
Bolivia, on Peru's southern border right now. . . ." I knew he
would arrange it somehow.

We tried various mining contacts to find how best to approach the source. This is marked on most maps as being Lake
Villafro, about fifteen miles southwest of Cailloma, a small
town near a silver mine. A representative of the company own-
ing the mine seemed rather more dubious. He explained that
the road to Cailloma was no more than a track, and that it was
often blocked by rock falls and snow. "It should be O.K. now,"
he said, but he really didn't seem convinced.

In England, the best way had seemed to fly to Arequipa,
then take what John Cowrie called "a native bus" the extra
couple of hundred miles to Cailloma. We now knew there were
no "native buses" and that the "road" climbed from seven
thousand feet to around fifteen thousand, over a pass that
might or might not be open. Nick suggested it would be a pity
to miss the opportunity of driving down the Pan-American
Highway the seven hundred or so miles from Lima to Arequipa
—this, particularly, since the road runs close to the Pacific most
of the way, and also through the coastal desert, with its remarkable green valleys, which are formed wherever a river runs
down to the ocean from the Andes inland. Everyone agreed on
this point when we discussed it during the fine, Peruvian-style
dinner that Consuela prepared for us that evening. Nick said
he would hire a *colectivo* for the Thursday evening, and that,
for twenty-five to thirty pounds, he thought this would be a big
American car and a driver, who would take us all the seven
hundred miles to Arequipa, then on and up a further two hundred miles to Cailloma. It seemed pretty good value to us.

The intervening three days were spent touring around Lima,
trying to find the various items that we had assumed we could
buy with no trouble at all in any city. By not purchasing such
items as sneakers, curry powder, nylon rope, and petrol lighters

in London, we had saved time and an overweight penalty on the plane out. Now we were to pay dearly: fishing tackle, large plastic bags, and nylon rope were next to impossible to find— and perhaps 50 per cent more expensive than British prices, when we did eventually track them down. Curry powder (every grocer has some) was found only after a tremendous search, but it was a most inferior variety, and we threw it away soon after the start. (Almost anything can be eaten if enough curry powder is mixed with it; without it, I wondered how we would survive.)

After careful thought, I telexed the paper in London with a proposed plan of action, giving dates of arrival at various main points along our route. I also sent a duplicate of the main map we expected to use, all marked up with routes and dates; this went with a BOAC pilot in his VC-10. The day before we were to set out for Arequipa, I was delighted to receive the paper's complete acceptance of the plan.

Perhaps the highest point of our stay in Lima was a lunch Nick and I had with Señor Antonio Bentin, a director of Faucett Airlines, the major carrier of air traffic within Peru. We drove from the airline offices in the centre of the city to the most palatial Chinese restaurant I have ever seen. Situated in the suburbs of Lima, it had at its entrance an ornamental pond filled with goldfish, and across this pond all the customers had to pass by means of a bridge. Plied with a Pisco Sour, the famous Peruvian drink, I was euphoric, and it turned into a meal I shall never forget.

We were lucky enough to be put in touch with Father Michael Smith of the Benedictine mission we hoped to visit at Sivia, about seven hundred miles down from the source. Father Michael kindly agreed to take film, medical kit, and clothing to Sivia from Lima, when he himself returned to the mission. This at least ensured a final change of kit when we reached the navigable part of the river.

4

To a Further Source

Thursday, 8 October dawned dull and misty, long after the Ashenhovs' crazy cockerel had waked us all in our nice, comfortable beds. During my short stay with Nick and Consuela, I often wondered whether any atomic fallout drifted from the remote test islands far out in the Pacific, pushed by the same winds that blanket Lima in sea mist for much of each year; this might perhaps have affected the cockerel's timing mechanism, for it seemed to crow long before any other cock in Lima. The day of our departure was spent packing our kit, while Nick made final arrangements for the *Peruvian Times* to continue production in his absence. I don't think the kindly figure of Don Griffis, the General Manager of the paper, saw it as too much of a problem.

We had all had the seams of our Lodestar high-pack rucksacks double-stitched before we left England. Now, in Lima, we taped the screw fittings of the aluminium frames, on which the sacks were mounted, with the black masking tape that is used in the motor trade to protect parts from paint during the spraying process. Although the rucksacks and frames were unusually light, I felt sure they would do the job if properly maintained. We oiled the fragile zips on the two side pockets, and lined the insides of the sacks with heavy-gauge polythene bags to effect a double protection against water. With far too much still to pack, in spite of having sent a large portion of clothing and film along with extra medical kit direct to the Benedictine mission at Sivia, we spent hours trying various combinations of load to make the best of every inch of space. Ideally, a rucksack should be packed with the heaviest items, such as tents and sleeping bags, at the highest point of the load, that is to say, last into the sack, but there is always a conflict with the need to get at such small items as food, maps, and gloves while on march. Quite clearly, if it is raining, and these things are packed at the bottom, then not only do the rest of the members of the expedition curse you while you fumble around trying to get to the bottom of the sack, but all your kit gets wet at the same time. The small side pockets can take only so much kit, and usually it ends up with some of the heavy kit having to be rolled up under the rucksack in a waterproof ground-sheet—which bangs about on my unfortunately rather large backside.

In addition to our enormous rucksacks, we each had quick-release webbing belts (except Anna, who had rather a chic leather affair) and these carried four bulging pouches and a machete. One pouch, on the left side, was full of emergency medical kit; the two at the back contained plastic water bottles, with other items such as water-sterilising tablets, fish hooks, nylon, spare compass, flint lighters, and insect repellent wedged in as best as possible. The remaining pouch, on the right side, bulged with sufficient high-calorie emergency food to last up to seven days, in the event that we were somehow split up from our rucksack and the other three members of the expedition. This food was largely made by Horlicks Ltd., and it was selected from food not used on my single-handed sailing voyage in 1968: hardtack biscuits, dehydrated meat bars, oatmeal blocks, and glucose tablets, in the main.

Finally, John Cowrie carried by hand a small aluminium attaché case containing his cameras, and Anna a similar smaller case. Mac and I each carried a none-too-small kit bag; these were full of film, medical kit, various perishable foods, a billy-can for tea, two Optimus petrol cookers, and some extra clothing. It was to be these two kit bags that were to go first if we were unable to hire guides or mules.

At eight o'clock in the evening, the *colectivo* arrived, just one and a half hours late. The car was a big and fairly newish Chevrolet with left-hand drive, which would, we thought, take the five of us with little trouble. The driver introduced himself as Humberto. He looked a big, phlegmatic, Peruvian version of

Broderick Crawford, clad in a brown, white, and black check shirt. The shirt was covered by an ancient, grey, woollen cardigan that had two coloured bands on each cuff, one white and one red. The faded, grey trousers and slip-on shoes looked pretty nondescript, but Humberto's whole appearance was updated by a smart, blue denim baseball cap, worn at a businesslike angle on his thick, if rather receding, black hair; his heavy, round, brown face wore a perpetually mournful expression.

Humberto established his personality at the outset by showing considerable displeasure at the amount of baggage we had. We were angry right back, all five of us, because he had been so late for the start of a long, and for us important, journey. Humberto responded with his doleful bloodhound look. We too lost a bit of our snap when we looked into the capacious trunk and found it nearly full of all sorts of parcels for Arequipa. Wrapped in brown paper, they could not be carried on the roof-rack, in case it might rain; instead, it was our own precious gear that would have to be lashed on top of a car for perhaps nine hundred miles, in goodness knows what weather.

At nine o'clock that evening—with Nick, Anna, and Mac wrapped in voluminous, blue driver jackets in the back of the car, John Cowrie and myself in the front, Humberto at the wheel, and all our gear on the roof—we set off for the source of the greatest river in the world. Consuela and the four children waved frantically in the dark, their faces lit red by the huge taillights of the car, as we pulled away from the kerb by the front gate of the Ashenhov home. Soon we were bowling south, along the greatest highway in the world, the Pan-American, which runs all the way from Alaska in the north, down the Western seaboard of the New World, to Chile in the south. However, this grand two-lane highway petered out not far from the outskirts of Lima, and with the huge, silent figure of Humberto brooding over the wheel, we rolled remorselessly through the night at a steady fifty miles an hour along a two-way road, which was little better than an average "A" class road in England.

With the long journey ahead in mind, Nick had taken a drink or two during the afternoon to ease the discomfort of the coming night. Now, with a half bottle of rum in hand, a huge floral tie loosened, revealing the unfastened top button of his fancy collared shirt, in classical editorial style and the green eyeshield, Nick told us the story of his life. Leaning forward to the back of the front seat, his narrow good-looking face alight with the liquor and crowned by a mass of slightly-too-long (to my way of thinking) curly fair hair, Nick whiled away the hours for us with a stream of hilarious stories. Occasionally, Anna would kick him, but nothing ever stopped him.

Educated in England, Nick had gone to Cambridge and then travelled as cheaply as he could to South America with a friend. For a while, he had stopped off in Lima and had worked for the *Peruvian Times;* this included an expedition into the jungle with the National Geographic Society. Nick liked both the climate and the good-natured people of Peru. He met and married Consuela before returning to England to pursue his career as a journalist. Nick then took a job for a while in South Africa, leaving Consuela and his baby son Igor in Sussex with his mother, and worked there as a correspondent for the Associated Press News Agency. Later, he went back to London to write for the *Daily Sketch.* It was typical of Nick to hire a plane and fly down to Cape Horn to search for and photograph Sir Alec Rose for the *Daily Sketch,* when *Lively Lady* rounded the Horn in 1968. Tiring of the climate and working conditions in Britain, Nick accepted the offer of a job on the *Peruvian Times* in Lima, when he called in there on his way back from Cape Horn. His self-assurance, vitality, and drive soon won him the post of Editor of the *Peruvian Times.* He has high hopes of developing it into a larger *Andean Times,* which would embrace all the proposed Andean Common Market countries—Colombia, Ecuador, Peru, Bolivia, and Chile. Nick told us of people who lived their entire lives on the huge rubbish heaps just outside Lima. These people eke out an existence simply by scouring the rubbish for scraps of food and materials with which to build and maintain the shelters they call home.

In the early part of the night, the road passed close to the empty shores, and we could see the mighty Pacific rollers brimming white as they surged in to the great stretches of sand or clawed high into the darkness against stark cliffs. Humberto was a steady driver, his pace seldom varied. He might as well have been at the wheel of a big truck as a Chevrolet, and we all felt safer than we would have if one of us had been driving.

With a large fuel tank, the car only needed to stop a couple of times for petrol, and on each occasion we crawled out into the garish light surrounding the pumps to gulp down a plastic cupful of hot, black coffee and perhaps munch a banana or a bread roll. I had known many nights like this on the A1, driving north through the night to Scotland. Only, here it was San Antonio and ICA, instead of Biggleswade and Scotch Corner; instead of Yorkshire and the North Sea, it was the desert and the Pacific. The agony of staying awake and the gravelly eyes were the same, but here the black strip of road was straighter and narrower, and the lorries came howling past at rather longer intervals.

Towards dawn, at around half past four in the morning, Humberto told Nick he thought we had better pull to the side for half an hour or so, unless one of us wanted to drive. We were drained with laughter by Nick's stories, and so we all fell asleep.

When I woke up, it was just getting light, and we were already on the move. The road stretched straight ahead, a thin, black ribbon of what seemed more like oil than Tarmac, and this reminded me of the waste oil roads of the Persian Gulf. On either side of the black strip lay the sterile desert, which was quite hilly. Burnt out motor tyres, tin cans, and derelict vehicles lay close to the road, the dry desert air acting on them almost like a preservative. The cold desert sunrise came quickly, the burnished copper shield rising swiftly out of the pale, biscuit dunes. Another day had begun. I felt rather like Lawrence of Arabia overlooking the An Nefud desert, and I smiled inwardly; the Chevrolet Impala was a bit different from a camel.

Before the early sun had a chance to heat the air over the land and start the daily onshore breeze, we reached the coast again, where the desert ran into the Pacific. The heavy rollers burst on the sand, as in any good painting in Harrods; the long stretches of beach were deserted, save for an occasional frail fisherman's shelter made of a few bamboo poles and palm leaves. We sometimes saw the men themselves in the surf, hauling straining nets against the suck of the retreating waves. In such a totally empty place of sand and sea, these lonely men seemed somehow exceptionally vulnerable and exposed to the elements; in the long run, life surely seems impossible.

Breakfast came twice that morning. First, we slowed to a halt in a cloud of dust before a whitewashed adobe hut in a little village that looked as if it were waiting for the "Magnificent Seven" to come riding in. Humberto groaned as he opened his door; then he mumbled at Nick that we should be able to get good fresh fish for breakfast. At six-thirty in the morning, we were the only customers, but the flies were there well before us. A couple of young Peruvian boys were scrubbing the place out, but stopped their work to bring us plates of firm, fresh fishsteaks and chips. We sat around rough wooden tables, on benches still wet from the scrubbing.

"Look at the desert flowers," said John Cowrie, peering out of the window, full of enthusiasm at the thought of really getting down to his photography at last. As soon as he could swallow the hot coffee, John was away with his special film and lens for insect and flower photographs. Soon, Mac and Anna joined him, and Nick and I laughed at the incongruous sight of three backsides stuck up in the emptiness of the desert as cameras were zoomed in for six-inch closeups of the snow-white desert flowers. Humberto rocked with laughter, and tears ran down his cheeks. "Crazy *gringos!*" he cried, holding his not inconsiderable sides. Some little time later, the intrepid photographers returned to the waiting car; all three had deadpan faces and spoke in serious tones of their art.

Soon after leaving the village, we were down by the sea again. Here the coastline had turned to dark, knotted rock, and we saw the traces of man's attempts at conservation. A small headland was coated glaring white with *guano*, the sea bird excrement so prized as a fertilizer; this small breeding ground for the birds was fenced off, and Nick told us of severe penalties meted out to those found inside the forbidden area. "Still, it's hard on them, really. What's the use of having a fertilizer-laying bird, if your family is starving to death?" he said. The poor Peruvians living on the desert coast appeared to be hanging on to life by only the barest margin. Sometimes, we would see giant figures coming down the side of one of the mountainous dunes on the inland side of the road; by looking carefully, we could see a few green plants dotted along the sides of the seemingly dry valleys. The bundles these lonely men carried on their shoulders were made up of these sparse plants. "For them it is harvest time," said Nick. Life was certainly simple and primitive: they didn't even have adobe huts to live in—only hopeless-looking shelters like those we had seen earlier at the beach. We had thought they were simply shelters for the fishermen to use during the fishing, but they were really home.

Further along we came to a small natural harbour. It was protected by a rugged island of rock on the seaward side of the narrow channel that led into a deep-water bay. The area of rocky land surrounding this little place had been developed into a smelly fishmeal plant for the anchovy fleet anchored in the bay. Its buildings emitted dense clouds of white steam from a complex of tanks, pipes, and concrete emplacements—the whole thing looked rather like an outlandish gasworks. On the outskirts of the factory, there was a cluster of untidy shacks belonging to those lucky or unlucky enough to have work in this evil-smelling place; at their doors stood little children brightly dressed in blues and reds, even if the clothes were rags. The men were away working in the factory.

The richest fishery in the world is reputed to be along the cold Humboldt Current, as it sweeps up the west coast of South America from the Antarctic. The islands just off the shores of Peru look just like icebergs, when their thick, white coats of bird droppings reflect the sun. There are signs, however, that these birds are declining in numbers, and that the anchovy shoals are being overfished by the fleets of the world. This steaming fishmeal factory and the attendant little float bobbing in the bay told clearly how seriously the Peruvians regarded the industry. While the others photographed the scene, I took the opportunity to have a close look at the boats. They appeared to be about eighty feet long and made of steel, and were about the same size, if a little narrower, than large tugs; the hull of one of them had once been white, but now there were only speckles of white showing through the red brown of the rust. The open box-like bridge and the superstructure were built around the rakish funnel, well up in the forward part of the boat. From the stubby mast running up the after side of the superstructure, a stout hoist for hauling the nets projected at about thirty degrees from the vertical. At least two thirds of the length of the boat was open deckspace; besides the carley float lashed alongside the bridge there was a small, black dinghy for safety. Although these boats lacked the smart appearance of the Scottish seine netters, they nevertheless gave a business-like impression. The skippers would have to be skillful enough just to navigate through the narrow channel at the entrance to the harbour, where it is swept by a heavy swell and foam from the waves breaking on the jagged rocks on either side.

Grim reminders of the perils of driving along this narrow highway are simple wooden crosses that stand at nearly every corner; these and the much smaller crosses at the foot of the main one commemorate the persons who have died in fatal accidents. At one point far below six such crosses, down some two hundred feet, just where the steep shale of the hillside bends out a little before plunging a further five hundred feet into the Pacific, the offside front door of a battered, white car swung to and fro in the sea breeze. "Last Month," were the words painted on the door. The placid expression on Humberto's face never altered.

Quite soon the road began to cross the fresh, green valleys of racing rivers that tumble down from their source ten thousand feet up in the Andes, only fifty or sixty miles inland. We must have crossed several of these desert oases during the course of the night without realising it; now, as the sun began to burn the day, we marvelled at the quality of the vegetation and the clear water in the rivers.

Superlatives rather tend to crowd each other in grand country, but when we stopped for our second breakfast that morning, we stepped out of the car into one of those memories that last a lifetime. The simple restaurant was a plain, white adobe building, complete with a ramshackle, sectioned, terracotta roof, just like the fish restaurant of a couple of hours before. But this time it was different. Our eyes welcomed the sheer freshness of the green willows along the riverbank on which the building stood, the simple arch of the high, stone roadbridge, and the sparkling water, as it rushed around the legs of a patient Peruvian peasant standing on the clear, gravel riverbed. The sun was just warm enough and the air fresh and clear. "He's after the freshwater prawns—just wait 'til you taste these," grinned Nick.

Again we sat at plain wooden tables in a bare room. The whitewashed walls hung with a few fly-blown calendars advertising cigarettes and Inca-Cola; no high pressure salesmanship here. Humberto was served first, for bringing the custom to the restaurant; we watched hungrily as he splashed sauce from a brown wine bottle onto a white soup plate full of the juicy, red prawns bathed in a clear vegetable soup. With a flourish, he replaced the twist of grubby paper which served as a cork for the sauce bottle; then he lowered his big, round face, now black with stubble, until it was but a few inches from the dish, and noisily spooned the soup into his mouth. "Yours will come soon," he laughed, cracking the curled red prawns with thick, brown fingers and mopping his face with a paper napkin.

I couldn't sit and watch, so I left the table and, sitting outside on a convenient boulder in the dust, let the sun warm my back and watched a solitary fisherman wading like a cautious heron through the shallows. Better than London fog, I thought, taking a deep breath and stretching myself. Everything was just right. In a few hours, the heat would haze the clarity of the mountains, and drowsiness would take the edge off this wonderful feeling of well being. How glad I was that we hadn't flown direct to Arequipa.

"Grub's up," called Mac through the open doorway. I stood up very slowly and threw aside a piece of grass I had been idly twisting in my hands. Looking around I thought to myself: I'll never forget how good it is to be alive at this moment in this place.

After the prawns were eaten, we drove on along the coast, the sun steadily raising the temperature. As we drove through the small towns and villages in the green valleys that alternated with stretches of empty, burning desert, we noticed that it must have been some kind of national celebration day. For nearly every building, no matter how poor, seemed to be flying the Peruvian national flag (of three vertical bars: red, white, and red). I asked Nick about this, and he explained that since the revolution, the military government had made a real effort to get the population to feel pride in being Peruvian. "*Arriba el Perú* is the slogan; it was helped a lot by the fine showing of their almost amateur team in the World Cup," said Nick.

Whenever we stopped in the green valleys, people were gentle and friendly; there were always crowds of children and chickens. Life seemed pleasant enough.

At midday, the road turned away from the coast and wound inland. "That's the last of the Pacific. The next time we see the sea, it will be the Atlantic— It's going to be quite a trip," reflected Mac. We all pondered the long distance we had to go, and not much of it by motoring. Nick had already told us how he hoped we weren't being spoiled by the Tarmac road. "Don't get the wrong impression," he had said. "Just about all the roads in Peru are unsurfaced, and when the rains come in a few weeks time every bus carries a set of shovels to clear a way through the avalanches."

Once away from the sea, we really felt the shimmering heat reflected from the pale sand of the desert. The road wound up through narrow passes into the foothills of the Andes; soon we reached a desert plain, and even with all four windows open and going at fifty miles an hour, the car was uncomfortably hot. Humberto began the upsetting trick of nodding his head from lack of sleep, which was particularly disturbing in the hilly places, where crosses marked the fate of other drivers—and passengers—who had nodded at hairpin bends. Nick tried all sorts of ploys to keep Humberto awake, from funny stories in Spanish to short digs in his ribs.

The arid plains would one day be fertile fields, Humberto told us. The government was going to drill a tunnel through the mountains and draw water from some of the Amazon tributaries on the other side of the watershed to irrigate the desert. Nick said it had already been done further north, with remarkable results.

"There's Misti," said Nick, as we sped along the dead-straight road through the desert.

"Where?"

"Straight ahead, just to the right of the road. See the snow-cap above the desert?" Sure enough, a faint, white patch seemed to be hanging in the sky far ahead. The main part of the mountain, clear of snow, was invisible in the heat haze. The extinct volcano was just as I had always imagined Japan's Fujiyama would look. It was like a vision.

About three quarters of an hour before we reached Arequipa, we had to stop at a kind of frontier post. Uniformed police, *guardia civil* as we came to know them, checked carefully and slowly through our passports, but Humberto came away from the little shed they used as an office with an even sorrier look than was usual. His driving licence and insurance were in rather a mess, and it seemed likely that he would have to pay a fine. After six hundred miles at the wheel, this bit of news took the last small puff out of Humberto's sails; he refused to be comforted and, despite the numerous sweet oranges John Cowrie had bought while waiting for the passport check, Humberto sadly insisted that he was just too tired to go on past Arequipa. Our chances of finding another car to get us up to Cailloma at half past four on a Friday night looked none too bright; all five of us felt tired, dirty, and decidedly dispirited at the idea of Humberto letting us down.

With a population of some 300,000, Arequipa, in the southwestern corner of Peru, is the country's second biggest city. A little over fifty miles inland from the Pacific, and 125 miles west of Lake Titicaca, Arequipa lies, at 7,000 feet, well into the foothills of the Andes. It is on the remarkable railway connecting Cuzco and Puno on Lake Titicaca. Although the land between the Pacific and the northwestern shores of Lake Titicaca rises to a height of nearly 12,000 feet, it still forms a sort of valley through the Andes.

We had little time to explore the ancient town. Humberto pulled in to the kerb in a narrow backstreet that was flanked by tall, old buildings on either side. He gave Anna the big straw hat he kept locked away in the trunk, and refunded us ten of the original twenty-seven pounds we had paid for the journey from Lima to Cailloma. We unloaded all our baggage into a small *colectivo* agency office, and suddenly Humberto and his car were gone.

"No, there is no *colectivo* service to Cailloma. Nobody goes there; I'm not even sure where it is," said the clerk behind the desk, poring over a rather tatty map.

"The mining company's office will be closed for the week-end," said Nick. "How much would it cost us to hire a car from you to go up to Cailloma tonight?" he asked the clerk in Spanish.

"I shall have to make enquiries. Can you come back here to this office in one hour—at six o'clock?" the clerk replied.

"O.K. We have got some shopping to do anyway," said Nick.

We left our gear behind the office counter and took the chance to look around the market, which is the focal point of trade for many miles around. The countryside provided the market with a variety of different goods. Nick bought himself a fine alpaca wool poncho to keep himself warm when we neared the source. A poncho is really a coarse woollen blanket with a hole cut in the middle for the wearer's head; it hangs down around the knees and looks quite mysterious until you realise that everyone else is wearing one, too.

Most Peruvian towns have a covered market built of stone or concrete; it is usually a large hall with rows of stalls, areas for the sale of different goods. Once familiar with a particular market, it is possible to make directly for the stall you want, for meat, fish, vegetables, fruit, clothing, or one of the many other items available.

The food is quite inexpensive by British standards, but various devaluations have closed the gap in recent years; most financial reckonings can be made in dollars if the Peruvian *sol* is not used. However, it is easy enough to make mental comparisons in price, with the pound sterling standing at about a hundred *soles*, at the present exchange rates.

The first thing about the Indians that strikes the visitor to the Andes is how short and weather-beaten they all look. They are small, broad people with a distinctly oriental look, which would seem to support the theory that they originated in Asia and made their way across the Bering Strait, then down through North America and into South America. The women either looked old or like young girls; there were few very old people at all. Peasant women at the market stalls wore voluminous skirts and gaily coloured ponchos in which they may have wrapped their produce, in which case, they brought it to the market slung across their shoulders. Almost inevitably, the women wore bright white "stovepipe" straw hats with high crowns and comparatively narrow brims, around which they usually tied a colourful ribbon.

There were always many young girls chatting happily to each other in the meat section of the market. Although the meat smelled fresh enough, the odour was nevertheless nearly overpowering; every last part of the cow, sheep, goat, or whatever animal, was carefully cut up and displayed for sale, and there was always an array of mangled heads gazing sightlessly from the slabs.

The market was closing as we went around in Arequipa. Just outside under the wall of the market itself, I found a crowd of people of all ages gathered around an astute-looking young man, who seemed to be selling strips of dark brown bark in lengths of approximately a foot. Since I was nearly late, I could only pause and watch for a few seconds. The strange thing about the bark was that when the man cut it with his knife it oozed a substance exactly like blood; I never did find out what this was or why such a large crowd was gathered around the man.

Having lost the others while trying unsuccessfully to buy a straw hat for protection from the fierce sun at high altitude, I was glad to find them all reassembled in the office when I arrived. "He wants thirty-five pounds!" shouted Mac. "He's trying to take us for a ride! I'll show him! Just let me look around for half an hour. Come on, Anna." Anna dutifully followed, also enraged by the cost. The argument concerned the new driver and car.

Nick and I were not too sure of ourselves and started the usual Peruvian haggling process to no avail. "He says it will be a hell of a journey and the car is bound to be damaged by hitting rocks underneath when it gets in among the potholes," Nick said. "Cars never go up there; it's usually only trucks or jeeps, and often even they can't get through. I reckon if we want to go, we should take it at thirty-five pounds—it would be cheap in England." Nick felt the same as I did, but we had reckoned without Mac's power to ferret out a good price.

While we were counting out the notes, Mac came running back up the street.

"There's a fellow down there who says he'll do it for eighteen pounds. It'll take seven hours to cover the hundred and fifty miles, which may seem slow, but he has to go over fifteen thousand feet, then down to Cailloma at fourteen thousand a hundred and fifty feet."

"Look Mac, we've just paid this fellow in advance," I said. "But still, we'll come down and see if your man will really do it for eighteen pounds."

Sure enough, we found the man only two hundred yards further down the street, in a dark and all-but-empty bar; he didn't look as if he had been drinking and he agreed that if we went on Monday, he would be pleased to take us in his American limousine for eighteen pounds. However, if we wished to go now, on a Friday night, the price would be higher—twenty-five pounds for the added hazards of night driving.

The five of us discussed the situation over a couple of bottles of beer. If we stayed in Arequipa, there would be the extra cost of a cheap hotel. We all wanted to get on, and the difference in price seemed small enough, compared to the air fare from London to Lima. We all agreed that twenty-five pounds was really more than reasonable and sent the man off to fetch his car while the beer was finished. The car, such as it was, turned out to be a really ancient Buick, and I quietly wondered if it would make the journey at all. Looking at the map of Peru, the dotted lines representing the road we were to take, I noticed, had more squiggles than any other road in the whole of Peru. The driver there and then agreed to do the job for twenty-five pounds, but he declined to come up to the office to collect our gear, saying there would be ill feeling if he appeared to steal the agency's custom. "I'll wait here by the crossroads," he said. "You bring your baggage down; it's only a few metres."

Our change of plan went down like a lead balloon at the *colectivo* agency, the *gringos* in their strange clothes and ridiculous hats must surely be *norteamericanos*, and with all those cameras, they would also be very rich. With petrol at a shilling sixpence a gallon and low wages for the driver, the thirty-five pounds was quite a good deal.

"I'm afraid we must keep five per cent of the thirty-five pounds you paid us . . . to cover our overhead in this matter." The clerk was not friendly. We just shrugged our annoyance and lumbered down the street with all our baggage. The car was empty.

"Come on, let's load up anyway," said Anna, struggling to rid herself of the heavy rucksack, and we all followed suit. The driver returned, a thin smile playing on his crafty face. "I've just been to see a friend. The price is now thirty-five pounds. You have so much baggage. My springs . . ."

"You crook!" Mac exploded. Nick and I grimaced at each other, but it's easy to be wise after the event; we had lost the five per cent and still had to pay thirty-five pounds. We were all tired from the cramped night and day with Humberto.

The driver was henceforward called "Fony." He continued to be friendly, even wheedling. I felt a tremendous flash of hatred for Fony and my hands itched to get around his throat.

First, we had to go to a garage, fill up with petrol, and get two spare drums filled as well (there were no more pumps along the way to Cailloma). We paid for all this. Then Fony demanded to have his dinner before setting out on the journey. Tempers were becoming frayed on all sides, but Fony had his way and we were dropped off at a chicken restaurant to have a meal ourselves; he would come and pick us up at nine o'clock. Mac refused to be separated from his kit and sat in the car outside while we ate. Fony had to walk home for dinner.

The restaurant was new—opened that week, the waiter claimed—but the fried chicken was old, very old. Picking at greasy wings and chips with slippery fingers in mock-romantic candlelight, we had the whole place to ourselves.

"We could just pay him the balance up to twenty-five pounds when we get to Cailloma; that was the price we agreed on." I was determined to get even with Fony. The discussion went on at such length that when John Cowrie relieved Mac in the car, Mac came in and started a whole new thing about his cold meal. We were all in need of a good nights sleep, and, foolishly, I thought the warm car would be just fine. I really had no idea what we were in for; none of us had, not even Mac, who had been quoting whole chunks on altitude from A

Traveller's Guide to Health over the Ashenhov breakfast table
back in Lima. Anna wanted a bath; John Cowrie was in the
middle of a cold and felt miserable; Nick wanted to get on and
kept mentioning newspaper deadlines; Mac was well up to his
forty-a-day cigarette mark, and I just wanted some sleep. Nobody was thinking about altitude.

"Are you ready?" Fony beamed as he came into the room.
We paid the bill and "the last supper" was over.

It was just after nine o'clock as the battered car rattled out
of the old town. Ahead the snowcapped mountains stood peace-
fully in the calm, moonlit night. Seven hours, I thought.
That'll mean about four in the morning—plenty of time to get
my head down.

Nobody wanted to talk, and I thought a bit about what it
was we were trying to do in this first phase of the adventure.
We were going to the source of the river that is furthest from
the mouth of the vast complex of waterways that make up the
Amazon River. I remembered sitting, as a small boy of eleven,
with ink-stained fingers behind a scarred, old wooden desk at
Windsor House Preparatory School, just across the road from
the Granada Cinema in Slough. Mr. Macarthur, the geography
teacher, had told us tales of mystery about Colonel Fawcett,
the Incas, El Dorado (the golden city), deadly blowpipes, and
the huge anacondas in the jungle. "The Amazon is the
mightiest river in the world," he had said, pointing with a cut-
down billiard cue at a large map of South America. "It starts
somewhere up here, in the eternal snows of the Andes, nearly
three miles up in the sky." But the tip of the cue rested in the
purple-and-white strip of the Andes, at Lake Lamicocha, the
source of another tributary of the Amazon—the river Marañón,
in the north central part of Peru.

With so many things to remember, my brain just stored
away a mental picture of a cold, blue lake, surrounded by snow
and called Lake Lamicocha. Now, twenty-one years later, I
knew Lake Villafro was more than three hundred fifty miles
further than Lake Lamicocha from the Atlantic by way of the
Apurímac, Ene, Tambo, Ucayali, and Amazon. This car would
drive us to within a stone's throw of Lake Villafro—there was
nothing to it. Just before I must have fallen asleep, in the back

seat this time, I remember the start of the climb: yellow head-lights picking out the boulders and steep rocky banks at each hairpin bend, as we bounced along the deeply rutted and pot-holed dirt road.

Next thing I knew, the car had stopped, and the front pas-senger door was open; the luminous hands on my new Smith's watch said twelve-fifteen. Outside Anna was being sick.

"I *said* that bloody chicken was bad," I muttered, groping for the door handle. "I've got a splitting headache myself. Fony's exhaust must have cracked on the bad road—it'll be the fumes making us ill, as well."

"It'll be the altitude. Anna's altimeter is reading just under fifteen thousand feet," Mac said quietly in the darkness, as I got out of the car.

Outside, everything was dusted with snow and ghostly. The moon still lit up the mountain, though now from behind a layer of thin, woolly cloud. The peaks didn't seem to be very much higher than the road, and the landscape was eerie, with stark rocks and grotesque, boulder-strewn slopes. It was still, and painfully cold. Even Fony was wrapped in a heavy poncho; only his bare finger tips poked through frayed, woollen gloves, and his balding head was covered by a thick, American Army-style hat with ear flaps. Anna stopped the harsh vomiting sounds and came back quietly towards the car, from behind a huge stone just a few feet back from the road. Just raggedly out of sleep, I didn't know what to say, so I just kept quiet. It seemed no place for a girl. I recalled an old military cliché about three-o'clock-in-the-morning courage, and shuddered. I was far from home. There was no warm croft in this desolate pass, and I felt a bit sick. We wouldn't be coming back in the car.

We piled back into the Buick and slammed the doors, our duvet jackets buttoned close, the hoods pulled down by draw-strings to cover our faces. No one said much as Fony bumped on across the ice-covered potholes. Through the windscreen, it was all boulders, bends, and snowdrifts.

As the hours passed, we were half-awake in the car, stopping every so often for Anna to be sick. Once we passed a big, six-wheeler truck, of the kind used instead of buses on the high

Andean plateau; they carry people, sheep, llamas, and any kind of load across the country. This truck was going the opposite way, and Fony waved it down to find out the way to Cailloma. Apparently, he had been using a kind of sixth sense in his driving and really had no idea where he was. When the cloud of dust subsided, the truck driver shouted down from his cab that we had come about two thirds of the way from Arequipa to Cailloma, and that the road was clear. Soon, we would go down about seven hundred feet and come onto the vast snow-swept pampas region, of which Cailloma is the main centre of population. On we went, on and on, the sump often scraping the roadbed between the deep wheel ruts; the occupants of the car all looked decidedly fagged.

At around half past three, we began to see a glow in the sky. "Cailloma!" said Nick. It looked as if it must be a pretty big place to light up the sky so, but we were all rather past caring. Mac and Nick didn't feel very bad, but Anna, John Cowrie, and I felt like death warmed over, with headaches and nausea. When we finally rolled into the large, empty, dusty square, the town centre, we just lay in the car until daybreak, hoping it would be several hours away.

Fony, Nick, and Mac left the car at five o'clock; Anna would not, or could not, move from her seat in the front, and John Cowrie lay huddled and groaning under his unzipped sleeping bag. I felt none too keen to do anything, at least until the locals showed some interest. All too soon, at ten past five, the other three returned, bringing with them the uniformed member of the *guardia civil*.

"Fony says he won't take us up to the silver mine, which is about ten miles out of here. What's more, he wants to be paid now, so he can get off home," Nick explained to me. "I told him we'd pay about the twenty-five pounds, and he is quite upset." I noticed that several locals had gathered around the grey figure of the policeman. They had wind-cracked faces and were clad in woollen hats and sombre ponchos.

"The policeman is bound to side with Fony; he won't want to lose face with the locals by supporting the *gringos*," I said.

"That's about it," replied Nick. "He says we've to pay the balance of the thirty-five pounds."

"How will we get to the mine if we let Fony go?" I asked him.

"Oh, there's a daily truck for the workers. It leaves at six o'clock; we can go on that."

"I've found a place where we can get fried eggs and coffee for breakfast," Mac said soothingly.

"Nick, please tell Fony we aren't leaving the car until we have transport up to the mine." My head hurt terribly, and I certainly couldn't face the idea of food or drink.

"John's cold looks a lot worse; I think we should get him bedded down in the café in his sleeping bag—something to eat and drink will help," Mac said, and he looked a bit worried about Anna as well. Nick seemed quite fit and strode around helpfully arranging our transport up to the mine.

At five-thirty, I choked down a cup of coffee, but couldn't face anything to eat. Instead, I looked around for some kind of lavatory. "Oh, they won't have anything like that up here," said Nick. "You'll just have to find a wall somewhere on the outskirts."

It wasn't far to the outskirts, just a hundred yards or so, but my heart thumped painfully, in the thin air, with the simple effort of walking. The town of Cailloma was only an empty patch of ground, about two hundred yards square, surrounded on all four sides by stone buildings—a few of them white-washed and two-storey, with tin roofs like warehouses. Around this, there was an untidy huddle of stone buildings with thatched roofs. The whole place gave a depressed, miserable impression. Just outside the main entrance to the square, I found a few small, tumbledown walls making small paddocks, in which there were clusters of the first llamas and alpacas that I had ever seen. Also, there were traces that showed I had arrived at the public lavatory.

After fruitless haggling with Fony and the *guardia civil*, we finally gave way and agreed to pay Fony the full price. Neither Anna nor John Cowrie said much at all; unshaven and unwashed for two days, we men felt grim, as did Anna. The talk now was all of *soroche*, the mountain sickness, which was certainly afflicting three of us. We transferred all our gear onto the back of an ancient Chevrolet truck belonging to Cía Mi-

nera Cailloma. It had steel scaffolding along the sides for the
passengers to hold onto, and about twenty mine workers clambered aboard, taking a couple of bicycles and a few stores with
them.

We had a last cup of coffee at the café, whilst calling to
collect John Cowrie. It was a bare, dark room with a counter,
and it was also a kind of general store. Outside, there were two
rickety wooden tables and benches on which a couple of llama
herdsmen and four old women sat draped in layers of clothing
that were covered by heavy ponchos. Every soul in Cailloma
wears a hat. Some wear woollen hats with ear flaps, others
straw hats or felt hats; very little of the body is exposed to the
sawing wind. We found a place to sit among the wicker baskets, black cooking pots, and other clutter belonging to the
women, and sipped strong, sweet coffee from chipped, white
enamel mugs that might have been made in England.

"I don't think the truck will wait much longer; it's five to six
now," Nick said, looking at his watch. We paid the bill and
trotted over to the waiting vehicle, under the curious gaze of
our fellow passengers. Mac clutched a small can of petrol that
the truck driver had kindly given him for the petrol cookers.
The truck started up and slowly rolled across the square.

"*Adiós, capitano.*" Fony, beaming, was waving a fistful of
notes. Only hours later did we realise that Anna had left a
Swiss Army knife, and I a machete, in the back of Fony's car,
and that he had made a sale.

We rumbled up the track towards the mine, and I had
plenty of opportunity to take in the scenery. Cailloma stands in
the middle of Pampa de Cailloma, a bleak, wind-swept plain of
sparse, grey-green and yellow icha grass, bordered by distant
mountains on all sides. These stand out clearly in the morning,
but, except in the June–September dry season, they are obscured in the afternoon by frequent snow, hail, or sleet storms.
Standing in the miners' truck, and hanging to a jolting rail that
was cold even through warm skiing gloves—in spite of the
bright, early morning sun—my impression was one of vast
spaces. The mountain peaks appeared to go on forever, for
there was always another one to be seen faintly, beyond any
gap between other mountains.

As we bounced along the track to the silver mine that roughly followed the course of a nearly dry river, I realised with a shock that this must be the Apurímac. We were nearly at the source of the Amazon.

"*¡Salud!*" I felt my elbow being tapped by something hard, and turned to look straight into the grinning face of a fellow passenger.

"*¡Salud!*" he repeated, and looking down, I smiled at the half-empty beer bottle he thrust towards me with his big, rough, brown hand. I took a swig from the bottle, while still looking into the bright black eyes. A real Red Indian brave, I thought to myself, for the face, which was dominated by a huge nose and gleaming, white teeth, was framed by a mass of black hair that pushed out beneath his battered, grey felt hat.

"I'm schoolteacher; I speak little English," he said deliberately.

"Pass the bottle on, and say '*salud*' to whoever you give it to," shouted Nick from the other side of the truck.

I passed it to a figure on the opposite side of the aisle, for my head felt as if it might burst, and I couldn't face a conversation. "*¡Salud!*" I said weakly to this much shorter, broadchested figure in a dirty poncho and peaked balaclava.

"*¡Salud!*" The impressive, red-brown face cracked into a smile as he took the bottle; "cracked" is the right word, because his face had deep creases across it, some of which were open wounds burnt by the wind. Low wages and a short, harsh life, the face seemed to say. After a good swig, the miner passed the bottle on around the truck. "A good way to get tuberculosis," I heard Mac muttering.

Below, as I suddenly realised, the Apurímac had dwindled into practically nothing. What if it dries up before we reach Lake Villafro? I thought to myself. Then, above us, I noticed a miner walking along what appeared to be an artificial canal cut into the mountainside, and I realised that even here in this desolate place there were "hydro schemes," as they are called in the Scottish Highlands. The silver mine and Cailloma would both be drawing electricity from water power.

By now, we had climbed another few hundred feet and were nearing the mine; herds of llamas and alpacas were being released from small, stone-walled paddocks that were blackened by their droppings. The Quechuan Indian herdsmen live in incredibly primitive, thatched stone huts, but above each one is a rough wooden cross proclaiming a sort of Roman Catholicism. The high pampa is strewn with stones, and these have been collected over the centuries to fashion in a rather haphazard way, low stone walls around huge areas of pampas. As one looks into one of these empty fields, there seems to be nothing in it but grey dust and a sprinkling of small boulders; yet, on a closer inspection, there are, perhaps yards apart, tussocks of the coarse icha grass, which is the food of the llama and the alpaca.

Suddenly rounding a bend in the dry river valley, we came into the dilapidated cluster of black corrugated iron buildings that go to make up the main part of the Huayllacho silver mine. The shafts are dug horizontally into the mountainside further up the valley, and the ore is then brought down in dumpers to be washed in the main buildings of the mine. It was six-forty-five in the morning; the air was still, and the sun, in a cloudless blue sky, warmed the bottom of the valley, as we piled out of the truck that then motored on to the living quarters a couple of miles further on at the head of the valley. We had been told by the schoolteacher that Señor Knapp didn't get up until seven, so we all flopped down by the truck on our sleeping bags for ten minutes doze in the sun.

"Come on. Let's go and see Knapp." I struggled out of sleep to find Nick shaking my shoulder, and sat up trying to look wide awake and full of enthusiasm. This was a bit of an effort, since my headache made it difficult to open my eyes to the glare, and I wanted to be sick.

"It's a quarter past seven. That looks like Knapp standing outside the house." Nick pointed to a fairly large bungalow with a low tin roof. On the gravel by the front door stood a slim, dark-haired figure clad in soft shoes, turned-up blue jeans, and a brown check lumberjack shirt under a loose, fawn windcheater; he wore glasses hornrimmed on the upper half only, and a tangerine-coloured safety helmet.

"Hi! I'm Dick Knapp, the manager around here," drawled the friendly American voice, as Nick and I came up to him. He must have wondered what was up, with me in my powder-blue duvet, Nick in his smart, new poncho, and the other three sprawled sound asleep in similar garb—among a jumble of rucksacks and grips, by the side of the track not thirty yards away from his house.

"This strange collection of people is an expedition. We actually call ourselves the British Amazon Expedition, 1970–71. I'm the leader, John Ridgway, and this is Nick Ashenhov, Editor of the *Peruvian Times*." (It sounded so impressive, and we still thought that we were going to do it.)

"Oh, I read that. Come on into the house; I'll help if I can." Nick grew at least two inches, and I knew I wouldn't have to do much talking. I hoped to hell Dick had some aspirins.

The three of us sat around a low coffee table of dark stained wood, lounging in easy chairs. There were three homemade-looking bare-element electric fires full on, spread around the floor of the long, depressingly bachelor-style sitting room; except for an end wall, brightly covered from ceiling to floor with magazine liquor ads, the decor was entirely yellow and dark muddy brown gloss paint. Cluttered with old geological magazines and chippings of rock, the room did little to alleviate the feeling of intense nausea from which I was suffering.

"*Soroche*," said Dick. "Here, take these two tablets and eat a good breakfast; it'll help a lot." The cook-boy came in with three plates piled with fried eggs, sausage, and bacon. I wondered where this kind of food came from in such a remote place, but I said nothing and made a real effort to force it down, while Dick and Nick talked on about the future of mining in Peru under the revolutionary government.

"These bastards just don't wanna work," said Dick in true "colonial" style. "They're gonna squeeze us *gringos* so hard we'll just leave their goddam country. Peruvianisation will mean the mines'll just go to hell." There was something passionate, even fanatical, about the way his eyes blazed behind the glasses; from my own fifty days sailing alone, I knew only too well how unbalanced a lonely man can become, and I wondered when Dick had last had visitors to the mine.

Forty-six years old and much younger-looking, Dick was born in California and still owned a little land there, to which he dreamed of retiring. Of Red Indian and German stock, he was, and I would think always had been, a fighter. He hit Iwo Jima on Day One with the U.S. Marine Corps and saw the Pacific War right through, before joining the California Institute of Technology to read geology; he claims to have been one of the finest students they ever had. From there, he moved to South America and had spent the past eighteen years up and down the Andes, in and out of numerous mines and deals, "fightin' wild Indians," as he put it.

"Villafro is not and never has been the source of the Amazon," cried Knapp, and I almost choked on my bit of sausage. "These maps were made up from air photographs—Villafro just looks a convenient place for it to start, from the air."

"Where is the source of the Amazon, then?" asked Nick slowly.

"Look. I've bin sick; I gotta get down to Arequipa with this bronchitis; I'm going down tomorrow morning—but we'll go and look for the real source today. We can take a pickup most of the way across country." His finger pointed across the map spread on the coffee table. "It's really the Hornillos river system, which runs into the Apurímac just below Cailloma. I reckon that the source is up here, in the Chila mountain range on the Continental Divide. I calculate it to be twenty-seven kilometres further than Lake Villafro, thirty-six if you include the artificial diversion where they have transformed the Hornillos water through the two lakes Parihuana and Huarhuarco to make a hydroelectric scheme which brings the Hornillos water back into the Apurímac above Cailloma. I've never been to the source and I'm damn sure no one else has, but I reckon I could get the pickup pretty close."

"We were thinking of taking a look at Lake Villafro, then just setting off to walk down the river until we reach the navigable part, about six or seven hundred miles away. Now, I'm afraid we just can't refuse the chance of getting to a further source than has yet been discovered," I said, feeling very weak at the whole idea of doing it there and then.

"I'll tell you this, if you set off from here, walking and camping out in the river valley, you won't get far in your condition. Some of you will die—the *soroche* will kill you." Knapp explained what Mac had been trying to tell us in Lima. Either the human body comes up the mountain slowly, pausing for acclimatisation, or it suffers from a lack of oxygen in the blood. Colonel Adam, in his book A *Traveller's Guide to Health*, recommends two days spent at 10,000 feet, then three days at 12,000 feet, then a further four days at 14,000 feet. He says the limit for permanent residence seems to be about 16,000 feet. It is recorded that of animals taken rapidly to 18,000 feet, 5 per cent become unconscious within 15 minutes.

We had come up to 15,000 feet in a day and a half.

In retrospect, I believe my thinking often became severely muddled during the rest of the time we were at high altitude. Of course, I didn't think so at the time.

Since 1965, I have tried to follow a maxim of the late Field Marshal Lord Slim: "When faced by two alternative courses of action, each of equal merit, choose the bolder course." In the situation in which I now found myself, there were two courses: either take the chance to look for the source immediately, or wait at the mine for Knapp's return. The latter might be some time, considering Knapp's ill health and often stated intention to resign his position with the company and return to America. In the meantime, we should be left without a vehicle or a guide with local knowledge of the area. It appeared to me that the best course of action was to go into "overdrive" and then to search for the source with Knapp, before he went down to Arequipa next day.

Going outside, I roused the others and told them of the need to act swiftly, before Knapp decided to leave the mine. Both John Cowrie and Mac were keen to come to look for the new source, although John looked wretched. Anna agreed to Mac's advice to spend the day in the warmth of the house. She had been sick five times and just wanted to be left alone to sleep.

Mac, Anna, and I set to to erect our two small, lightweight, yellow mountain equipment tents and pack into them all our gear; we found an ideal site on a dry, grassy bank by the little brook that is the Santiago River. It wasn't long before we attracted half a dozen inquisitive, young Quechuan Indian boys; gaily though poorly dressed, they were the children of some mining families that live in grim poverty, in primitive accommodations provided by the mining company just by the main mine buildings. Although only eight or nine years of age, these little boys already looked old, their faces creased and burnt by the wind. Each one had marks where crusted blood tried slowly to heal these wounds of nature.

Above us on either side, the mountains rose bare and steep; a herd of alpacas, black and white and silly-looking, grazed quietly on the few patches of icha grass near the brook, which is only half a dozen feet wide and ankle-deep at this point and time of year. The mountains looked awfully savage and unrelenting, stark red, brown, grey, black, and even green; the stratas of crumbling rock, mingled with strips of snow, rise up to around seventeen thousand feet. This is the area of the Continental Divide, the very ridge of the backbone of the mighty Cordillera Range, and thus also of South America. Half a dozen kilometres to the west, on our side, the streams all drained to the Pacific; they drained into the Atlantic, nearly four and a half thousand miles away to the east, and nearly three miles below.

While we prepared the camp, Nick and John Cowrie went with Dick in the pickup to see Lake Villafro; on the way, they were lucky enough to see and photograph some of the rare vicuna, nearly extinct now, owing to the depredations of the hunters who seek what is reputed to be the softest wool in the world. These fleet miniature versions of the alpaca are, by law, protected animals. Nick and John, just on the other side of a hill from the mine, found Villafro to be smaller and greyer than they had expected; it is backed only by a series of gaunt, shale-covered cliffs; these, soaring perhaps thirteen hundred feet from the level of the lake, are ribbed white with a few strips of snow in the gullies. Perhaps a mile long and two or three hundred yards wide, the lake rippled dully under the sky, already greying in preparation for the afternoon snowstorm.

There it was, the patch of water that for the last seventy years and probably many more, had been marked on atlases and maps everywhere as the source of the Amazon. In Lima, we had reassured ourselves with an official Peruvian government map that marked Lake Villafro in bold lettering as *Origen Del Rio Amazonas*. Now, by a stroke of luck, we would change all this—or would we? Who is the international arbiter,

I wondered to myself, who could order the alteration of all the different maps and atlases that mark Lake Villafro as the source of the Amazon? After all, someday perhaps, as with the Nile, a monument will mark the source of the Amazon and a road will lead to it—it would be a pity if they put it in the wrong place.

At the lake's bottom end, there is a small dam from which a pipe leads across and down to the Huayllacho silver mine. Its nine hundred feet of lead served to run a small hydroelectric plant; after that the water carries on for another few hundred yards to a beat-up old cyclone that used to be part of a fishmeal plant, but now, with the Villafro water, cleans out the tailings in Knapp's mine. By the time Villafro's hosepipe-full of water has done this, it is a dirty, washed-out grey colour, and seeps and trickles vaguely downhill to join the Santiago brook, some little distance down from where Mac, Anna, and I erected our base camp.

When they returned to the mine, Nick and John were impressed, not with Lake Villafro, but with the extraordinary flair and ease with which Dick Knapp drove the pickup. "He says it is the only relaxation he has," said John Cowrie. "Whenever he feels lonely or frustrated with the miners, he goes out and drives the pickup like crazy across the open pampas—we are going to have quite an afternoon." Poor John's face was grey with fatigue, cold, altitude sickness, and from not having shaved for two days. I was glad I couldn't see mine.

We left Anna in the house and piled into the pickup a little after noon. Nick and I sat in the cab with Dick, while Mac and John clung to the sides of the open platform on the back. In spite of a lot of engine coughing, Dick drove in a sort of frenzy, and I was thankful we were in a new vehicle. The weather looked anything but good, and flurries of fluffy snowflakes often filled the air and cut visibility to only a few yards. If the pickup got stuck or broke down, we would be in a bad position. Looking through the window in the back of the cab, I could see both Mac and John. Their faces were haggard and both had their eyes shut with exhaustion; even the wiry Mac, who had been born at six thousand feet and had spent much of his childhood in South Africa, was clearly feeling the sudden change from sea level to fifteen thousand feet. Beside me, Nick was saying less and less and admitted to a headache and nausea; this was a bad sign, because his spirit and enthusiasm had contributed much to our reaching the mine before Dick Knapp went down to Arequipa, and had that happened, we never would have learnt of the Further Source.

After a bone-shaking drive of about eight miles, along a track that was smooth when compared with the one to come, tens of miles across country, Dick stopped the pickup by the Represa dam at the northern end of Lake Huarhuarco. "This dam was built by the mine about twenty to thirty years ago," Knapp said; he wasn't sure of dates. "It is about ten miles south of here that the Hornillos River is diverted along an artificial ditch to Parihuana Lake, and then through a couple miles of tunnel to the Callamayo River and so into Lake Huarhuarco. This system provides us with about nine hundred kilowatts for the mine mill, and we'll drive on along it until we reach the Hornillos. It's pretty cold, and I reckon we could get another person in the front of the truck."

"I'll go on the back," I said, and there wasn't much argument as Nick, Mac, John Cowrie, and Dick Knapp all squeezed into the cab. With my duvet buttoned right up, I hung on as we bucketed along the faintest trace of a track until we came to the tunnel. I felt like death. Two miles of tunnel, dug by hand at fifteen thousand feet, seemed incredible. Every few hundred yards, we got off the pickup to look at the sinister open craters that act as inspection holes.

"Occasionally we dig it out, and the local kids crawl up the tunnel to get the trout left behind; they've had them up to a yard long," Dick told us.

By the time we reached Lake Parihuana I realised full well that unless I got a firm grip on myself, I wouldn't make it to the source, so I had a few stern words with myself on the question of leadership and related matters. Crouching alone in the back of the cavorting pickup as it lurched across the vast, empty pampas, I had on the huge straw sun hat Humberto had presented to Anna what now seemed an age before, crammed down on my head; and as I was muttering away to myself, the scene reminded me of "The Goon Show"—perhaps I really was a crazy general reviewing the troops standing in long imaginary lines across the pampas.

At the head of the tunnel is Lake Parihuana which, as the name implies, is a favourite place for flamingoes. On one side of the lake was a low, forbidding-looking group of isolated stone walls and small huts, some unenthusiastic people, and grim, wide-eyed little children. Distant mountains stood out clearly many leagues away, and numerous small snowstorms moved slowly across the horizon, blotting out the mountains in their course. At the squalid huddle of three or four houses near the lake, an odd alpaca skin lay, with the animal's insides dumped in a heap beside it. There was a dead flamingo; these are killed, I learned later, both for their feathers and their blood.

This may be the simple, uncluttered, back-to-nature life, but it's also simple, sullen poverty. A little girl of somewhere between two and five had a crinkled-up, dark, dirty face, which would have passed for the face of someone of forty. Looking across that cruel plain, I imagined the life ahead of her: images of her tending the scattered herds, of primitive childbirth, regularly repeated during her teens, of moaning her grief, as her fourth and fifth children are left to die because the family hadn't food to support increased numbers, and then of her own rapid aging and early death. Such is the relentless cycle, part of the effort to maintain man's grip on the fringe of his world.

Two groups of pink flamingoes of about thirty in each flight started to stalk carefully away as we approached; suddenly, they all exploded into the air together, an astonishing sight in this yellow and grey land, for flamingoes are a bright red and black when they're in the air, a marked contrast to the deep green and blue of the lake, the yellow and brown pampas, and to the snowpeaks in the distance.

Dick had never been further than this point. There was no track, but he pushed on, sideslipping up steep little slopes, skirting around numerous logs, and generally using the pickup like a light tank. The afternoon was well advanced; it was a race against time to beat the darkness: if we should get stuck at sixteen thousand feet, the night would be deadly cold. . . .

I think it was the monotony of the vibration in the back of the truck that was the worst; headache and nausea tended to dull the senses, but the vibration had to be overcome all the time; if it had not, I would be thrown either out of the vehicle or against something hard inside it.

Frequently we stopped to take bearings from the various features of the landscape to ascertain where we were. It was like some kind of nightmarish map-reading exercise; Knapp seemed to place some value on my skill with map and compass, and feeling as ill as I did, I found this most unsettling. I was carrying the map, and when the pickup jarred to a halt, Knapp would fling open his door and yell, "Let's take a look at the map," and we'd spread it across the bonnet. It was the worst kind of map-reading situation: bad weather, fatigue, and haste all conspired to cause a mistake that could prove fatal in our condition. One peak looked much like another; streams and pools seemed far from accurately placed on the map, part of the cause of which may have been that a number of pools and streams dried up at the end of the larger-than-usual dry season.

The whole situation certainly didn't lack interest. Few people had ever been this way before, and even the alpaca and llama population had thinned out to next to nothing. But lurching and spinning the pickup up and down through gullies, between axle-shattering boulders at thirty miles an hour, trying to squeeze as much distance into the fast-disappearing afternoon, made the whole venture far from dull. Everyone apart from Knapp was too far gone with altitude sickness to be particularly frightened, and Knapp himself seemed too concentrated on finessing the truck across the *altiplano* to feel scared of what he was doing.

We were now skidding along at around sixteen thousand feet. At the head of the valley, in front of us to the southwest and about eight miles distant, lay the snowcapped peaks of the Chila mountain range, eighteen thousand feet above sea level and the true furthest source of the Amazon. To our left a few hundred yards away, flowed the shallow waters of the river, so young (it seemed) that it hadn't even had time to cut a proper valley, even just a little one, but tended instead to meander all over the place.

After another hour or so of crashing across the country, we came to a place that Knapp and I identified from the map as the first main tributary of the Hornillos. We were now right up against the wall of the Chila mountain range, on the far side of which all the water drains into the Pacific. From the map, we couldn't tell which was the mainstream and which the tributary, but at the junction it was clear that the branch coming in from the west was the big one, providing a considerably greater volume of water. "I reckon that one from the south dries up in the dry season," said Knapp. "It does not look as if it could go far with that little trickle."

I suppose he could have been wrong, but certainly the stronger flow from the west, the Ancollagua as it was now called, looked far from promising. If the southern stream had been the big one, it would have been very awkward for our purposes, since we had planned to run alongside the river by keeping to the ridges. If the southern tributary had turned out to be the main one, Knapp would have had to drive the pickup across the river and navigate a bog, or we'd have had to walk something like fifteen miles at the wrong end of the day, and at a height where the pressure was quite insufficient to get enough oxygen into our unaccustomed lungs, insufficient even for just riding in the pickup, much less for a major slog up to over seventeen thousand feet.

We followed the main broad valley, with the mountain wall on the left and across the end culminating in peaks of eighteen thousand feet, and rolling, barren hills rising on the right. Across this valley meandered the river Ancollagua, glinting like steel in the hard, clear, but suffused light of the late afternoon. About five miles up the valley from the point at which the southern tributary comes in, the Ancollagua rounds a small spur, and at that point it seemed to be just a little brook. "Can you get us up to that spur, Dick?" I asked Knapp at the next map-reading halt. "It looks to be just to the west of Ccascana— those huts up there on the opposite side of the river." I felt sure that if we could get the pickup close to the spur, then we would be able to see the source by walking a short distance to a point from which we could see over or around the spur.

"The time's gettin' on, we'll sure have to move it," Knapp drawled, but the look in his eye showed he was going to drive even harder.

Rising up at the far end of the valley, there was a fine peak. Dominated by a great snow field or glacier, it stood out quite clearly above the main wall of the Cordillera. Our map was one of the 1:100,000 photogrametric series, issued in 1968 by the Peruvian *Instituto Geografico Militar*, and Nick said it was the best series ever produced in Peru, as far as he knew. From this map we concluded that the huge 17,875-foot snow-covered peak was Minaspata, and on its slopes, the true furthest source of the Amazon. It was a great sight, and we were lucky to catch it when we did because the peak was lost a few moments later behind another snowstorm.

For a time, with the excitement, we even forgot about the sledgehammers throbbing in our heads from the altitude sickness; it was now only a question of Knapp's ability to get the pickup closer to the spur. The remarkable thing about Dick's driving was the ferocity with which he approached each new obstacle, be it a hillside, a bog, or a narrow gap between boulders; once he had decided what to try, he always pinned everything on momentum, as if any obstruction could be overcome if it was hit hard and fast enough.

At one particularly difficult slide of shale, Dick thought it better for us to get out of the truck. Then, while he tried difficult angles and places along the side of the ridge, Mac and I dropped down onto the floor of the valley to investigate a rather curious "object" we had seen from above. At this point, the river Ancollagua had dwindled away to about ten or fifteen feet in width and was shallow enough in parts to jump and splash across without getting wet feet: the "object" we had seen from above lay in a huge bog several hundred yards wide and a mile or so long. It was a black and white alpaca. Mac and I were able to reach it by hopping from island to island; in the bog, only its head, neck, and the very ridge of its back were clear of the chill, black pool in which he was stuck fast.

"Just like the sheep on the Sennybridge Training Area in Wales," said Mac.

"Yes, you can usually pull them out, so I suppose we can do the same with this," I replied, and we both grabbed the animal's long woolly coat where it showed black and white above the surface. Because Knapp was showing signs of reaching the top of the ridge, we pulled with some desperation and soon had the alpaca on its side on the island with us. Its wool had that hopelessly sodden look, and the poor animal was unable to stand.

"Come on, he's done it," cried Nick from above. Sadly, we left the alpaca alone on the island and trotted, gasping for breath, around to meet the pickup as it came down the far side of the ridge. On the way over, we noticed several bleached skeletons around the margin of the bog; other animals had made the same mistake as our alpaca.

"Oh, it'll never last the night when the temperature drops," said Knapp. "You might just as well have left it where it was. If we don't hurry we'll end up the same way too."

A mile or so further on, we reached a point just opposite a ruined stone hut, on the other side of the river, marked on the map as Ccascana; it was perfectly clear to us all that if Dick pushed the pickup any further, it would roll over. "That's fine, Dick, we'll get to the spur in about half an hour if we walk from here," I said. Nick and Knapp agreed to stay with the truck and turn it around. I told them our route along the river and said that we should be back in an hour and a half; if we failed to return, then they should make the best of a night in the cab and come looking for us in the morning.

Mac, John Cowrie, and I felt very ill. But it was clear to me that we were faced with one of those rare opportunities in life that make all the grey, forgotten days seem worthwhile. Whatever happened now, we would remember it for the rest of our lives.

"There's no need for you to come, if you're feeling rough, John," I said to Cowrie.

"If you're going, so am I," he replied. From the look in his eye, I could tell there was no need for further talk.

"I'll be O.K. too," said Mac grimly.

Away we went, all three buttoned up to the eyes in our duvet jackets; although we were not carrying kit, both Mac and John Cowrie had cameras swinging awkwardly around their necks. By walking fast and trotting a little now and then—as much as the painful thumping of our hearts and throbbing heads allowed—we covered about two and a half miles in half an hour, and this

brought us around the bottom of the spur, where the river Ancollagua was only four or five feet wide; we were able to jump
across it at will. Directly in front of us, we could see the valley
floor rising in a cleft "V," straight up into the ridge. It was indeed a sight to remember—even as I was being violently sick.

We all three sat on a long, grey boulder, trying to summon
enough energy for the dash back to the pickup—three men who
barely knew each other, three men who had been in such a rush,
and who had no time to size each other up. Now, in those few
moments of calm on that cold, grey boulder, I felt we all
realised we had left behind the mechanised protection of
planes, hired cars, and pickups: we were alone in a most desolate place, with only. ourselves to depend on. Perhaps we
looked at one another for the first time. From here there were
about four and a half thousand miles to go, and for us, and
Anna who we would soon be joining, the world had suddenly
shrunk. We certainly were not sure of each other.

On the two-and-a-half-mile walk back to the truck, I was not
at all surprised when the pace quickened. There was an unusual
dream-like quality about this walk. A sharp, knocking pain in
my heart and my gasping breath pushed into the background
the dull drumbeat in my head, while my knees felt weak and
my straining legs quivered with the effort to force my body forward. There was nothing new in this situation. It had happened on countless occasions since my school days; we were not
just trying to beat the gathering darkness but were out to beat
each other, to establish a sort of physical pecking order that
we could fall back on whenever the going got hard in the coming months. To my way of thinking, this is natural human
competitiveness, but it does nothing to help the building of a
team. The Army exhorts a young officer to perform every skill
better than his soldiers. Personally, I had been unable to do
this. Particularly in the field of weapon training, I had failed
lamentably to develop both the memory and dexterity necessary to strip and assemble the various smallarms as fast as even
the least resolute members of my platoon; and yet there were
times when I felt I had a pretty good team going.

Now here, racing across the windswept pampas, although
keen enough in spirit and physique to crush the other two, I

was certain that the best course of action was to slow down and walk steadily towards the two figures waiting on the bare ridge above. No pecking order was established.

"Let's go. You've been an hour and a half; it's almost dark," cried Dick as we clambered up to the top of the ridge, our hoods down to keep cool. "I reckon I'll have to cut across country instead of following the river; that's the only chance of reaching the track before dark," he added.

A snowstorm had again blotted out the mountains and half the valley; I knew only too well the risks of cutting across country, and so navigating up and down gullies and along curving ridges by "instinct." We stood a good, or should I say bad, chance of getting lost miles from nowhere.

We piled into the truck, and again I found myself alone in the back. The weather worsened perceptibly for a while, then cleared again as Knapp raced up and down, in and out, and even sometimes around and around in a frantic effort to cut the corner formed by the river, and so reach the track before darkness or before a snowstorm caused us irrevocably to lose our bearings.

Sitting, standing, and sometimes hanging on the platform of the truck, I had my back wedged against the rear of the driver's cab, and I tried to sit on Nick's new poncho, which covered a collection of fuel drums lashed down against the cab. The stops became less frequent as it grew darker, and twice the front axle crunched sickeningly into solid rock. For the first time, I began to feel the numbing cold in spite of the skiing gloves and warm clothing, but there seemed to be no way of warming myself. In this kind of situation, I have always found the best thing is simply to withdraw into my inmost self and wait for some sign of improvement in conditions.

Finally, it got completely dark, and still we had not reached the track; Dick never stopped now, but just kept on going in the direction he thought the track must lie. With nightfall, the temperature also lowered, and this, combined with the wind chill effect of the moving truck, made it pretty grim on the back. When eventually the pickup did emerge onto the track, it was at a point much nearer Lake Huarhuarco than Lake Parihuana. Then Dick was able to make much better speed, and this made it even colder on the back. The wheel ruts on the track were often filled with water covered by a thin layer of ice that crackled as Dick tore on through the night.

It was a quarter past seven when the truck finally stopped outside the low bungalow at the mine. The journey back had taken an hour and three quarters. Stiff with cold, I could barely lift myself over the edge of the pickup.

We had taken the chance and achieved the aim. Now we had to pay the price.

5

Remember Huayllacho

"John's looking pretty sick. I think we should ask Dick if the mine doctor will come over and see him now," said Mac, looking worried, as we sat around the electric fires in the sitting room. Dick had very kindly offered us the use of his house while we stayed at the mine and he was showing Anna where she could have a bedroom to herself—she had been sick nearly a dozen times in twenty-four hours and she now complained of vomiting blood. When he came back into the sitting room, Dick agreed immediately and sent the cook-boy off to find the doctor. Although Mac and I felt desperately tired, Dick was keen to play his guitar and talk. I looked around for Nick, who had been saying less and less for the past three or four hours; like John Cowrie and Anna, he had also retired to bed.

Dick produced a half bottle of whisky. I just couldn't bring myself to touch a drop, so we just sat and talked while we waited for the doctor to arrive. I'm afraid we were poor company for Dick; after his long spell on his own, he must have found us surprisingly dull to talk to. Yet it was all we could manage just to keep our eyes open, and we were mightily relieved when the doctor did eventually come. Mac went off to Cowrie's room with the doctor while Dick and I started on a fine sort of Peruvian hotpot that the cook-boy had kept in the oven while he was out looking for the doctor. Although I made a big effort, I didn't get very far with the meal.

"Well, I'm glad we called the doctor. He says John Cowrie has bronchial pneumonia," said Mac, as he came back into the sitting room with the friendly, young Peruvian doctor (who didn't look too worried in spite of the diagnosis).

"Bronchial complaints are common up here. The surest remedy is to go down a few thousand feet—a few days in Arequipa and he'd be right as rain," said the doctor. It was now late on Saturday evening, and clearly the doctor wished to be elsewhere. He soon wished us goodnight and left saying he would return next afternoon to see how Cowrie was responding to treatment; within half an hour we were all in bed.

In spite of the previous two nights in cars and the business of finding the source, I still found it difficult to sleep, owing to the splitting headache and nausea from the *soroche*. At five in the morning I switched on the light in the bedroom I was sharing with Mac, who was out to the world in his dark green Army sleeping bag. For me sleep was impossible, but being consciously awake was little fun, so I switched out the light and dozed fitfully until seven o'clock.

On Sunday, 11 October, we all got up—all except John Cowrie, who looked and felt dreadful in the darkened little bedroom that he had all to himself. He was on a course of penicillin injections, tetracycline capsules, and various other pills. Nick Ashenhov and Dick Knapp were both leaving for Arequipa at midday and they were both ill, Nick with *soroche* and Dick with bronchial troubles. However, Nick had agreed to take my account of the trip thus far to Arequipa, for the *People,* and also some movie film for ITN. Anna, Mac, and I all worked on this in the morning, and although Anna was sick again, I felt not especially bad and managed to eat my lunch all right when Nick and Dick had left, the latter saying he would return on the following day to help us with our plan for a forward move down the Apurímac valley.

The best thing about the house we were in was undoubtedly the Quechuan Indian cook-boy. He always greeted us with a smile, and none of our increasingly peculiar dietary habits ever caused him to complain in any way. The house itself, a long, low L-shaped bungalow made of stone, with a tin roof, was probably built in the early part of this century. It is quite likely that no woman ever had a hand in its decoration, and the resultant depressing yellow and brown theme gave it the atmosphere of a musty, provincial boarding house. This was particularly so in the dining room, with its varnished glass case for china, forty-kilowatt lighting, square table with plastic tablecloth, and glass salt, pepper, and mustard pots with plastic tops —all this surrounded by severe, straight-backed wooden chairs. While this was certainly not conducive to our rapid recovery from the depressing effects of the *soroche*, nevertheless it was far better than our tents.

We spent the rest of the day simply sitting around forlornly, hoping the *soroche* would go away as we became acclimatised. Needless to say, we felt sure we *would* become acclimatised. All we had to do was to keep quiet, warm, and well fed; then after a few days the headaches would go away. This is a perfectly reasonable line of thought, and in any case Dick Knapp would be back next day with transport. That Sunday night passed reasonably well for me, but not so well for Anna, whose aching head prevented her from sleeping for a large part of the night.

Next day, John stayed in bed in his darkened room, although he looked and felt much better. Everyone else got up and puttered around the house; we each thought how groggy the other two looked. No matter how hard we tried, neither Anna nor I could eat our breakfasts. Porridge and fried food at that time encouraged a feeling of acute nausea, which came on the moment we entered the dingy dining room; at lunch we tried again, and this time I stared grimly at the soup for a while, but then had to make a dash for the bathroom to be sick. Anna decided her condition would improve if she got on with something constructive instead of mooning around, waiting for Knapp to return from Arequipa. She persuaded the foreman engineer of the mine to lend her a truck and driver for the afternoon to take Mac and herself out to photograph the pink flamingoes on the foreshore of Lake Huarhuarco. I stayed in the house, desperately hoping Knapp would show up.

It was around that time that Mac showed definite signs of getting better. Although still suffering from severe shortness of breath when he tried to walk up the side of the valley, he had no further trouble with either headache or nausea. Mac was, of course, analytically interested in finding a reason for his recovery and thought that several factors might have influenced this improvement: a light, wiry figure combined with an abnormally large lung capacity developed during his swimming days, and the fact that he was born and spent his childhood, as I have said, at six thousand feet in South Africa. Finally, he perhaps felt that heavy smoking had accustomed his lungs to rather less oxygen than would otherwise be the case at sea level, and as he had for reasons of supply been forced to cut back on smoking at Huayllacho mine, this might have compensated a little for the reduction of the oxygen content in the air.

My own belief was that Mac's rapid recovery was caused more by psychological than physical factors. Chay Blyth and I had noticed, while we were rowing across the Atlantic, that whenever one of us was depressed, the other welcomed the opportunity to comfort him and set an example of good spirits and optimism. Now, with Mac finding himself rather less affected by the *soroche* than either Anna, John Cowrie, or myself, his concentration was not on thoughts of himself but on his task, as medic, of speeding the recovery of the others, and by thus forgetting himself he accelerated his own recovery. Whatever the cause of Mac's better health, we none of us lacked the time to consider and discuss at length the causes and effects of the *soroche*.

Anna and Mac returned from the lake in time for supper; Knapp did not. Once again, Anna and I looked at the food but couldn't eat it, though John Cowrie got dressed, came to the meal, and started to eat like a horse. If only Anna and I could have forced down—and kept down—some food, I feel sure it would have helped us. We were both suffering from vomiting and diarrhea, however, and this had its consequences: not only did we lose the benefit of the paracetamol tablets Mac gave us to ease the headache, but without food we began to feel weaker, while the headache lessened not one jot.

That third night in the bungalow passed only very slowly indeed. No longer physically tired, I found it nearly impossible to sleep; my headache was like some sort of clamp on my skull, and no matter which way I turned, whether lying down or sitting up in my sleeping bag, the pain was never relieved for long.

In the morning, Mac became interested in the symptoms of

cyanosis displayed in Anna and myself. Across the breakfast table, I could certainly see in Anna what Mac was describing as the result of oxygen starvation, for her skin had taken on an almost translucent look, and her fingernails and lips had become blue. The last time I had seen this was in Aldershot, six years before. One night, when I was orderly officer of the 3rd Battalion, the guard commander telephoned to say that one of the prisoners in the guardroom had been found hanging by a lanyard from the bars of his cell. On my arrival a few minutes later, I found the unfortunate soldier stretched out on the floor. He had succeeded only in strangling himself, since he had swung off a chair instead of having fallen in a sharp enough way to break his neck. The result was a starvation of oxygen in the brain, which showed in the pronounced bluing of his lips and fingernails.

I felt rather uneasy when I realised Anna and I were both looking blue. Mac suggested that when the doctor called to see John Cowrie, who was now much recovered, we should ask him whether Anna and I could have some oxygen from the small hospital supply; that would give us temporary relief from our headaches. The doctor kindly agreed, and we all bundled into a battered truck and went bouncing up to the head of the valley, where the main living quarters for those who worked in the mine is situated.

The rough track ran in a steady incline, right up the right-hand side of the valley for a couple of miles, until it all but reached the wall of stark, bare, red rock, which caused the track to wind this way and that in its effort to pass on to the shafts beyond. A side track to the left brought us down into the small mining settlement, a bleak collection of whitewashed stone huts nestled at the source of the little hook known as the Santiago River. Directly above, where the side track had left the main track, there was a gaping cave, the mouth of the uppermost shaft in the valley. The two main buildings were the hospital and the school, and at ten o'clock in the morning we found the settlement deserted save for the numerous children and the women, many of whom had babies at their breasts as they went about the household chores of sweeping, cleaning, and fetching water from the stream. In spite of the obvious poverty and extreme hardship of life at this outer limit of human settlement, the women still managed to wear brightly coloured and voluminous clothing; some of them sat out in the open air, working away at primitive weaving machines on which they made thick, heavy, multicoloured ponchos from the dyed wool of the llamas and alpacas grazing on the few tussocks of coarse icha grass by the streams and on the lower slopes of the narrow valley. Above the distant peaks, the sky was etched blue in the crystal air; occasionally, huge eagles slid back across the lonely precipices; patches of fresh snow melted in the strong sun around the huts on the valley floor.

The hospital was severe. We sat on scrubbed wooden benches, sharing the bare room with its whitewashed walls and cold stone floor with other patients of the day. Every so often, the cold became so intense inside that I would walk outside to let the sun warm me. The glare hurt my eyes, however, and it wouldn't be long before my head would feel about to explode, so that I would return to the waiting room to pace up and down in an attempt to ease my aching head. In such a predicament, it is hard to study the exact behaviour of others. Yet as far as I could tell, Anna sat in a coma, with her eyes shut and saying nothing, while Mac and John Cowrie discussed the reasons for the unusual appearance of our fellow patients.

There were only four main rooms in the hospital. On one side of the waiting room, there was an open door leading into another room for dentistry—the old-fashioned chair and drill gave it the impression of a Nazi torture chamber. In the far corner, opposite the dental room, a closed door led off to what I thought was a small ward for in-patients, while another open door, also opposite the dental room, but on the front side of the building, led into the consulting, and probably operating, room. There was the usual collection of medical paraphernalia: eyesight charts, scales, height rulers, and wall charts of skeletons; an additional piece of furniture was a six-foot table painted clinical white—but rather spoiled by the dark brown trickles of dried blood on its legs.

Before us in the queue for the doctor's attentions, there was an old-looking young Quechuan mother who cried softly as she hugged a seemingly lifeless baby in her arms. The doctor explained that the child, the girl's sixth, had pneumonia and that everyone expected it to die because her husband simply could not afford to feed a large family.

An Indian miner of indeterminate age arrived with a badly gashed left hand; it was rapidly stitched, as the impassive, ruddy-faced patient looked on without comment. Mac persuaded the doctor to ask the unfortunate miner to measure his lung capacity by blowing into a measuring machine. The man had a typical Quechuan miner's figure—short and stockily built, with a reddish complexion indicating, the doctor said, a high iron content in the body. We expected a high measurement from the powerful Indian's barrel chest yet both Mac and John Cowrie comfortably exceeded his lung capacity; sadly, this experiment to prove the spurious superiority of the Aryan race was somewhat impaired when Anna and I had a go: we barely had enough lung capacity to make the machine work at all.

Anna and I had little time for such experiments, for we both wanted to get on with the business of the day, which was the temporary banishment of our headaches by taking a few good whiffs of oxygen. But we were appalled to learn that the cylinders were empty and that the nearest oxygen was down at Arequipa. "Your headaches and nausea will not get better," said the young doctor emphatically. "For you there is only one cure—go down to Arequipa for a week!"

Anna said nothing, and I didn't want to talk about it, either. The doctor gave us some milk of magnesia for the nausea and injected me with penicillin, to halt the advancing tonsillitis that threatened to make my life even more uncomfortable. Then we all got into the truck, which took us down to the bungalow for lunch. I took one look at the fine meal and dashed off to give up the benefit of the milk of magnesia.

Mac and John went off to photograph the mine in the afternoon, while Anna stayed in the sitting room, writing letters and reading magazines—in an effort to save up sleep for the coming night. I retired to bed and began to worry about dying: the headache was not improving, we were steadily weakening, and by now I knew very well that people died of the *soroche*. I considered the stupidity of sitting and waiting for Knapp, until pneumonia or some other complication set in and polished us off. No telephone to the outside world; a hospital hundreds of miles distant—to reach which, we would have to make a seven-hour truck journey that climbed higher still before starting to descend. It would be just the sort of stupid fatality that one read of every day in the newspapers.

Knapp did not return to the mine.

I spent the fourth night in misery—sitting up, lying down, being sick kneeling over the toilet bowl, and just holding my head. Anna fared no better.

On the fifth day, Wednesday, 14 October, the ground outside was white with snow as first light came. We didn't know what to do with ourselves. In the dining room, we sat facing out from the table so that we wouldn't see the food, or we'd ask the poor cook-boy to prepare dishes we thought we could eat, such as boiled potatoes or a small dish of tinned fruit salad. In the sitting room, Mac would spend long hours patiently recounting the detailed history of the Zulus in an effort to prevent us from going to bed, which could only lead to an even more sleepless night to come. Anna and I agreed that whether Knapp came back or not, we must go down to a place on a lower altitude on the morrow. Mac set off to make enquiries and returned within the hour with the foreman of the mine. "There is a truck going down to Yauri in the morning; another truck from here connects with it near Cailloma at nine o'clock in the morning," the foreman told us.

Knapp still did not return to the mine.

The fifth night was spent like the fourth. At one point, Anna feared she was getting pneumonia and panicked when she felt unable to breathe. Hearing a movement outside her room, she called for Mac to ask for help; it was in fact John Cowrie, who unhappily went back to bed, thinking Anna was just having a nightmare. It was like some dreadful plot in a novel: Anna choking for breath in the darkness of her lonely room, her call for help unanswered, and imagining herself collapsing and dying. Fortunately, it didn't come to this; she started to breathe normally and got through the night in much the same state as myself.

Next morning, we tidied the house and left a letter for Dick, thanking him for his hospitality and telling him of our plan to go down to Yauri. At eight o'clock, we heaved all our belongings onto a battered truck that came to the front door to take us down to the connection with the Yauri truck. Anna and I sat miserably in the cab with the driver, while John Cowrie and Mac stood in the back with a couple of miners who wanted a lift for part of the way down the valley. The sunlight was already melting the thin snow on the ground as we set off. We would always remember Huayllacho!

The jolting truck followed the same course down the track to Cailloma that we had come up only six days previously—parallel with the grey, dirty trickle of the mingled Villafro and Santiago. When the truck debouched onto the grey-green Pampa de Cailloma, however, the driver headed more to the south and then east, crossing the tiny Apurímac and keeping to the left, as he sped along a great, flat area of pampa.

We passed lonely Quechua Indian women who were sitting on the ground, spinning loose clumps of llama wool with primitive hand-operated spinning wheels, which they set in motion with dextrous flicks of the fingers. These women sometimes had babies on their backs and young children playing about them, as they kept a careful eye on the grazing herds of llama and alpaca.

The track was by now a sort of highway, perhaps a hundred feet wide, and the driver could choose any one of a dozen tracks, all running in the same direction. Occasionally we passed an isolated stone hut with a wooden cross on the roof and a huge field marked off by a stone wall, but often these holdings were in ruins, as if they had been deserted long ago.

Eventually, after driving east for about ten miles, the truck driver stopped at a junction in the tracks. He called the place something like "Angostura"; it was where the track running east–west meets the track running north–south. Anna and I didn't greatly care; we just crawled out of the cab and lay down on our backs in the sun, with our heads resting on our packs and our hats tipped forward over our eyes to keep the sun off our faces. There was another truck standing empty and deserted at the junction, so we were not too worried when our original driver turned his truck and headed off back towards the mine.

It was good to be out in the sun; there was no wind, and in the distance we could see a sort of mill-cut running back into the Apurímac River to our front. Two impressive Quechuan women appeared from nowhere with a little boy of about four, who dropped his trousers and proceeded to turn our sunny enclave into a public lavatory. As the mother buttoned up the shoulder straps of the boy's trousers, I noticed she wore a bright, white stovepipe straw hat with a broad, red ribbon around the base of its crown; her black skirt and white blouse were covered by a heavy, black-and-red-checkered poncho, and on her feet she wore plain black shoes that were in the last stages of dilapidation. The woman's face was proud and hawk-nosed, and her expression, sufficiently cruel for me to thank goodness I hadn't had her for a schoolmarm. The other woman was dressed and looked much the same, except that her hat ribbon was green and her poncho a rather duller red and brown; she looked as if she might well have been the aunt of the little boy with the diarrhea. He himself wore the simplest rags and ran barefoot; his scabby face and feet bore witness to how tough a child had to be to survive in the hard world of the *altiplano*.

At a quarter past nine, the driver appeared, a tough Quechuan with a ragged poncho and a woollen hat, with flaps to keep his ears warm. Thrusting his poncho back over his shoulders, he set about loading our gear onto the back of the truck in a purposeful manner, and we followed suit; clearly, we would soon be off. This truck was far and away in the worst condition of any we had seen; it appeared to be a sort of privately owned, all-purpose bus or taxi, an ancient Chevrolet with a crude wooden cattletruck sort of frame in back and a separate wooden luggage rack on top of the cab. The walls of the tyres had big chunks torn out of them, their treads nonexistent, which was probably caused by driving hard across the boulder-strewn open country. The cab was decorated with a frilly curtain along the top of the windscreen, and a little toy dog made of llama wool bobbed and danced from the rear-view mirror. Anna and I sat in front again, wrapped up in our duvet jackets; once we were in, the driver walked around the front of the truck and tied the door shut from the outside with an old piece of twine; then he walked back around the front and jumped into the driver's seat. At the third or fourth attempt, the engine started, and we rolled off across the plains.

At the beginning, Anna and I felt only half conscious, but we made a big effort to take in the passing scenery. We crossed the Apurímac at a shallow ford and set off in the general direction of Yauri, which was further down the Apurímac valley. We had not gone far, however, when the driver stopped to pick up a couple of women wearing black stovepipe hats, and a powerful-looking fellow, wearing only one shoe roughly made out of an old motor tyre, who had been waiting beside the track. There was now some delay because as the fellow with the one shoe pointed out, we had a slow puncture in one of the four rear tyres. This meant a great deal of hand-jacking of the offending rear end of the truck; needless to say, the jack was kept under the seat in the cab, and Anna and I, although still tied in, had to keep leaning forward to allow new pieces of the mechanism to be brought out to aid the wheel change.

At last the job was done, and the driver started the truck. But to our consternation, he did not follow the track for Yauri, but instead turned off to the right, across the rolling pampa. While we were bumping across country, I kept thinking of something I had read somewhere about camels being "ships of the desert." It seemed to describe us; as long as the driver kept off the mountains themselves, it looked as if he could take his groaning truck anywhere on the pampa. After a lifetime of following roads in vehicles, it was a peculiar sensation to be in a huge truck that meandered at will across the countryside. The driver behaved rather as if he were riding a horse, picking his route across streams and between boulders, and angling up and down the sides of ridges. "He'll get stuck; then where will we be?" asked Anna. Her face wore her resigned look, but her knuckles were white on the dashboard in front of her.

"In a pretty pickle," I replied as flippantly as I could manage, for the headache was still master of my life.

Eventually we came down to within just a few hundred yards of the Apurímac and stopped. Anna and I looked at each other in alarm. We really weren't anywhere at all. "Look at that herd of llamas! The woman is getting the dog to drive them over here. I do believe John and Mac are going to have company in

the back," Anna laughed. At least her headache must be a little
better, I thought.

The driver got down from the cab and unstrapped a bicycle
from its place on the outside of the wooden framework near
the back of the truck. Then a little boy of about fourteen, who
might be described loosely as the driver's aide, mounted the
bike and rode off expertly through the boulders to play his part
in the roundup. More Quechuan herdspeople appeared, seem-
ing to pop up from behind boulders. They tied a rope to the
back of the truck, then held it taut, at about waist height, as if
it were a thirty-yard extension of the truck. We had our corral.
Half a dozen sorry-looking sheep were herded into the back of
the truck, and I could hear John Cowrie calling to Mac to help
him stack our kit well clear of the sheep's "evil intentions."
Meanwhile, the bicycle roundup was proceeding with a great
deal of female cursing from the tough-looking woman in charge
of the herd; the llamas had coloured strands of wool in their
ears, which act as marks of ownership and look much better
than the splashes of dye used on the sheep in northwest Scotland; but the haughty faces of the brown and white llamas
wore expressions of greatly offended dignity.

As the herd breasted the rope, everyone gathered around to
give suggestions on the selection of the beasts to be sent for
sale in Yauri. The herdswomen became even crosser, starting to
slash the air indiscriminately with switches of what looked
rather like willow. "She's chewing coca. Look at that wad in
the side of her mouth," said Anna, for even we had got down
from the cab to watch the event. True enough, there was a big
lump on the left-hand side of the raven-haired witch's face, and
her lips were flecked green with the juice from the leaves. The
lady was on a trip. When two llamas were dragged up a couple of planks onto the back of the truck, the herdswoman
started to shriek with such vigour that the men dragged them
back down again. The process of selection went on for at least
another twenty minutes before four chosen beasts were hustled
onto the back to join the six sorry-looking sheep; five women,
three men, and two boys also clambered aboard to join Mac
and John. The bicycle was strapped back in place, and the

driver, after tying us in once more, set off again across the pampa in the direction of the track.

We followed the track, which in turn followed the Apurímac valley, sometimes grinding up hairpin bends thousands of feet above the river, and at other times driving right beside the water, fording the tributaries as they came in. The track appeared to be a fairly new development, for some of the rocks near the river looked as if they had been blasted only a short time before. One thing was certain—the road would be impassable during the rainy season that was due to begin in November.

All the time, we were slowly but surely descending, and, imperceptibly at first, Anna and I began to feel better. In Anna's case, the improvement showed in her enthusiasm to take photographs; when we stopped to discharge one of the passengers, Anna had me sit in the middle of the seat so that she could use her camera through the open window. In my case, the fading of the headache allowed me to think more clearly; it was as if, by leaving the Cailloma *altiplano*, I was leaving a land of grey fog behind me.

I thought of the Quechuan Indians chewing *coca* in the back of the truck and felt I could understand why they needed a drug to get them through life. "If coca did not exist, neither would Peru"—so wrote a Spaniard in 1550. And not only Peru, but all the Andes and the Amazon basin. Today it is thought that there are five million people addicted to cocaine, the alkaloid yielded by the coca plant.

Coca (genus *Erythroxylon*) is cultivated on the slopes of the eastern Andes. It is a low, thick bush with glossy, dark green leaves that look quite like tea. These leaves are picked four times during a period of fourteen months; they are carefully spread out in the sun to dry, then shade-dried in order to keep the green of the leaf. The leaf itself contains the alkaloid methyl-benzoyl-ecgonine, which is cocaine; it was used not so long ago as a local anesthetic by dentists, I remember, but its chief medical use now is as a pain killer in the last stages of terminal cancer.

The drug, in precisely the same form as it is used today, has been found in tombs and graves reaching far back into pre-Inca times. Small woollen bags containing the leaves were found in the tombs, and with them small gourds containing lime (which was made by burning seashells or limestone). Now, as then, the method of taking the drug is to make a wad of coca leaves about the size of a Brazil nut. This is stuffed into the side of the mouth, and a pinch of lime is added to help extract the juice. When this juice is swallowed, the chewer becomes less susceptible to cold, hunger, thirst, and fatigue—the very things you don't want to be susceptible to if you live on the *altiplano*.

Precisely what coca does to the human body is no longer in doubt; plenty of medical evidence is available. There is, among those long addicted to coca-chewing, high frequency of degeneration of sensory perception, disturbances of the eyes, enlarged thyroid, and general physical breakdown—the list of the moral and physical maladies caused by this addiction is frightening. Coca may well sustain the Indian at these high altitudes, but eventually it breaks him, and he is left an addict, apathetic and stupid.

Meanwhile, during Anna's frenetic photography and my own meditations, life was proceeding in the back of the truck in the way it always had since the *gringos* brought the big Chevrolet trucks up onto the pampa. John Cowrie and Mac, standing in the back of the swaying truck, quickly made friends with their fellow passengers, in spite of a complete language block—English and Quechua are about as dissimilar as it is possible to get. Bursts of laughter echoed in the cab. But although the humans got along well enough, the animals did not. Llamas and sheep are like petrol and matches. To the disdainful, rather stiff-necked llama, the stupid sheep is something to be held in contempt, and our llamas showed their contempt by spitting and then urinating on the unfortunately much smaller sheep, whenever they ventured out from the corner in which they cowered, away from their superiors.

Wherever there was some surface soil, the land was speckled a brown-yellow by the icha grass, or *paja brava*, as it is sometimes known (literally, "wild, tough grass"). When the truck stopped, I examined the grass anew—without the headache, life was much more interesting—and saw that it grew close to the track in round clumps as much as eighteen inches high and two feet in diameter, with hearts of blue-grey, turning to brown-yellow as they neared the tips of the individual blades of thin, sharp grass. We passed through places where there was very little grass but much grey rock, often standing in smooth, twisted pinnacles and blocks, as if it had been polished into shape by some giant hand.

The river was clear again, the grey sludge from the Huaylla-cho mine long since filtered away in gravel shallows and pools. As it leapt and splashed its way down the valley, it still seemed a very young river, but old enough to be a fine trout stream, and I looked forward to pleasant hours with the glass spinning rod and threadline reel I had bought in Lima and idly boasted would help catch our breakfasts.

At one place, about two hours after leaving the llama roundup, the dusty truck stopped to pick up another passenger from a village in the river valley just below and to the left of us. Looking down, we had a fine view of a cluster of stone huts with thatched roofs and of seemingly illogically shaped fields. In the whole village, there was no indication of any kind of cultivation—just bare areas of pampa bordered by straggling stone walls that thus transformed them into "fields," and smaller walled paddocks blackened with the llama and alpaca droppings. In the centre, facing us high on the track above, was a tin-roofed, single-storey building, with two windows, two doors, and a smutty whitewashed wall. This was the school, symbol of education and the future of Peru. At the back of the building, on a patch of empty ground, stood the football field, an essential of any self-respecting Peruvian village; two poles served as goal posts at either end, and the school children played the game with an élan that could not be bettered anywhere in the world. On the walls of the schoolroom, there would certainly be a coloured photograph of at least one member of the Peruvian team. To the Peruvian poor, these men are supermen—peasants like themselves, yes, but nevertheless men who have fought their way out of poverty into stardom, "stardom" meaning anything better than bare subsistence living.

Rolling down the valley, the river gathered other tributary streams along the way, all crystal clear and tinkling out of rock. A few small green trees, rather like coarse willows, sprouted on the banks, and numerous swallows and little diving birds shared the rushing rapids and still pools with ducks. There was little sign of human life. Occasionally, we surprised a lonely herdsman gaily dressed in an intricately woven poncho and the typical cone-shaped woollen helmet with ear flaps; usually he would be moving his llamas along with a big bundle of kindling wood, collected from the riverbank, strapped to his back. Always he would wave back to the passing truck in a friendly manner. We passed a place in a tumble of rocks where grey bluffs, shaped like the pipes of a cathedral organ, fell sheer to within a few yards of the riverbank, where another tributary of almost the same size as the Apurímac came in to shape a "Y". Knapp had told us these were the ruins of an Inca settlement from which the Incas are reputed to have governed the headwaters of the Apurímac. I wanted to investigate, but as I felt far from fit enough to go scrambling about among rocks, and time was passing, I made no attempt to get the driver to stop. We pushed on down the valley, halting every now and then to negotiate a tricky passage between huge boulders, some of which seemed eroded by the floods of centuries.

After about seventy miles of winding through the cliffs beside the river, the track emerged into another huge, open plain, so large the snowcapped peaks on the furthermost side from us rose only just above the horizon. Here the river meandered so much that the truck took a straight line instead of following it, and so saved much time. Our driver increased his speed as the track broadened, until, like the stretch we had covered on the way from the mine to the junction point, it was perhaps a hundred feet in width. The only reason I could see for the increased width was that in the rainy season the area might become so muddy that each truck would tend to choose its own course. The earth on the plain became a richer brown colour, and the whole vast area seemed to have been under cultivation at one time or another. It was as if there was so much land that the oxen pulling the primitive wooden ploughs worked in a new field each year, leaving a gap of perhaps many years before a field was used again. The fields were not at their best because it was early spring and they were still drab with the barley stubble of the previous harvest. Some miles out in the plain, we stopped in a small village where the houses, although still thatched with straw, were adobes, built with heavy blocks of sun-dried mud mixed with straw, blocks that shrink a bit in drying. "Surely this isn't Yauri," said Anna. "It's too small—there's nothing here at all."

Luckily she was right; it wasn't Yauri, but a small hamlet where some of our fellow passengers wished to get off. "I'll see if I can get something to eat over there; it looks as if it might be a store," said Mac enthusiastically, as he jumped off the back of the truck, and suddenly I felt hungry for the first time in days.

A few minutes later, Mac emerged clutching four bottles of Inca-Cola and four packets of Santa Maria plain tea biscuits. I wolfed down my biscuits—and most of Anna's—but I gave the Cola to the driver, and it cheered him up a bit. As we were leaving the village, we crossed a river over a narrow wooden bridge, and I realised with a shock that it was the Apurímac; this time it ran dark and silent fifty or sixty feet below the level of the village, through a black gorge only a few feet wide.

Out on the open track again, we could see in the distance what looked to be a small town. "Yauri." The driver uttered the only word of the journey; taciturn, I suppose, would be the word to describe him.

As we neared the town, we crossed the river again, but not over a bridge on this occasion, for it had spread out across the plain in perhaps a dozen little streams, and comprised an area of water and gravel of about a quarter of a mile. The driver rammed the truck across as if there were no river at all. On the other side, the track pointed wide and straight at the squat towered church on the crest of the mound on which Yauri is built, and we began to pass groups of Indians still working in the fields, for it was still only four o'clock. They looked like family parties, each bent over its own patch of ground, breaking the surface with tools resembling mattocks.

Once in the town itself, we were among simple mud houses, some thatched and some roofed, with the terracotta sections familiar in Latin countries; a few buildings, such as the school, had shiny tin roofs. The truck drove straight up the side of a small mound, which was rather like an island in the plain, and then headed up a small side street scattering a few llamas and pigs in its path. Most of the passengers left the truck at a storehouse on this street, and all their livestock was unloaded. Anna tried her Spanish and a young Peruvian appeared, explaining that he was the schoolteacher. He said the truck would take us to a restaurant in another street, and opposite this we would find an inn where we could stay for the night. We had come only about ninety miles in the eight hours since leaving the mine at eight o'clock that morning, but even so we were all pretty tired.

"The cyanosis has gone, but I still think we should try and get down to Sicuani; it's over thirteen thousand feet here and nine thousand feet would be much better," advised Mac, while we sat waiting for our meal in the dark room that was the "restaurant" in Yauri.

"I feel a lot better, but I wouldn't mind going down a bit," Anna said absently.

John was outside in the street photographing the "typical *altiplano* town," as Yauri is often described—to anyone who has ever heard of it. The only place of any size at all in the almost empty district of Espinar, itself only one of more than a dozen districts in the vast mountain province of Cuzco, Yauri is an ancient market town. In spite of its small size—it is not even as large as a good size English village—the little town is so far distant from anyplace else that it has quite the air of a capital, and its people have a certain pride in living at the heart of things. Pigs wallowed in the open sewers in the streets, and crowds of children and chickens were as abundant here as in all the little places through which we had already passed in our journey from Lima. Shawled women in white straw hats sat on their doorsteps, looking like small tents in their great black skirts. A lot of gossiping and scolding of children seemed to go on, but all the time the women's fingers absently twirled the spinning whorls, and balls of wool grew larger and larger, while little girls of four and five copied their mothers and spun smaller whorls of the same coarse wool.

Inside the restaurant, our meals arrived at last, and John came scuttling in from outside. Huge bowls of peasant soup were made up of trout from the river, potatoes, rice, meatballs, spaghetti, onions, tomatoes, and various herbs. The soup was served with big cups of strong black coffee, and fresh bread rolls made a good ending to a long fast. I managed to eat most of my food, but Anna only picked at hers. Mac and John Cowrie soon finished theirs, and John then ordered a steak and more potatoes. He didn't say whether it was llama steak but was eating so fast he probably didn't notice. Throughout the meal, we were closely watched by a sinister group of four men who looked like rustlers and sat at a table in a dark corner of the room. I think they thought we were rich *norteamericanos*, and so they looked none too friendly. There were others in the room who didn't watch very closely, for in the main their heads lolled drunkenly on their chests. When we were halfway through our tasty meal, a horribly disfigured dwarf crawled in from the street and dragged himself across the floor and through a door that opened into a yard behind the restaurant; then, while crouching under a wall in the yard, he was given a plate of scraps, such as might be given to a dog. It was one of those scenes to be repeated again and again in South America, which made me thankful for my own lot in life.

We asked if the light might be switched on; it was dark, and the restaurant clearly had the luxury of electric light. "At five-thirty it is dark—then the light comes on," came the polite answer. The electricity plant in the town was for lighting only, and although it was almost too dark to see at five-fifteen, there could be no question of light until it was "officially" dark.

A jaunty narrow-faced man of about forty, dressed in European clothes, came into the restaurant and joined the four men in the corner. Outside in the street was parked his new Simca station wagon; it looked strangely out of place among the pigs and grubby children. On the windscreen we could see *Hoy Yauri* written in white chalk. "It means it's a *colectivo*, and he's just arrived from somewhere else; the *Hoy Yauri* is to advertise that he was coming to Yauri today," Anna told us.

"Does that mean he could take us to Sicuani tonight?" asked John Cowrie, munching his steak.

"Well, we could give it a try," Anna replied. "How much do we want to pay?"

"It can't be more than about sixty miles. About a pound a head, I reckon," I said, and everyone nodded.

Anna said a few words in Spanish and the owner of the car looked at his friends, who nodded their agreement to the price. "He'll do it. We leave at six o'clock." Anna looked triumphant.

The road to Sicuani was much better than the track from Cailloma. We all squeezed into the new car and, after a stop to fill up with petrol, started on what turned out to be a pleasant drive on a bright, starry night with a full moon. At high altitude in the clear Andean air, the stars seem nearly close enough to touch. Just outside Yauri, the broad, well-maintained red earth road crossed a large tributary flowing in from the southeast; then we climbed up onto a long ridge, keeping the Apurímac in the valley on our left.

Our plan was to continue to the northeast for about twenty miles, following the ridge above the river all the while, and then to turn sharply to the right and east, then dropping down to Sicuani in the valley of the Urubamba River on the other side of the ridge from the Apurímac. The driver of the car introduced himself as Augusto and told us he was a solicitor by profession and that his father was the mayor of Yauri. After welcoming us to his country, he asked what it was we might be doing in such a remote place. When he found we were *ingleses* and not *norteamericanos*, he became very friendly; in fact he hardly stopped talking for the remainder of the journey, much to Anna's annoyance, since she had to do all the translation. "I am sad you have suffered from the *soroche*, but you have followed the course of the river all day and seen it on the pampa. After a few days in Sicuani, you will be well again, and then you will be able to come back up here onto the ridge and follow the river down through the mountain gorges," he said.

"What about our baggage?" asked Anna. "There are no roads."

"It is true there are no roads, but the people in the villages are friendly. They will lend you mules and guides; it will be no problem," said Augusto. I thought he looked as if he hadn't walked more than a few steps in his whole life and had no idea what the remote, roadless, Apurímac mountain gorge would be like. This was confirmed when we came to a point in the road at which he had to swerve to miss some boulders, which didn't exactly look as if they had rolled onto the road by themselves.

"What are those doing in the road?" queried Anna.

"Ah, the locals put them there hoping for a wreck—then they can rob the car," replied Augusto.

"That's not my idea of 'friendly villagers,'" muttered John, from deep in his duvet.

By nine o'clock we were at the head of the steep valley that twisted down towards Sicuani; although it was night, the full moon made it easy enough to see a good part of the surrounding country. Soon we were driving past the first real trees we had seen since leaving Arequipa. Small groves of tall and elegant eucalyptuses lined the narrow road and the tumbling stream on our right. We passed through several little villages of adobe huts, and once, the bright lights of a hydroelectric plant glared up from the banks of the stream. Within the hour, we crossed the Urubamba River and the railway that runs south from Cuzco, through Sicuani to the distant northern shores of Lake Timcaca, and then southwest through Arequipa to Mollendo on the Pacific coast.

Sicuani by night seemed ablaze with multicoloured lights, after the endless blackout of the surrounding mountainous country. It appeared to me rather like a Mexican town in a Western film, with narrow mud streets and ancient overhanging buildings. Even at ten o'clock, several stores were still open, and John Cowrie dashed away to buy some coarse chocolate to last him through the night. We booked into an inn for the night—Mac, John Cowrie, and myself in one room (at five shillings each), and Anna in a room of her own (nine shillings). After saying goodbye to Augusto, we all turned in, exhausted.

6

The High Walk

Next morning I woke at six with one of those startled feelings, not knowing where I was and wondering what was wrong. I looked about the small windowless room with its high ceiling and bare whitewashed walls and saw John Cowrie sound asleep in a bed by the opposite wall. Across the way, Mac was flat on his back puffing away at the first smoke of the day. I lay back and smiled, remembering we were in Sicuani; what was "wrong" was that there was no headache—I felt fine.

"You know, if Anna is O.K. today, I think we should get right back on the Apurímac and get on with the job. Anna's trouble is that she has had a hell of a shock with this *soroche*, and she's beginning to have doubts about her ability to make the trip. If we get going straight away she won't have time to think about it." Mac had been lying there, working all this out for quite a while.

"Well, I feel O.K. The misery is in the past; nothing lasts forever. I agree the best thing is to get out and get walking," I replied.

John Cowrie and Anna stayed behind to look after the gear while Mac and I went out to look for breakfast. The sun shone from the cloudless blue sky, and again I felt it was all much better than London fog. As we made our way slowly across the small plaza, with its inevitable bronze, sword-clutching statue of a liberator, we could see that the small town of Sicuani was ringed by hills, several of them inscribed with political slogans. In the further distance, lofty peaks, some of them still capped with snow even in October, provided a grand backdrop for the busy market scene within the old town itself.

Neither Mac nor I were much good at Spanish at this stage of the expedition, and we had great difficulty trying to persuade the boy behind the counter of the empty poolroom where we went for breakfast to serve us boiled eggs. "¿Huevos, señor? Sí, no hay problema." The only words I knew in Spanish were señor and huevos. "Scrambled huevos" had been Chay Blyth's favourite Tuesday morning breakfast during the Altantic rowing project, even though ancient powdered eggs don't really compare with the fresh ones.

In the end we gave up, firmly convinced the only way eggs are ever eaten in Peru—and a lot are eaten—is fried. We sat at a small table by the wall, eating fried eggs and bread rolls, with cups of black coffee to wash them down. The boy who did the cooking by the cash register sent an even smaller boy into the poolroom to clear up the empty bottles and general debris of the previous night.

The bat-wing doors clattered open, and in strode a young policeman, smartly turned out in pale grey-green uniform, complete with pistol in a holster at his waist and sharp creased trousers tucked into calf-length black boots. It was breakfast time for the law. He also had fried eggs, bread rolls, and coffee, but with the added touch of the daily newspaper—clearly the senior boy had concluded quite rightly that the *gringos* could not read Spanish. Next door, a radio blared the peculiarly unpop sound of Peruvian music from Radio Sicuani. All around the square outside the poolroom, the pace of daily life was beginning to quicken.

On the way back to the hotel, we passed through the open market place, its ragged stalls covered by strips of faded canvas or bright blue plastic sheeting. As always, the hardy shawled women, with straggling black pigtails and toothless grins under black or fawn felt hats tipped up at the back and down at the front, squatted in the dirt of the cobbled square with their wares. One old crone in a huge cherry-coloured skirt cackled away as she tried to get Mac to buy a bag of coca leaves; another, with a baby wrapped in a poncho on her back, tried to interest us in small white sacks of eggs, rice, wheat, raisins, and strange-looking herbs. We passed a row of stalls where hot bowls of vegetable soup and juicy morsels of meat on wooden skewers were being served and eaten. At the far corner of the market, just as we were leaving, we passed the ironmonger's section, and Mac bought a couple of enamel mugs—hoping that we would have mules to carry all our kit once we got back into the mountains. Back at the inn, Anna told us she felt much better and agreed to join us after we had bought various basic foods for the coming high walk.

The day passed pleasantly enough as we searched around the town for the items of food and kit we thought we would need if the villages were not quite as friendly as Augusto had assured us. At four o'clock we clambered onto the back of another truck, this time bound for Yanaoca, at twelve thousand feet on the ridge overlooking the Apurímac. As a final gesture of joie de vivre, John Cowrie bought a litre of cheap red wine and we rattled across the cobblestones thinking the whole affair most satisfactory. The truck was empty, save for a couple of Quechuan women with a baby; they gave us a length of sugar cane to chew on in return for a few swigs of our wine. Anna was delighted with the large bars of coarse chocolate, full of grains of crude sugar, which she found most of the Sicuani stores had in stock. We also had a total of ten second-hand sacks made of a tough plastic mesh, and widely used throughout Peru for carrying salt; a couple of these sacks were full of new items, such as two flexible machetes, Tupperware-like bowls stuffed with rice, sugar, and tea, cans of tuna fish, and a few loaves of bread.

We were just a little surprised when, on the outskirts of town, the truck pulled off the road and bumped a hundred yards or so across an empty field towards a group of two or three houses. "Well, we couldn't really expect to have the truck entirely to ourselves," proclaimed Mac, expansive now with the dreadful wine.

We all climbed out to see what was in store. The valley was darkening with the coming night and the mountains were already blackened by lowering rain clouds; the end of one of the smaller valleys was completely obscured by the grey skeins of a slow-moving rainstorm. There was a smell of wood smoke in

the evening air, and Mac declared this was definitely eucalyptus
—he remembered it from South Africa. Surprisingly, we found
ourselves in the middle of a group of small kilns that were
being used for baking the terracotta sections used for roofing;
the red wood used in their construction came from the floor of
the valley itself, which looked as if it were divided into a series
of paddy fields.

An Indian worker began to load the tiles, straight out of the
kiln and still hot, neatly onto the truck. Women, children, and
old men stacked them with surprising speed, until the foreman
arrived dead drunk; then there began a long argument between
the foreman and the driver of the truck. The driver had com-
mitted the unforgivable mistake of snapping a tile across his
knee, at the outset, to show all concerned what inferior tiles
they were, and how it would not be his fault if many were broken on the journey up into the mountains. There was cursing,
gesticulating, falling over and being helped up; the work was
stopped and started a dozen times, while the foreman's wife
plied him with more crude spirits to soothe him. When one kiln
was empty, the lorry was backed up to another, to take on even
more tiles. At this point, long crocodile-lines of adolescent
boys came trooping along both sides of the road, heading in the
general direction of the town. Dressed in off-white shirts and
trousers, they all wore white paramilitary helmets. Garlanded
with eucalyptus leaves for "camouflage" and carrying Army
packs on their backs, they looked as if they were nearing the
end of the Monte March. John Cowrie ran out into the middle of the road to photograph this strange sight, as the lines of
boys straggled past him on either side of the road in the fading
light. The whole idea of being photographed in their uniforms
apparently delighted the boys, for they broke what little semblance of ranks there was and mobbed their photographer,
knocking him to the ground in their eagerness, but he recovered his poise and escaped unharmed.

Darkness came and with it heavy rain. The loading continued and the passengers were allowed back on board the truck,
which had a good strong tarpaulin roof. At length, the loading
was completed and the workers drifted away, some to their
homes and some to bank up the fires under the kilns with euca-

lyptus leaves. The hopelessly drunken foreman remained to count the total number of tiles, but this task was quite beyond him, and he was dragged from the truck. In his place, a young girl of perhaps ten or eleven years of age came aboard and with nimble fingers rapidly totted up the number by the light of a gutting candle she balanced in her left hand. Unfortunately the girl dissatisfied the driver, for he discovered that she was the daughter of the drunken foreman, and after a short delay the third count began, this time by an independent arbiter. We all heaved a sigh of relief when this was accepted.

The whole length of the flat bed in the truck was covered with warm tiles, stacked vertically; all our gear was piled on top of this. Then more Indians joined the list of passengers. The heavily laden truck had been backed right up against the second kiln during loading, and this meant that the rear wheels were high up on a mound formed of broken and discarded tiles. Since the rain had soaked the ground, there was danger of the mound's collapsing. Crouched on the hot tiles with our duvet jackets loosened, and our sleeping bags under us to act as insulation, we heard the driver clamber noisily into the cab. Gay lights made the cab look like some kind of Christmas decoration.

There was a long pause.

"You know what? The engine's not going to start!" cried Mac. Sure enough, the starter was jammed, and it became clear the only chance was to push the truck. There wasn't a hope; even though the second kiln was nearer the road than the first, we were still at least fifty yards from the harder surface.

None of us had any ideas. The driver didn't seem the least bit worried as he organised the remaining workers to push the vehicle back a few yards from the mound and onto level ground. Then he produced his jack and worked away at it until the rear side wheel was well clear of the ground. Everyone but the *gringos* appeared to know what was going on. Half a dozen men gathered around the rear of the truck and began to wrestle with the wheel while the driver sat in his cab at the controls: it seemed an ingenious way to start a truck. Once it was going, we lumbered across the spongy ground, narrowly missing a ditch with the back wheels; the road wound away into the night, back up into the mountains.

The higher we climbed the colder it became in the back of the truck, and we were glad of the warm tiles beneath us. Once more in the dark, away from the lights of the town, we fell silent, each wondering, I suspect, what lay in store for us in the Apurímac valley. For my part I was more than glad the headache kept away from Anna and me.

It was after eleven o'clock when the truck pulled to a halt in a little village square, high on the ridge. Everyone filed out, so we followed to stretch our legs a bit. The driver ushered us into a little hovel which, although badly lit by a single candle, we could see doubled as both a home and a store. We were given steaming bowls of lamb stew and chunks of bread, and black, sweet coffee was served in badly chipped enamel mugs of the same kind Mac had bought in Sicuani. The storekeeper told us we were in the village of Tungasuca, the altitude of which measured twelve thousand feet on Anna's altimeter; we also learned that Tungasuca is nearer the Apurímac than Yanauca; in any case, the truck was not going any further that night. Finally, there was no objection to our sleeping in the back of the lorry, but we would have to share it with two Indian men, two women, and a baby, all of whom were going on to Yanauca in the morning. The tiles were much hotter than we had realised.

At four-thirty in the morning, when we were waked by the driver, the first flush of dawn lit the eastern skies. We lowered ourselves drowsily from the back of the truck onto the puddled track below. There wasn't much comfort in the empty grass square, but Mac quickly had the little petrol cookers roaring in a comforting fashion in the shelter of the covered entrance to an ancient village church. We breakfasted well, on boiled eggs, porridge, and mugs of scalding tea, and the men followed this with a good wash and shave at the communal tap, which worked from a standpipe just a few yards up a lane that led back the way we had come in the truck on the previous night. After breakfasting and washing, we packed our gear into the ten salt sacks.

"Get the stuff all ready and packed up for loading on the mules," Mac said. And that was when our troubles began.

At first, we tried to do our hiring through the Quechuan owner of the store in which we had had the lamb stew on the night before. He told us that the nearest point to the river was Surimana, only ten miles away, but to get there, we had to go into another small place called Cochapata; there were no roads or tracks but there was a footpath. He also thought we might be able to hire donkeys from the village, but he couldn't possibly arrange anything like that; it would have to be done through the policeman and the headman, or *gobernador*, as he is officially called in the village. They would decide what beasts were required for the work of the day in the village; if there were any to share, the storekeeper told us, he was quite sure the *gobernador* would arrange for us to hire them, with a guide.

We took this information philosophically enough; after all, the distance was only ten miles altogether, and it was not yet six o'clock in the morning.

At six-thirty, there was a drumming of hoofs from one of the lanes on the other side of the square, and a fine white charger galloped into sight bearing a noble figure who was draped in a big brown cloak. It all reminded me of an advertisement of Napoleon brandy, but I felt a little guilty about this, since the others were clearly impressed by the evident return of the Equestrian Age. Once he was rid of his poncho, a policeman was revealed, arriving for duty. Anna approached him, looking quite fetching in the large straw hat Humberto had given her long ago in Arequipa.

"*Sí, sí, señorita. No hay problema,*" the policeman kept repeating, as he brought Anna back across the square towards us. I thought to myself: last time I heard that, we got fried eggs instead of boiled.

"There'll be no problems; the *gobernador* will be here at eight o'clock. This kind gentleman will have a word with him, and we will have hired guides and donkeys as we require. They can't let us buy mules because they are all needed for work in the fields." Anna sounded quite sure that everything would work out all right.

"O.K. I'll buy some rope to lash the loads onto the donkeys, if you want to look around the village and take photographs," I said. "We'll meet here at ten to eight to discuss the hiring with the *gobernador*." The others then went off to see a horse being broken in in a paddock to the side of the square, and I set off for another store to buy the rope.

The adobe huts of the village of Tungasuca sprawled untidily about the over-neat grass square, which is paved with smooth concrete in the shape of a St. Andrew's Cross. A schoolteacher I met on my way to buy the rope went to great lengths to show that the great Tupacamaru had lived in Turyasnea for a great part of his life. Needless to say, the statue in the square was of Tupacamaru, a crusading Peruvian who took the name of one of the Incas to symbolise his ambition to rid his country of Spanish oppression.

Walking back towards the church with a spool of new hemp rope, I could not help but wonder at the way it rained only at night, leaving the sun to shine, though not too warmly, through the day—rather like Camelot weather, I thought. There were plenty of people and plenty of horses, mules, and donkeys around the village, to say nothing of pigs, chickens, and herds of inquisitive, barefooted, little children. Ten miles walk on such a beautiful day, with all these people to help us, really should present no problem at all.

The plateau on the mountain ridge stretched away to the north towards a large shallow-looking lake that lay blue under the peaks in the distance. Already the dusting of snow on the mountains was disappearing in the morning sun. The air was filled only with silence, as the village settled down to another day in the strong, if not very warm, sun.

A little after eight o'clock, the policeman came across the square with a straight-backed, slim man in his late forties whom we all took to be the *gobernador*. He had a good felt hat in his left hand, and his poncho, although not new, had fine embroidery around its sides. "*Buenos días, señorita, buenos días, señores,*" he smiled gravely at us all in turn.

After a short discussion, barefooted little boys were dispatched to all corners of the village, and we heard the first notes of warning from the *gobernador:* "The men will be all out at work in the fields at this hour of the day . . ."

Soon the boys returned, one or two with old men who looked as if chewing the coca had aged them quickly. Three boys brought donkeys with them, and one brought a mule; the rest looked crestfallen and ashamed to admit they had been chased by their mothers. "We'll get it all on three donkeys and a mule," said Mac cheerfully, already quite the professional hostler. So we started to repack our gear into the rucksacks under his direction. His own kit split nicely into two panniers and fitted evenly, one on either side of the mule's back; our rucksacks were lashed crosswise one to each donkey. Mac said the guides could carry the camera case and food bags separately. John Cowrie muttered something about his having "ridden for thirty years to hounds and never seen girths tightened like that." Anna let us all know that her opinion of horses was that they terrified her, and that she would have nothing to do with them. "Why can't we just have guides?" she asked.

I felt uncomfortable in the knowledge that I had no experience whatsoever of horses; I was extremely wary of being near the back of them, for fear of getting kicked—particularly by the mule, which had been blindfolded for loading. I didn't have anything to say at all. The most dangerous possibility seemed a row between Mac and John Cowrie over the question of equine leader.

The loading was really going quite well, if a little slowly. I was just beginning to imagine myself in the role of John Wayne heading a troop of U.S. Cavalry against the Indians, when I noticed a small knot of hard-looking Quechuan women bearing down on us. They were walking so much faster than usual. . . .

Next thing I knew coarse female hands, like claws, were tearing at the lashings on the animals, and all our gear was dumped unceremoniously back on the muddy ground. Weakly, I stood back and watched as Anna, dressed like one of Hemingway's safari heroines in the movie *The Snows of Kilimanjaro*, tried desperately to reason with the five Quechuan harridans. It was quite hopeless from the start. There was much wringing of hands on Anna's part, and she was almost reduced to tears, but the cruel-faced women showed no sign of sympathy for the *gringo señorita*, and simply led the animals away, back up the lanes leading off the square. Only then did it dawn on me that the little boys must have taken the animals without asking their mothers.

"John, I think you should do the talking, and simply use Anna as an interpreter. These people have no respect for women in any business sense," said John Cowrie. I sensed a lack of confidence in my leadership. Mac was muttering something about getting a grip on things, and said that "if we'd been quicker we'd have been away long before they arrived."

Standing there on the edge of the deserted square, I felt uncomfortably short of ideas. It was now after nine o'clock, and the sun was already high. Ten miles seemed rather farther . . . "Come on, Anna. Let's go and see the policeman. We'll see if this newspaper cutting from *La Prensa* will get him moving," I said. It was my trump card. What a cunning fellow I am, I thought to myself, as we crossed the square on the way to the little police station with the oval-shaped, tin *guardia civil* coat of arms fastened on the outside wall above the door.

While the impressive cutting from the pages of Peru's largest daily newspaper didn't have quite the effect I had hoped for, it got the policemen moving, once they had wiped the tears of laughter from their eyes. Unable to read Spanish, I had not realised just how dramatically the newspaper had described the expedition: Anna was an Olympic champion; Mac, John Cowrie, and I were ex-commandos, and I was presented as a karate expert as well. To the *guardia civil*, it seemed a hilarious way of carrying on, but the article did result in a much sterner line with the villagers. Fresh orders were issued and the barefoot messengers scampered off, to return this time with more than half a dozen sorry-looking down-and-outs. The kit was hastily unpacked from the rucksacks and thrust into the salt bags once more; then Anna and Mac set off with the advance party in the direction of the little village of Cochapata, halfway to our destination. This left John Cowrie and myself with more than half our kit lying at the edge of the square with absolutely no way of carrying it; we looked at each other, but it just was not possible for the two of us to carry it all.

The expedition was split, and as the minutes ticked by, the split grew larger. This was the result of the idea I had conceived in London—of a dozen sturdy porters of Inca pedigree, bearing our loads with a grin as they skipped across the Andes, immune to the raging tempest. "Hang on a minute, John," I said. "I'm going to get that horse standing outside the police station."

As I ran across the square, a picture of Anna, caught in a snowstorm at nightfall, with no tent for shelter, flicked across my mind. I really must get a grip on myself, I thought. The whole thing was turning into a shambles . . . "British Amazon Expedition indeed!" It was preposterous.

"*Bonito caballito blanco*," I purred to the policeman, pointing at, but not daring to touch, the doleful, dirty white nag that was weighed down by nets full of empty bottles.

"*Sí, bonito*," the policeman grinned hugely. He was firmly on our side; indeed, he had just slammed the cell door on two unfortunate teenage boys who had steadfastly refused to carry our kit. Now, gesturing, he showed that the horse was to be lent to me, and that the grubby little boy by his side would lead him for us.

"I got the horse," I told John Cowrie proudly, when we reached the other side of the square. Even if his head did hang a bit, he was still a fine horse. " 'Noddy,' I think we'll call him, for the way he nods his head as he goes along," I said to John Cowrie, as we lashed a huge mountain of kit on the poor creature's back. The friendly policeman gave me an official-looking note for the *gobernador* of Cochapata and pressed a few more little boys into our service. In spite of his friendliness, I could see he was pleased to be getting us out of the village.

"I'll carry the camera case; that's everything," said John Cowrie, keen to be off in pursuit of the other group, which had all his kit.

We waved goodbye to Tungasuca and marched out—Noddy, three tiny boys, a green-lipped old coca chewer in motor-tyre sandals, John Cowrie and myself, but few people in the village showed any interest at all as we left. At first, we wound slowly through flat pastures that ran smooth and green into the waters of the lake; cattle, pigs, horses, donkeys, and even llamas all grazed together on the cultivated quiltwork of the plateau. The blue sky was already dotted with fleecy white clouds in preparation for the night's rain, and the mountains rimming the horizon lent the scene the atmosphere of an old English mural painting. This was soon dispelled when we turned to the west and climbed a steep, winding hillside path; the little boy in charge of Noddy gave him his head and threw small pebbles at the unfortunate animal's hindquarters to make him move faster. Halfway up the hillside, where the grass had turned to brown and Noddy kicked little puffs of red dust from the narrow path, we passed a horseman coming down. Riding tall in the saddle and swivelling from his hips to greet us as he passed, I noticed he had the pale fine-drawn good looks of a true Castilian. The smart black felt hat, the poncho draped across the fine, chestnut back of his horse, and the big leather stirrup cups left me in no doubt that the horseman is the proudest figure in the High Sierra.

Near the top of the hill we slowed a bit. The old man was finding that even the coca couldn't help him climb faster than a modest speed. Somewhere above and ahead of us, John Cowrie and I heard the thin, quavering wail of a *quena*, the Quechuan flute, its plaintive notes drifting across the *altiplano* as a lonely shepherd watched over his herd. At last we gained the top, and found ourselves in a land of smooth rolling hillocks where llamas and alpacas browsed quietly on the sunburnt grass.

The little boy said something, pointing back at the old man, who was bowed and grunting under his load.

"I think he means we've got to take a break," said John Cowrie, who had already taken at least one roll of film. We sat on the grass and I wondered if the headache would come back. Far ahead of us, I could see a straggle of ten or eleven figures who were the advance party, winding across the plateau. It reminded me of the "nick-nack-paddy-whack" scene from the *Inn of the Sixth Happiness*, the one with all the mission children fleeing across China under the benevolent guidance of Anna in her straw hat.

After about an hour, we came down into a sort of hollow near another lake, and passed through a collection of little adobe huts, each with its wooden cross on the roof and a small walled garden full of pigs and chickens. Down by the reed-fringed lake, oxen grazed and flights of ducks arrowed across the calm surface that was sometimes dimpled by rising fish. At the far end of the lake, I could see the advance party gathered in front of what looked to be a schoolhouse. A football game stopped, and the curious villagers of Cochapata crowded around to see who these visitors might be. We had come five miles in an hour and a half, and what with one thing and another, the day was fast slipping away; already it was three o'clock. On the journey across, I had been taking a look at Noddy—in an amateur sort of way "judging a piece of horseflesh," you might say. Cautious enquiry in broken Spanish had revealed that Noddy might even be bought for about ten pounds, cash down. I had asked John what he thought of the idea of buying the horse, thus cutting down the daily hiring problem—I knew it was Mac's idea to buy a complete stable to enable us to be independent of the locals for all but guides and food. John had a vague sort of look at Noddy's mouth and said he didn't look too old, but that he was unshod, which wouldn't be too good if the "going was bad."

When we all assembled outside the school, I presented the young and energetic *gobernador* with the "official letter" from the police, with the result that eight new guides were rapidly selected from the football team—short, bronzed, smiling men with barrel chests and powerful shoulders. While all this was going on, I shattered the calm, easygoing atmosphere by losing my temper in the most outrageous fashion, almost causing Anna, who was interpreting, to break down in tears. The hacks from Tungasuca were demanding double the wage stipulated by the policeman back in the village. This latest example of demanding "*gringo*-prices" so enraged me that I threatened to send them all packing with nothing at all—until I noticed some of their football-playing replacements sidling towards the edge of the crowd. The altitude is sending me round the twist, I thought to myself, immediately trying to soothe Anna's badly ruffled nerves, but agreeing that in the present situation we really ought to pay the Tungasuca people a bit extra.

"I want to make it clear that I want no part of that horse; if you buy it, there will be no contribution from me," said Anna, for John Cowrie was already riding Noddy around the football field, and telling us that he meant to take the saddle home for his daughter. "Look, if we don't get going soon, these fellows won't take our gear because they say it will be dark before we get there and we might get caught in a thunderstorm." Anna clearly meant what she said: there was to be no horse. Mac and John Cowrie both thought differently; they agreed with me that having Noddy would mean less hiring of horses at each halt. Furthermore, the little boy was keen to take ten pounds, so I agreed and gave him a roll of ten one-hundred-*sol* notes and took it for granted we owned the horse.

"He's taking off the saddle," said Mac. I was paying off the Tungasuca guides in such a way that they would have to sort it out among themselves when they returned to their village, owing to the large denomination of the notes I gave two of the men.

"Hey! What are you doing with my saddle?" I shouted.

"Your horse, my saddle," replied the little boy.

"How much?" I cried in exasperation.

"Five hundred *soles*." (Five pounds.)

"Four." I trembled with rage.

"O.K.," smiled the little boy sweetly, holding out his hand for the extra notes. We saddled up and off we went, moving much faster with our new guides. We were back on the *altiplano*, with John Cowrie leading the unenthusiastic Noddy with five feet of plaited leather bridle. Everything seemed to be going smoothly now, after the fireworks at Cochapata. Even Noddy seemed happy enough to plod along in back and follow the rest; John Cowrie just hung the bridle over the horse's neck and let him follow at his own pace, tapping him on the rump every now and again with a piece of bushwood to keep him up to the mark. We covered the distance in good style and soon appeared to be nearing the enormous gorge down which the Apurímac flows, a little white ribbon far below the sheer grey precipice.

"Help! I've lost him." I turned and saw John Cowrie in hot pursuit of our newly acquired white horse. Noddy had taken it into his head to bolt up a separate and much smaller valley, in an attempt to make his way home to his less arduous and infinitely more preferable life as a Tungasuca empty bottle carrier. Luckily for John Cowrie, a llama herdsman cut off

Noddy's escape and soon had the unruly stud under control and restored to his rightful owners. Needless to say, the Cocha-pata guides found the incident sidesplittingly funny—whatever would the silly *gringos* do next?

Noddy seemed to find it harder going downhill than up, and so John Cowrie and I fell further and further behind, as the expedition followed the narrow trail along the Apurímac valley. In the failing light of late afternoon, Noddy slipped and slithered down the treacherous rocky trail. On the far side, we could just make out a similar path; it clung to the side of the precipice, winding thousands of feet up from a crossing place on the riverbed. The river was so far below there was never a sound from the white torrent. Up and up like a writhing tentacle the path climbed towards a tiny cluster of red-roofed huts near the top of the valley wall. Far away to the south, in the direction of the Yauri pampas, flashes of sheet lightning illuminated rainstorms. "We must hurry. Anna says the guides reckon those rains will be here within half an hour," Mac warned, having waited behind for us to catch up. "If you like, I'll take the horse for a while; he may go faster for me," he added.

"O.K. I'm frightened that if I push him, he might go over the edge," I replied. I realised that not only might the rains come, but it certainly would be dark in half an hour. Mac might well be able to do something with Noddy; I remembered he had told me tales about the paths in Swaziland being so narrow that the ponies are trained to put both left legs forward, and then both right legs, as they walk almost in a six-inch line.

As we travelled on down the path through occasional scrubby bushes, quite suddenly, just as the rapid tropical dusk was making it difficult for us to see, we came to the little village of Surimavia, which clings to the side of the valley about three quarters of the way up from the riverbed. In the gathering darkness, the primitive red tiles on the roofs of the adobe huts below us made the village look as if it were one of those high-walled towns I'd seen in books about the Himalayas.

Once in the village itself, the guides followed the main path, which had a little water channel running full beside it, until we seemed to be about in the middle of, if slightly above, the main bulk of the houses. They then opened a simple wooden gate on

the left that led down into a small, steeply sloping paddock in
which there were a couple of trees that loomed quite large in
the dark. On either side, low white-walled buildings sloped
down the sides of the field. Mac gave all the guides cigarettes,
while their chief went off to find the *gobernador* of the village;
then, when it was quite dark, it began to rain—slowly at first,
but with big heavy drops that soon fell thick and fast.

"Come on, let's get in here!" cried John from the open doorway of an empty barn-like building at the edge of the paddock.
We all picked up our gear and went into the dark, windowless
room, lighting the way with our torches. Anna quickly lit
some candles, and we arranged our gear on the uneven earthen
floor on which we would sleep for the night.

"Hey! Look at the saddle sore on Noddy's back," called Mac
from somewhere outside. I had a look, and sure enough there
under the sackcloth that shields the horse's back from direct
pressure from the saddle, were two open sores, each about the
size of a milk bottle top, right on top of the spine. "I reckon
he's had those for years," Mac said, "but we'll have to be
careful."

Anna called from the barn doorway that an old man had appeared saying he was the *gobernador* and that he would take
Noddy away to a stable for the night and give him a feed of
maize leaves. This was just what we'd hoped for; having fixed
Noddy up for the night, we paid the guides from Cochapata,
and the four of us were left on our own to cook up a meal.
Using both petrol cookers, Mac and Anna prepared a welcome
meal of boiled rice and tuna fish, with a little fried onion added
to make a dish that more than filled us up—but at the same
time convinced us all that Peruvian tinned tuna could really
only be considered an emergency food. Under Mac's careful
eye, the tall, enamel billy-can soon boiled enough water for a
good cup of tea for us all; we used half a small tin of sweetened
condensed milk and kept the remainder for the morning brew.

The flickering candlelight picked out places in our barn that
we had not noticed previously; there was in fact a small
wooden window on one side of the room that opened like the
doors of a cupboard. Also, in a corner stood a primitive mud
stove with a round hole in front for refueling with wood and a

similar hole on the top for heating purposes. It wasn't a barn at
all but an empty house; the dark mud walls were blackened with
soot and the dusty floor was bumpy, and a great variety of bugs,
attracted by the heat of the petrol cookers, began to crawl
across it from their nooks and crannies in the walls. "We're
lucky it's so high here. When we get further down, we must
avoid these places—they're infested with hookworm, 'the
scourge of the Americas,' it's been called," said Mac, and Anna
started to shiver with cold and horror.

Since we were all tired, the night passed quickly enough and
without untoward incident, although Anna never slept on the
floor again, but always found some kind of table or bench to
keep her off the ground. At five-thirty in the morning, daylight
streamed in under the door, and we crawled out of our sleeping
bags to get ready for an early start. The old rascal who had
looked after Noddy appeared at six with half a dozen eggs for
our breakfast; they made a supplement to the porridge, tea, and
stale bread.

"I'm pretty sure this fellow is not the *gobernador*—he's just
trying to deal himself in for some business by arranging
guides," Anna reported. She was having a lot of difficulty because the Indian really only spoke Quechuan; he knew no more
than about a dozen Spanish words. It appeared the real *gobernador* was away visiting another village and that the hiring of
guides was going to be done on a sort of private enterprise
basis, particularly as it was a Sunday, which is the day when no
self-respecting Quechuan Indian goes anywhere. Saihwa was
the next village down the valley, some four hours distant, and
four hours beyond that was San Juan; naturally we were keen
to reach San Juan in one day, but guides will only work to the
next village down, at which point local etiquette demands that
the chance of employment be handed on to the next village for
the next stage of the journey. All the talk about guides that we
had read in books on the Andes had somehow led us to believe
that the Indians did a lot of guide work. Of course, they had
never done any such work before in this area—the Indians were
just being polite!

After much marshaling by Anna, which was rather ineffectual because of the language problem, we set off with six guides

at eight-thirty. It was lucky we had no animals with us except Noddy, because the guides from Cochapata had gone off with our newly purchased rope during the night. The magnificent scenery was rather spoilt for me by another burst of temper about halfway towards Saihwa. The guides started to act up, demanding extra money; they threatened to leave us and our kit on the path and walk home if they didn't get it. Luckily it never came to this, despite much shouting and gesticulation—all of which I regretted later, when I had cooled down. On top of this, there was a lot of bickering among the four of us about the chores— cooking, washing up, lighting fires, fetching water, and all the other small tasks. We were still far from acclimatised to the altitude, which certainly showed in our ill humour.

The Apurímac valley slopes down steadily for over hundreds of miles, but even in four hours of walking on that Sunday morning, we were able to notice a marked change in the temperature and vegetation; in among the yellows and browns we detected a steady thickening of a much greener gorse-like bush. The improvement in temperature was, I suspect, caused by the fact that Saihwa is situated in a sort of "sun trap," while Surimana, on the side of a hill, was often in shadow.

It was just after midday when we toiled into the little village of Saihwa. There was something about the way it nestled in its own tiny valley that gave it an impression of total self-sufficiency. Even the few scattered adobe huts appeared quite independent of each other; with its own little field, shed, animals, and implements, each in its own way seemed self-reliant. No rates, no water and electricity bills here.

The tantrums of the morning had passed, and we were all four keen to press on through the village to San Juan; when we flopped down in the Saihwa village square, we had meant to stop only for a quick snack but had not reckoned on the problem of getting new guides on a Sunday afternoon. And the square was enchanting. There was something overwhelmingly peaceful about that gently sloping and thinly grassed patch of earth, with its one thick eucalyptus tree right in the middle, offering us shade from the sun at high noon. We led Noddy to the mossy stone wall on the upper side of the square that offered a patch of bright green grass where a little communal water channel trickled its way down through to the houses. To one side of the square was an impressively ancient mud church with whitewashed walls; it was the only building in the village with tiles on its roof; all the others had straw. The church had a big bronze bell and a fine arched entrance, but it seemed to be empty and locked up.

On the other two sides of the square stood mud huts and sheds. Strangely, there was no sign of people. We sprawled on the ground and waited, while Mac got the cooker going in the shelter of the roots of a tree. We ate the remaining bread, cheese, and some cake Anna had brought along. The guides from Surimana showed no particular haste to return home, but instead lay around smoking Mac's cigarettes and talking broken Spanish. One of them went off to find the *gobernador*, but returned instead with an unusually short fellow with an intelligent weasel face who told us the *gobernador* was away in Pomacanchi and was not expected back for at least another three days. Also, we learnt there was no chance of getting guides on Sunday, but that we were welcome to stay at his house; he would also look after Noddy.

All our good resolutions had melted away, as we lay in the shade of the eucalyptus tree; across a maze of small terraced fields, we could see Surimana further up the valley. In the clear mountain air, it hardly seemed a days walk. I thought to myself that we'd have to do better in the coming weeks or we would never reach the mouth of the Amazon. But the smiling faces of the guides, so completely recovered from the silent recriminations of the morning, and the warmth of the sun that I felt through my heavy woollen pullover persuaded me to lie back and relax in the warm, peaceful atmosphere. After lunch, we all wandered over to "weasel-face's" house; he told us his name was Ernesto, or something very close to it. The guides left for Surimana with fond goodbyes and more cigarettes, and Ernesto produced a small bottle of gentian violet and a little swab. He brushed the healing liquid onto Noddy's back, and we settled into a small annex room, once used by his two sons, who were now grown up and away. There was a table on the side of one wall for Anna to sleep on. It was a much better place than the barn at Surimana. As soon as we had everything sorted out, we crossed the small farmyard and found Ernesto's wife and mother-in-law doing the cooking. Guinea pigs scuttled around the floor like tennis balls; they were not really pets— Ernesto told us they were the finest delicacy and that everyone prizes them for their meat. Several mud ovens were dotted around the kitchen, and on these, big square tins that once had contained cooking fat bubbled away amid the wood smoke, while the women crushed maize to be fermented and used to brew the local beer. In another hut, we were shown huge racks of maize that were ready for the mules to carry on to the nearest market, two days away, across the *altiplano* at Poma-cancon. Apparently, very little food was brought into the village, apart from basics like sugar, salt, and tea; there was no shop, and communication with the next village, by foot or mule, seldom occurred more than once a month. When compared with life up at Cailloma, the people of Saihwa lived quite comfortably at 11,500 feet; with the harvest of maize and potatoes in, they were ready for the rains and snow of the coming months. To us the simple, sunny life seemed close to idyllic.

In the evening, we were just starting our cooking when Ernesto appeared with a plate of hot clear soup and small-grained rice he called *arroz de la sierra*; Anna, in turn, made scrambled eggs, a dish that had never been seen before in Saihwa and that the two Quechuan women thought hilariously funny, for some reason. There is no bread in the village, and although the people keep cows, they never have any milk, butter, or cheese. At around nine o'clock we turned in, to be ready for an early start the following morning, pleased with the confident assurances given by Ernesto on the subject of guides and mules for the journey to San Juan.

The day got off to a bad start when John Cowrie woke first at five o'clock and then proceeded to kick Mac and me into wakefulness, as we lay fast asleep on animal skins that were scattered on the bare earthen floor of the hut. Anna suffered the same brutal treatment, and the sense of outrage never quite left me for the rest of the day. We had an early breakfast of cold tuna fish, a hard-boiled egg, and cup of bad tea, and were completely packed up and ready to go at six.

It had rained heavily during the night, and poor Noddy looked decidedly *"infirma"* as he stood moodily stamping the maize straw under the dripping eaves, for whichever way he moved, it was impossible for him to get all of his body out of the water running from the roof. The sore on his back had run during the night, and poor Noddy looked a really sorry sight. The mountain Indians start their day when the sun first touches the lofty peaks, but on this particular morning the rain seemed to keep everyone in bed. It was well past six when Ernesto scurried across the muddy yard; he didn't even spare a glance for Noddy. When questioned by Anna on the horse's condition, he simply shrugged his shoulders and dismissed the matter. Instead, he bobbed up and down like a little sparrow in his efforts to assure us that the guides and horses would come into the yard at any moment.

At 11,500 feet there was still a chill in the air—as well as in our relations with Ernesto—when we finally stalked out of Saihwa at a quarter to nine that morning. Guides, mules, horses, and donkeys had all come into and then gone out of the yard; either prices were not right, or it was too wet, or the urgent call of ploughing prevented recruitment for our cause. Luckily, the rain had begun to slacken as a little party of one *chico* (boy), two ancient, coca-chewing guides, Noddy, and a hired black stallion, started to slip and slither up the steep muddy path out of the village.

After climbing sharply for about five hundred feet, we were already sweating under our duvet jackets and rainproof cagoules. Suddenly, the path levelled out, and we were out of the little side valley that contains Saihwa and were heading down the main Apurímac gorge. We paused on a rise while we adjusted our clothing to allow for easy walking on the level ground and the warm sun that had broken through the dusk of the early morning. Our two old guides eased their burdens by leaning back on smooth grey boulders; then with groping fingers, they fiddled in small leather pouches for coca leaves and lime to help them through the day. They were gasping for breath through blackened teeth and muttering about *dolor de cabeza*, so we sat on the rocks and wondered at the staggering magnificence of the river gorge, set amid endless mountains, many of them dusted with snow during the night but now sparkling in the early sunlight. Just when we were thinking of moving on, Ernesto and a small party of boys, women, and a horse scrabbled up the path and overtook us; they were carrying heavy wooden hoes, and the horse had a primitive wooden plough slung across its back. We all smiled politely at each other; there was no love lost between us, for old "weasel-face" had charged us not only for the use of the hut, but also three times the going rate for his horse. While I have had rather more than my share of being duped, I have never yet managed to overcome the little sense of injustice that goes with the experience.

Our path led gently along the side of the valley, and the sun lit up the increasing green of the vegetation; bushes bordered the drab yellow-brown of the stubble in the tiny fields, for hoeing and ploughing was only just beginning around Saihwa. For more than an hour, there were no minor valley streams coming in from the east, and we were able to make good progress until around eleven o'clock, when we all began to feel the hours since our paltry breakfast. We came to a small grassy spur, cropped close by passing mule trains and wandering llamas; ahead, the valley widened, and our path led sharply away from the course of the river. We would have to make a lengthy detour to cross an incoming tributary stream.

"I'm starving. What about some elevenses?" I said, hoping everyone would agree.

"There is the rice pudding," Anna replied. In a flash everyone had their packs off, and Mac was lighting a fag for himself and offering some to John Cowrie and the guides. The rice pudding was contained in two small plastic boxes that Anna and I had bought in Sicuani; the mixture was rice, condensed milk, honey, and raisins, with a little milk powder added. We shared a box between two, and the pudding was unforgettably delicious.

"Someone's coming along the path," called Mac from his perch a little further along the track. A lone figure was labouring up the hill towards us, looking curiously out of place in shabby European-style clothes. He was leading a small, chestnut brown horse.

"How do you do? I am Señor Modesto Casapino Auros and I own the part of this side of the valley ahead of you. I would like to welcome you to my land." The rather plump little man was sweating profusely, but his manners were impeccable; he addressed Anna with charming courtesy. He told us that he was a poor lawyer from a small town some distance away, and that he loved this remote place, even though it brought in practically no money at all. To me, it seemed rather unfair that the Indians should not only have to scratch a bare living from the rocks but also have to pay dues to absentee landlords; but then, perhaps I was just becoming indoctrinated by the policies of the revolutionary government and was impressed with its declared goal—to give "human dignity to the *campesino*."

Señor Auros spoke very good Spanish and told us of the numerous pumas, the mountain lions that leave their caves at night to raid the poor Indians for their dogs, chickens, and pigs. Ahead of us, where the path wound back towards the Apurímac on the other side of the tributary stream, there was a long isolated spur that Señor Auros told us held the remains of a pre-Inca fortress. We were keen to push on to San Juan, but the señor was equally keen to give us his visiting card, and to this end he started to bellow a message in Quechuan to the small adobe hut far below us. A none-too-young Indian come racing up the slope bearing a piece of paper in one hand. When he arrived puffing at the top he discovered that he had brought the wrong thing and was sent racing down again, only to return several minutes later with the news that there were no cards in the hut, which was hardly surprising.

Soon we were on our way once more. Mac and Anna saw a hummingbird, and as we came across the stream and through some bushes, Mac came suddenly to life, leaping around with his butterfly net, to the hysterical cackling of the guides. But he soon caught a variety of insects. These were either dropped in little "killing bottles," or killed and neatly folded in pages torn from an old copy of *Reader's Digest*.

When we reached the outward end of the spur, it had begun to rain again, but the long climb up the path from the stream made the place a welcome rest in spite of the gentle drizzle. Perched crazily at the very tip end of the ridge, the ancient fortress Señor Auros had mentioned commands a fine position overlooking the ribbon of tumbling water thousands of feet below. The ground falls sheer away on three sides, leaving a narrow path back along the spine of the spur, where it joins the main valley path at right angles. Looking down from the moss-covered stone ruins, I wondered whose hands had laid the stones with such care. Perhaps some copper-skinned noble had once felt here some of the pride I feel, in my own little way, looking down from my lonely eyrie, high above the *Loch à Chadh-fi* (Loch of the Spindrift) in the northwest Highlands of Scotland. We didn't stay long at the ruins. It wasn't the sort of place you can photograph, but was a place that inspired thought.

After the ruins, where we had a small snack of cheese and a few raisins, we pushed on, for it was still a long way to San Juan; Señor Auros had told us the end of the spur was only about halfway from Saihwa. Just as we settled down to a steady path along the main valley, there was another side valley to detour; that the path snaked up and down the valley side, sometimes clinging precariously to the walls of a precipice, sometimes flat along the narrow edge of a ridge, but in general the path was descending. The vegetation always continued to "expand." Far away above us now were the harsh, cold lands of the *altiplano* around Cailloma. There, living was stark, in little stone huts; here, even on the almost sheer sides of the gorges, there were little plots of land, perhaps with rather poor soil, but all carefully looked after, even if with the primitive wooden plough and hoe. Along the pathway, there was now spiky cactus and a crocus-like little flower; in the stream beds, crystal water burbled and tinkled from pool to pool down among the rocks. Lining the banks were green bushes and patches of bright grass. Above everything, in every direction, huge mountains towered and glowered; sometimes frozen in weird pinnacles of misshapen rock, sometimes classically majestic.

Much of this grandeur was wasted on me as the day wore on and the journey seemed longer and longer. The guides were good enough, but both of the horses needed a lot of care and attention to keep them going at even a snail's pace. We seldom walked together; more often than not, one would be in front and one behind the horses, while Anna made best speed on her own up the steepest places. As the hours passed, I began to feel increasingly hostile towards the other three; I found myself planning and rehearsing a brief vitriolic speech that I intended to deliver when the moment was right.

At last we arrived on the outskirts of the village of San Juan. Ploughing was in full swing, with perhaps fifty men, women, and children hoeing away and exhorting cattle to drag their wooden ploughs through the soil. We were greeted with shouts of pleasure and dirty tin cups full of evil-looking *chicha*; this is a grey homemade beer, which is distilled from maize and a few other ingredients. Quite clearly, many of the workers in the fields had been drinking *chicha* all day long; now they were delighted to welcome yet another diversion from the labours of the day. We didn't want to stand around too long because we felt hungry and footsore, so we only had a few cups of the drink and politely insisted that we had to get on. The sun had already lost some of its warmth by the time we struggled down the path to the last stream, before a steady climb led up to the village, which lay astride a well-rounded spur. Tall eucalyptus trees lined the way, and we were overtaken by a proud, arrogant Indian from the fields who, mounted on a handsome brown horse, galloped ahead to give warning of our coming.

On the last gentle climb uphill, I waited for us all to close up so that we could make a reasonably cohesive entrance to the village. It may have been the unaccustomed drink on an empty stomach; it may have been the altitude, but whatever it was, I chose this time to make the short, vicious speech that vented my feeling towards each of the other members of the expedition at that time. We were all tired, and standing by the side of the dusty path, all three of them looked at me in a very unloving manner. There was a short pause, then John Cowrie made his own carefully thought-out reply. "Not only do you look like an ox, but you think like one," he said. Choking with rage, and utterly speechless, I stared back, imagining my hands stretching his neck like a rubber band. With this little outburst over, we all walked silently together for the last half-mile into San Juan.

Although we had come down about five hundred feet from

Saihwa, the river had also done so, following the course of the valley, but the village of San Juan clung to the valley wall thousands of feet above the riverbed. There are many more people living in this pueblo than in either Surimana or Saihwa, and the whitewashed walls of the adobe huts appear to be laid out in a semblance of order with a grassy square or plaza in the centre. When we arrived, it was already past four in the afternoon, but an intervillage football match was nearing its climax, and we were asked to wait on the sidelines until the result was clinched. A young schoolteacher wearing a straw hat and curved dark glasses ushered us into his room, which opened onto the plaza; he gave us each a handful of *maíz tostado* (toasted maize) to nibble, while we sat on a bed and watched the game through the open door.

The village is built on a small spur projecting out from the side of the valley towards the river, thus commanding a position similar to the one commanded by the pre-Inca fortress we had visited earlier in the day. The faded white walls of the single-storey huts with their thatched roofs made a peaceful and reassuring setting for the football match. Although the buildings surrounded the field, only those higher up on the side of the valley actually overlooked the plaza. From somewhere higher, the village water supply trickled down through numerous dirty farmyards in an open gutter before finally emerging through a stone wall in the middle of one end of the plaza. Like the lip of a jug, a carefully placed, narrow green leaf projected the tiny stream clear of the wall, and there was always a queue of grubby children with pitchers and wooden buckets collecting water for their mothers. Any water escaping the buckets splashed quietly on the stones and then meandered across a corner and down one side of the plaza.

The football field occupied most of the square. Although there were no actual lines to mark its boundaries, natural features, such as walls and the brook, did. The goal posts, fashioned out of two straight sticks, were placed about six and a half feet above the balding grass; these were connected by a plaited leather thong, representing a crossbar. It was really more of a tournament than a match. Boys of all ages up to about twelve represented the distant villages of Saihwa, Santa Lucia,

Pomacanchi, and San Juan itself. The teams had roughly eleven members each, and the barefooted players wore red jerseys and shorts. The main support came from the serried ranks of thirty barefooted little girls clad in rags; throughout the series of matches, they sang a variety of Peruvian songs in a most delightfully happy fashion. Other "support" was provided by black pigs, white chickens, a horse, and several dogs that wandered onto the field from time to time.

On the far side of the field were the buildings belonging to the village *gobernador*. After a bit of a rest and a snack of maize, Anna and I left John Cowrie and Mac to go and pay our compliments to the headman, who was watching the football match from a bench on his side of the plaza. Augusto, the *gobernador*, was an old man; unlike all the other villagers, he did not wear a poncho, but favoured tatty old clothes of a semi-European style. Slumped alone on his bench, he was a sorry sight. A battered, off-white Panama hat crowned a dirty, lined face that had watery brown eyes, and a stubble of several days pricked white from his cheeks and jowls. His mouth sagged open, revealing a solitary blackened tooth in the middle of his upper jaw, and the tooth moved slightly when he played with it with the tip of his tongue. We chatted for a while in a desultory fashion, but Augusto wasn't really Anna's kind of man; all the same, we did go with him to take a look at the Apurímac from the end of the spur, where it cascaded through the rocks far below. He told us of huge trout in the pools and mountain lions in the caves, and warned us that ahead the way was *"muy accidentale"* which, roughly translated, means "awfully up and down."

When we returned to the plaza after a short visit to the seemingly unused little chapel, we found the football match was over, and after bidding Augusto goodnight, we rejoined Mac and John Cowrie in the teacher's room. We had the inevitable cup of tea brewed in Mac's billy-can; after tea, we were taken to the main schoolroom, just a few yards off the plaza; this old mud-walled building had a rough grass forecourt. John Cowrie and Anna decided to try a night in one of our little yellow tents, rather than risk the bugs on the dusty schoolroom floor,

while Mac and I decided to clean the old desks and spread
them with the saddle cloths Noddy didn't need in his stable.

Quite suddenly it was dark, and the flickering light from our
candles and the two petrol cookers lit up wall charts of human
skeletons as well as portraits of bearded generals and admirals
who had been the liberators of Peru in the nineteenth century.
We were fast running out of grub. There were only packets of
Maggi instant soup and a few boiled potatoes for supper; luckily this was supplemented with some toasted maize that had
been given us by the young schoolteacher. I drifted off to sleep,
warm and snug in my down-filled sleeping bag, in the middle
of a heated discussion on comparative methods of mounting insects and butterflies. The teacher, who was on a three-month
tour of duty from Cuzco, had a prize collection of insects and
Mac was adamant that he had mounted them in the wrong
manner. At around three in the morning, I was rudely, if
briefly, awakened by a frantic scurrying and muttering in the
darkness; heavy rain had flooded the tent, and Anna and John
Cowrie were taking refuge in the schoolroom. They hadn't
thought to dig a small drain trench around the tent; somehow,
this sort of vital precaution doesn't seem necessary at the end
of a long day.

It was still raining steadily at dawn, which made for an even
bigger effort to get up than usual. Fortunately, Anna found a
little more porridge somewhere, but there was nothing else left
excepting our emergency rations. When the teacher called at
six o'clock, I was quite ready to join him on a search around
the village for eggs; we crossed the plaza and climbed a roughly
cobbled path up the course of the stream, pausing every now
and then to poke our heads into various huts and ask for food.
Already, the smoke-filled rooms were nearly empty, for the men
had left for the fields at first light, and our enquiries met with
no success. The old crones crouched over their blackened cooking pots and shook their heads; quite clearly, there was no spare
food in the pueblo of San Juan.

On my way back to the schoolroom, I met a Castilian-look-
ing Indian who wore a beautifully embroidered poncho and an
old, white pith helmet, and this incongruous figure offered to
bring us some *maíz crudo* in half an hour. My arrival without

food and only a weak promise of guides was met with long faces and badly over-stewed tea.

"Uncooked maize is as hard as iron; the Africans wouldn't eat it in Kenya," said Cowrie. I winced. I really couldn't face any colonial reminiscences at that hour.

"We mustn't give it to Noddy; it's very bad for horses," muttered Mac. Silly old goat, I thought. Anna sat there looking glum—something she's hellishly good at.

"I see all the school children set off back to their villages at first light; they avoid the heat of the day that way," I volunteered cheerfully—anything to change the subject of no food.

Children began to appear in the forecourt in readiness for the day's schooling, and Noddy was led in, looking as mournful as ever. But at least the rain had stopped. Slowly, we gathered support for the day, a horse for three shillings and two men at four each; it was going to be a long, gruelling climb up out of the pueblo.

Just before we left, the school assembled and gave us a little display of drill, singing, and dancing; there were perhaps forty ragged boys and girls ranging in age from about four to twelve. The school at San Juan seemed to be run on disciplined, almost martial, lines. Balancing learning with play, there was football, played with frantic enthusiasm; coloured pictures of football teams hung on the walls, and the teacher, describing England, not only mentioned "Los Beatles" but also "Bobby Charlton" and "Bobby Moore."

After the display, it was midmorning before we finally got away on the long haul out of San Juan (at 11,050 feet), up across a ridge (at 13,500 feet) that cuts a corner where the river bends at right angles. Just above the village, we were overtaken by a gaily dressed little girl in tatters of red and yellow; she laughed as she gave us a small cloth bag full of toasted maize. We thanked her and stuffed the food into our back pockets, planning to nibble it on the journey. Up and up we climbed, passing through herds of llama and alpaca that were usually tended by old women who looked from a distance like walking handbells, dressed as they were in voluminous black skirts, shawls, and stovepipe hats. When at last, around one in the afternoon, we gained the crest of the ridge in bright warm sunlight, the thin, clear air enabled us to see almost infinitely far, and the lonely peaks in all directions gave me a peculiar sense of freedom. Here there was time to think in an objective way. We were free from all the petty cares of income taxes, gas, electricity, and water bills, mortgages, insurance, business transactions, and all the other agencies designed to pursue a man to his death and beyond. No matter what the emergency, we would be pretty hard to track down here. We lay basking in the sun, eating cold boiled potatoes, toasted maize, and the last remains of stale rice pudding. So secure did we all feel up on the ridge that we just fell asleep and let the future take care of itself.

"Hey, where's Noddy going?" It was Mac who brought me back from my slumbers. Noddy had gradually pulled the pack attached to his reins until it started to slide down the hill of its own volition. Our two guides were lying flat out, silently chewing away at their coca wads, quite unconcerned about the present.

As is usually the case after falling asleep in the sun, we all suffered from a rather unpleasant thick-headed feeling, but this soon disappeared, for the two guides began to discuss mutiny after we had only been going again for half an hour. They'd been pressed into service by the schoolteacher at San Juan and their hearts were not really in the job; thus, when we came into a small group of two or three huts, about halfway from the ridge to Santa Lucia, they stopped and took off their packs, making it quite clear they wanted to be paid and go home. We just left them standing there and took the packs ourselves. After about a quarter of an hour, they caught up with us and put on the packs again; there was no more talk of higher wages or of not finishing the job. I smiled smugly to myself—one small victory at last!

Santa Lucia is a tumbledown little pueblo at about 12,800 feet above sea level; and one reason it is much smaller than San Juan is that the water supply is practically nonexistent—just a small fetid trickle down one side of the cluster of shanty-like mud huts. We waited, sitting against the outside wall of the schoolroom, content to doze in the sun until the classes ended for the day, while John Cowrie wandered around the little village taking photographs. He was soon accosted by the *gobernador*, who came to ask us all up to his house for a mug of cool *chicha*. Mac said he thought we were in for a bit of overcharging if we accepted the *gobernador*'s pressing invitation to stay the night in his spacious hut, which did seem littered with spare beds; Anna felt the same, so we said it was vital that we meet the schoolteacher and insisted on taking all our kit with us as we left.

The teacher proved to be an exceptionally pleasant, slim, dark-haired man of twenty-nine years whom we had met only briefly at the San Juan football tournament on the previous day. He had set off from there at first light in the rain, arriving here in time for lunch and afternoon lessons. Although he spoke no English, the teacher made it quite clear in Spanish that the *gobernador* would take us for as much money as he could get if we stayed with him. As an alternative, he offered us the schoolroom, and this we gladly accepted. Our food stocks had finally run out because it had proved much harder to purchase food in the villages than we'd expected; we did not want to use our emergency rations unless a really tricky situation required it. When John Cowrie suggested we try to buy a sheep, we began negotiations with the *gobernador,* finally fixing on the bargain price of sixteen shillings. I went with the old rascal when he set off with an emaciated mongrel dog to take a sheep out of a thin, tattered-looking flock gathered on the hillside just outside the village. Tatty though they looked, the sheep turned out to be extraordinarily wiry and fleet of foot. Half an hour passed, and I was feeling uncomfortably breathless in the thin Andean air, when at last a reasonably young-looking sheep was caught, hogtied, and slung across the *gobernador*'s back.

"Um diddle diddle." In the little grass yard behind the schoolroom, John Cowrie invoked a deity from the White Highlands of Kenya before plunging his commando knife deep into and across the poor animal's throat. Both Mac and John Cowrie were experienced butchers, and in no time we had a pile of joints ready for cooking. Anna, who couldn't bear to watch, had been lighting the fire during all this. Every single part of a sheep is used by the Indians, and so we gave away the

stomach and the head, offering the teacher the fleece. At this
point, the *gobernador* asked us for a tip; this gravely offended
the others present—they saw it as an insult to the lofty position
of *teniente gobernador*.

A couple of hours later, the four of us were seated around a
small blue table about four feet square in the otherwise empty
mud hut that served as the school kitchen. With us was the
teacher. Two small mud fires roared, for we had found kindling
outside in the schoolyard. A tall Indian candle guttered in the
middle of the table, which was now littered with the charcoal
remains of four legs of lamb, the tops of six onions, a packet of
salt, in addition to two sheath knives. The flickering light
glinted on five greasy chins, and the air was filled with the
crackling of fiercely burning twigs and the hiss and splutter of
fat dripping from yet more meat cooking on top of the fires.

The teacher was delighted to see us, for he had spent two
years almost entirely on his own in the tiny mountain village,
with no one to talk to about the outside world. His chief
enemy was the *gobernador*, and just across the yard we could
see two little schoolboys sitting by another candle in the
teacher's own store; they were there for the night, their task
being to guard the small supply of dried milk and semolina
that the U.S. government had presented to the school children
of Peru. "Those sacks come up by mule train, and the *gobernador* is always trying to steal them," the teacher told us, as we
took some meat over to the two diminutive guards.

Next morning we awoke with the light at five-thirty and
Anna, who had slept on a long, narrow, school desk, was clearly
suffering from badly cracked lips. The reason everyone wears
hats in the Andes is that the sun, although not as hot as at sea
level, is harder on the skin; no matter how many tubes of high
altitude cream Anna used, the sun still burnt her cruelly. John
Cowrie, Mac, and I were also all burnt, though to a lesser ex-
tent; perhaps years of soap, water, and the razor toughens the
skin rather better than cleansing cream.

For breakfast, it was lamb stew, followed by fried heart and
liver, which really set us up for the long walk down the valley to Huayqui. For company we had a desperately stubborn
black mare, a good brown stallion, Noddy, and a strong teenage

guide who was clearly high on coca even before we set out. We left behind us the best part of a huge pot of lamb stew for the school children, who all gathered to give us a noisy farewell.

Our six-hour trek was the furthest distance we had yet attempted. We were growing daily stronger—and thinner—particularly Anna, whose once neatly tailored fawn slacks now needed, she said, a lot of support to keep them from falling down about her ankles. The Apurímac "Grand Canyon" at this point was in an area of erosion quite extraordinary even for this remarkable valley. To complete the scene of the old Wild West, it only needed a band of rustlers or a sheriff's posse galloping out from behind one of the brown rocky buttes. Quite clearly, few if any *gringos* had ever passed along this point of the valley, and I'm sure the American government would be gratified to learn how well their gifts of dried milk and semolina have been distributed to the school children and how zealously the teachers carry out their task of protecting these precious foodstuffs. I spent much of the day trying to puzzle out how the Indians managed to ride bicycles along these impossible mountain trails. We had seen no bicycles, but their tracks were clearly to be seen in the dust. It may have been the altitude again, but it took me hours to come to the correct solution—the imprints were made by the sandals the Indians wore; these were made from old motor tyres that are lovingly shaped into footwear by specialist cobblers in the Peruvian towns and then exported to the tiny pueblos by mule train.

In the course of our long walk to Huayqui, we passed another ruined Inca fort and descended more than three thousand feet. Two thousand feet of this was done in an almost vertical final descent to the village, where we were greeted by an entire school. The tall, handsome, young teacher wore his poncho in an elegantly disdainful style that was only a little spoilt by a pair of new American basketball boots. He told us over bottles of Fanta orangeade that the villagers had known we were coming since midday, when a messenger on horseback had arrived from Santa Lucia. We had arrived just at the end of the lessons of the day, and the teacher insisted we stay at his home rather than in the school. He escorted us up a dusty lane that ran between the tumbledown mud houses, and we came to a huge wooden door, large enough to allow a man to ride through on a horse. This covered entrance led into a roughly cobbled court-cum-farmyard alive with pigs, chickens, and a pair of angry peacocks that strutted around in rage displaying their brilliant fantails. In one corner, draped across a large wooden box, lay a brace of dead scarlet and white flamingoes. There were buildings on three sides of the small yard, and a wall with an arch leading to a small paddock, beyond which towered massive peaks on the far side of the valley. We were still far above the river itself.

Noddy, hitched to a post in the corner of the yard close to the flamingoes, was given a good feed of maize stalks and leaves. We were shown into an empty room close by a huge wooden door that looked as if it might be used for meetings. While we were unpacking, the teacher introduced us to his pretty, young Indian wife and her mother, a venerable lady of over seventy with a cloud of snow-white hair and no teeth. This old lady possessed a sort of Dresden china-like dignity, and had a fine, new, broad-brimmed straw hat with a pale green ribbon that we later found had been made in Paisley in Scotland.

First there was a sweet, thick chocolate drink and homemade bread rolls, after which we were asked to have supper with the family. "Surely we'd better try and buy something to drink, a bottle of wine or something from the village," said Mac, who had noticed the first little store we had seen since Tungasuca as we'd come down into the village. Mac and I made a tour of the village and although we could find no wine, we did manage to buy eight dusty little bottles of crude brandy for about a shilling each at the almost empty little shop, which was lit by candles and seemed to cater only to the very drunk. Indeed, several patrons were slumped down on the earthen floor, close to a large metal drum, which at first I took to be full of paraffin, but which I soon realised contained a raw spirit drink much favoured by the Indians.

Our dinner had a dramatic setting. As on the night before, candles flickered again, but this time the table was bigger and even had a cloth. The room was classical seedy South American —high whitewashed ceiling with faded yellow walls and pale pink window and doorway edged with green. Outside, the nightly hail drummed on the courtyard cobbles, and through the open door we watched the lightning pick out the peaks across the valley, while claps of thunder rolled back and forth. Every once in a while, the teacher's white mare would try to push her way through the door to join in the appreciation of her master's fine, Latin-American guitar music, while the rest of us sat well back in our chairs, sipping brandy after the meal of vegetable soup, potatoes, and more bread rolls.

Next day, the first party of strangers, besides ourselves, that anyone ever remembered was coming up the valley to decide the fate of all the privately owned land, of which there were over ten hectares in the area; four officials under the auspices of the vaunted reform movement of the revolutionary government would split the land into smaller portions and dispense it among the Indian *campesinos*.

Sitting there in the candlelight, I felt sure the teacher and his family didn't really have all the cares that Western civilisation had given me, but next morning we were to see the heavy cost of this simple life. Our breakfast was three hard boiled eggs each and more of the hot chocolate drink; this was provided by the grandmother. When we were packed and ready to go, at seven in the morning, it was obvious that something was wrong in the family, for the schoolteacher's wife was weeping openly. At last, just as we were ready to leave, they told us that their baby child was extremely ill with bronchial pneumonia; its breathing had become so difficult that it looked as if it might die at any time. Sadly, the only way they could get to a doctor was by horseback and it looked as if the child wasn't strong enough for that. "There must be something we can do; they've got the stuff for an injection but no syringe," said Anna, wringing her hands with anxiety.

"The trouble is that our medical kit has nothing suitable for a baby, and I just can't guess at a dosage—it's far too risky; but we could let them have a syringe," Mac replied, looking at me. I agreed. We had more medical supplies waiting for us at Cuzco and with the Benedictine monks at Sivia, much further down the river. No national health program in Huayqui; death is a frequent visitor to every family. Word about our medical kit soon spread through the village, and our departure for Acos was again delayed by a queue of Indians suffering from ailments as varied as bronchial pneumonia in babies to blindness in old men. Sadly, we just didn't have the medicines to treat them all.

The short three-hour walk down to the little town of Acos, which is actually at the end of a dirt road, was made on one of those unforgettable mornings when everything is just right. The sun shone clear from a deep blue sky, framing the pure white snow on the mountain peaks. At first, we followed the village water supply along an artificial channel that was lined with tall eucalyptus trees; it wound around a side valley through green meadows that were near the water. We had good guides and two mules. Soon after we left, we were overtaken by a little barefoot boy who raced after us; he was clutching in his hand his grandmother's straw hat, its ribbon trailing in the wind as he ran. It was a present for Anna, a token of their thanks for our help with the baby. Mac had a field day with the beautiful butterflies and even caught a couple of wingless wasps in his net—although that wouldn't seem to be very difficult since they couldn't fly.

Before long, we came to the first large tributary river we had encountered on the east bank, and had to drop right down the side of a cliff on a desperately narrow path that hairpinned down to the muddy brown riverbed. The horses found this particularly hard going, and on one or two occasions we recalled Sebastian Snow's accounts of his journey down the Marañón River further to the north; he had lost a horse and all the equipment it was carrying when it stumbled and plunged over a precipice. Luckily for us, Noddy was quite steady on his feet, even if he was painfully slow. Our two guides found a broad stretch of shallows where we forded the tributary at a run; our running, combined with the puttees bound around our ankles, prevented much water from getting into our boots. After a steep climb up the other side of the river valley, we emerged onto a rough dirt road that led us down a steady incline into the village of Acos. In a little store there, we had a light lunch of Fanta orangeade and some biscuits while Noddy rested outside in the shade of the only tree in the dusty square. We were back again in the land of two-storey mud houses, each with fancy, carved wooden balconies below rickety terracotta roofs. In the midday sun, there were few men to be seen, but several Indian women and little children wandered about the square, the women working spinning wheels to make wool from clumps of loose llama hair.

The small office of the *guardia civil* was on the opposite side of the plaza from the store, and here we tried the trick of showing the newspaper cutting, so successful in Tungasuca, to see if it would get us transport across the Apurímac to the little town of Pillpinto just on the other side. "The road only goes as far as the bridge; there are no vehicles on the other side," said the policeman. "You can wait for the bus. It will be here in one hour, at three o'clock."

We used the available time to try selling poor Noddy, who had worked valiantly, but now looked as if he had gone about as far as he could go; at fourteen pounds, we felt we would have had a bargain, and I honestly believed I was about to make the first profit of my life in selling something. Soon, a small crowd of interested onlookers gathered around the entrance to the store. "*¡Bonito caballito blanco!*" I shouted to them all, and there was a titter of response; then the storekeeper said the horse and all the tackle was for sale, while Anna, John Cowrie, and Mac joined me to show broad smiles of honesty to all potential buyers.

"I think you should offer him for sale at nine pounds," muttered the porky storekeeper out of the side of his mouth. I noticed all the others nodding their agreement, so I muttered a miserable "*Sí, sí.*"

After about five minutes, the storekeeper suddenly gave up and stumped back into the shop: "It's no good; the horse is old and unshod; he is no good."

Nothing could persuade anyone to buy Noddy, not even for seven pounds. This meant someone would have to lead him to Pillpinto on foot; nobody was going to let Noddy onto a bus, not even in Peru. After some discussion, John Cowrie set off with the poor animal carrying only the heavy aluminium camera case, while the rest of us settled down by the side of the square to write letters home; mine actually found its way home to Scotland in just under four weeks. The antiquated bus did eventually arrive in a cloud of dust; it was a long single-decker with great piles of luggage and chicken baskets piled high on its roof. But the driver refused to take us and all our kit. "There'll be another one shortly," he said. Anna didn't mind very much; since she'd found a place where she could buy several bars of the rough chocolate with coarse grains of sugar in it, she just sat in the dust munching away; and Mac was too busy writing to the British Embassy in Lima about his insects to care much about missing the bus. No other bus came, and time went by. I began to think of John Cowrie, alone with Noddy and the camera case; at least he had a hundred pounds in new hundred-*sol* notes worn around his waist in a money belt his mother had made for him out of soft brown cloth.

When at last a battered Ford pickup rolled into the shimmering heat of the square, I was feeling pretty desperate, but luckily the young driver and his girl friend agreed to take us on down to the bridge; it turned out that the truck belonged to the Ministry of Agriculture. Although the journey was not much more than a couple of miles, I didn't think we'd make it with all the kit. The narrow track wound down to the river in a series of sharp hairpin turns, and we could see Pillpinto surrounded by a patchwork of fields and woods as it nestled at the bottom of the deep valley, just on the other side of the river. When we got down to the bottom, we found a small hut that served as a sort of café, but that was all, apart from a turning place and scattering of eucalyptus trees. Anna stayed to watch part of the kit, while Mac and I shouldered all we could and staggered past a few Indians who were fishing from the bridge. From there we made our way towards the school, where we hoped John Cowrie would be waiting.

Pillpinto is in the Department of Paruro, whereas Acos is in Acomayo, and it seemed strange to be in what is really a large village, if not a small town, that had no vehicles, but instead only houses and mules. Walking beside the Apurímac, which is about seventy-five yards wide at this point, we found it flowing fast with rapids, and there were pools and large islands of gravel along the way. We passed several little stores, all of which appeared to be selling goods of the same general nature.

Coming into another dusty square, dominated by a crude football field, we saw Noddy tied up in front of a long, low building with a tin roof, which was clearly the school. "The headmistress has kindly offered us their building next door," said John Cowrie, pointing at an old two-storey building complete with balcony and clay-pipe roof. "Noddy is very tender. I came straight down the hillside and missed the hairpins," he added.

"We could leave him with you, and Cowrie and I can go back and get Anna and the rest of the kit," volunteered Mac.

And so it happened that I was left alone outside the school, while one of the masters explained to the children that I came from the country that is responsible for providing their dried milk and semolina. The result of this was that I was mobbed, and there were cries of "Washington! Washington!" Since John Cowrie evidently hadn't told them we were English, we were naturally taken to be *norteamericanos*. After a while, the master led me into the schoolyard, and a special display of Peruvian folk dancing, complete with sticks, masks, and fancy costumes was put on there and then for my sole benefit, while the smaller children swarmed around me, still muttering "Washington" and pulling at my clothing.

When at last school ended for the day and the children burst in a flood from the yard gate, I set off down the lane towards the bridge, having first locked up our gear in an upper room with a heavy padlock and key given me by the master before he left. I hadn't gone half a mile when I met the other three, struggling along towards the school with the rest of the gear. Although it was almost dark, we managed to get all the kit up to the room safely. While Mac got the petrol cooker going, Anna and I went out to try and buy more food, leaving John Cowrie to curry favour with the locals, in readiness for the hiring of guides for the morrow, by joining in the football match; even though it was practically dark, the game went on.

Later, over an ample supper of soup, eggs, rice, bitter chocolate, sweetened condensed milk, and coffee, we all agreed that the friendliness of the locals seemed to stop once we were back near the road. We were all keen to be away early in the morning to get back into the wilds. A problem in a large place like

Pillpinto is that although there are no formal latrines as such, it is much harder to find a secluded wall or grassy paddock than in the more remote mountain pueblos. On the other hand, the piped water supply enabled us all to wash our clothes that night under the school tap, in the privacy of the empty school-yard.

Next morning, we got up at first light and set about the usual sordid quarrels with people who said both yes and no about hiring themselves or their pack animals for the day. The *guardia civil* office was on an adjacent side of the square to the school; I had visited it on the previous evening and received the usual assurances of help. At five-thirty in the morning, I was knocking on their door in an attempt to forestall the usual excuse that "everyone has gone to the fields." The duty police-man responded by showing me a small stall at the back of the police station that held four healthy looking mules, of which he said we could have three—the fourth apparently was pregnant. The catch for that day lay in the problem of finding a guide, and this could not be resolved until eight, when unemployed men came to the station to report for various odd jobs.

At eight-thirty, we were loaded up, after a fine breakfast of eggs and a couple of tins of sweetened condensed milk, and the room in which we had spent a comfortable night was swept out and the key handed back to the headmistress. The duty po-liceman had not found us a guide, and the school children were chanting "Washington" again, but all this was topped when the senior boys began their recruiting for the days lessons: this entailed scouring the hovels in the area of the school and liter-ally whipping stray children through the schoolgate with leather belts. The lack of a guide was our undoing. If only we had got on our way instead of waiting! One by one, our mules were unloaded and led away by old crones who totally ignored the young policeman's threats. The indecision was nobody's fault but my own, and I was more than relieved when Anna and John Cowrie persuaded an Indian woman to rent us her horse as far as Capa, a little village only an hour further down the river. So with this hired horse and one remaining mule, to-gether with Noddy, and with three little boys who had some-how dodged school for the day, we staggered out of Pillpinto.

Our path lay along the bottom of the Apurímac Canyon and beside the west bank of the river. After an hour, we reached the squalid little pueblo of Capa, perched only a hundred feet clear of the water, in a valley that ranged sheer up into mountain peaks many thousands of feet above. The lower slopes were a maze of small terraced fields of all shapes and sizes; these stretched up towards the sunlit peaks, and beyond the shadowy depths of the valley, the fields grew into larger open parks of grassland; then at the top all was dust and rock.

The crunch came at Capa, when the woman held out her hand for the money due her for the hire of her horse, and the little boys began to unload the mule. We broke into a few savage cries about hiring the mule for the day, even if the boys didn't want to come on up into the mountains, to Pampacucho far above; this scared the boys, but the woman led her horse away. Anna meanwhile went down to the school to plead with the teacher.

But twelve o'clock came and we were no further on; the sun burnt down hot from directly overhead. Then a couple of middle-aged Peruvian doctors appeared on foot from Pillpinto, saying they were going to inoculate the children in Capa against whooping cough and diphtheria, and after that walk up to Pampacucho before nightfall. We had been on the point of giving up for the day, but the sight of the two portly doctors in faded old pith helmets, each clutching a battered leather attaché case, shamed us into action; after all, they would be at least two hours in Capa before they could set out for Pampacucho, and by then we would be far on our way.

The plan was that John Cowrie, Mac, and I would take turns carrying the packs belonging to Anna and myself; the rest of the gear would be loaded on Noddy and the mule. Anna was to lead Noddy, and whichever of us was not carrying a pack would goad the incredibly idle mule.

And so we set out on what was by far the steepest, longest climb we had yet been faced with. Quite soon, the beautiful river with its gravelly shallows, long, deep pools, and white rapids dwindled away to a silver ribbon far beneath us. We did half-hour stints on the packs, two carrying and one resting; the path was narrow and steep, and at one point we heard a bell ringing up ahead. But this only turned out to be the lead animal in a mule train of ten, bringing heavy sacks of maize down from above.

At two o'clock we collapsed under a tree, which, I saw, through my sweat and fatigue, resembled an English Alder. Although it gave us little shade, it was better than nothing and at least offered support for our aching backs. We soon gulped down the big bowlful of Anna's now-famous cold rice pudding, and we each emptied the contents of a tin of sweetened condensed milk; needless to say, there was no enthusiasm to get going again, and we all lay too long in the warm sun, watching huge eagles quarter the barren wastes around the towering peaks.

When at last we did set out, we faced another two hours of pain before we eventually gained the crest of a spur and found a level path running before us along the wall of the gorge. Once at the top, I began to feel the old pleasure of a hard days walk with a heavy pack on my back; I even managed the steady, loping half-trot I had used so many times in the past. There comes a point when the sheer pleasure of rhythm inspires a belief in oneself, that one can go on forever.

The sun was already beginning to cast long shadows from the grey boulders, when I came upon a little trickle of clear water bubbling out from among a tumble of rock close to the path. Remembering the trick at San Juan, I picked a narrow green leaf and stuck it on a ledge in such a way that it produced a thin stream of clear, ice-cold water. When the others arrived, they thought I might as well have discovered gold, for barring our emergency bottle, our water had run out long before and we were desperately thirsty. Poor Anna, who doesn't like horses, was in despair, for Noddy kept leading her off the path, or stopped to graze instead of getting on with the job in hand.

Far below us, we could see two tiny figures winding their way up along the path towards us; the telltale white dots of their pink helmets told us it was the doctors. Just after we got underway once more, we met two little Indians who muttered "*cerca, cerca,*" in response to our urgent enquiries about how much further was it to Pempacucho; I remembered from history lessons

at school that *circa* means (in Latin) "about," which led me to
believe that Pampacucho was not far away. The only snag was
that *cerca*, to an Indian travelling light, could mean a pretty
long distance. In fact, it was almost dark when the two lively
doctors scampered past Anna, myself, Noddy, and the hopeless
mule; they told us the village was no more than two kilometres
ahead.

It was quite dark when we passed a tiny cluster of mud
houses, and we could see the lights of a village at the far end of
a valley at least an hour away. "Down here, this is Pampacucho"—I heard John Cowrie's voice from somewhere
below us. He and Mac had gone ahead with the packs and
presumably got in before dark.

We were greeted by the teacher in a little, open patch of
ground that passed for the square, but was in fact triangular in
shape and too small even for a football field. The doctors must
have gone on to the further village, for we saw no sign of them;
but then, of course, we were far too tired to ask. As honoured
guests, we were installed in a whitewalled adobe on three
different levels; at the top, we found a small room with a rough
wooden table and a bench, and in there Mac and Anna set
about cooking a packet of soup and a can of *sardinas*, which are
a pretty grim sort of pilchard. Since the middle-floor room was
tiny, we left it to Anna for a bedroom; on the ground floor we
decided to leave nothing, in case our friendly hosts should be
overcome with the temptation to steal such prized items as the
nylon rope used for lashing loads to the pack animals.

The young teacher was unmarried, as are the majority of
teachers on their first tour of duty, after finishing at the training
college, in the mountain· villages. He had been in Pampacucho
for three years, and early next morning he was going down to
Pillpinto to discuss a possible relief. For us, the idea of no
teacher in the morning meant that all the promises for guides
offered during the evening would probably evaporate in the
cold light of dawn. Anna, however, hit upon the idea of paying
a deposit to potential guides there and then, thus booking their
services for the morrow.

With everything settled, the villagers began to appear with
little packages of food, in response to our earlier enquiries, and

the soup was soon thickened with potatoes and onions. It had been a long, hard day and we had all walked well, so our little dining-cum-bedroom was full of the *bonhomie* usually found after a big effort in the open air. The plan for the morrow was another long haul through two villages, all the way to Paruro, from which we hoped to hitch a lift on a truck to Cuzco on the following day. Full of good intentions, we laid out the sleeping bags on the cold earthen floor and drifted off to sleep, after having first snuffed out the candles.

Breakfast was cold boiled potatoes and weak tea; we kept three hard-boiled eggs each and a few pieces of stale bread for lunch. Although we were up as usual at five-thirty, the teacher had already gone, and we were left, as I had feared, with the *gobernador*, a squat, brown-skinned little man with aquiline features and black hair, whose eyes burned liquid-black, and a wad of coca leaves jammed into the side of his mouth. He was now fantastically devious about the price and availability of animals and guides, while all had been plain sailing the night before. Now we saw our deposits handed back one by one, and the only guide we got was a slim, cheeky-looking youth with a flute and a nasty scar on the left cheek of his narrow, arrogant face. Even this boy jibbed at the idea of going all the way to Paruro, and we had to agree to stop for the night at the next village, Arepalpa; this was a pity, since it was Saturday, and we knew only too well that there was little hope of getting help on Sunday. Even my last minute ploy of offering to swap Noddy for the *gobernador*'s faded poncho failed to win us the offer of a mule for the day. "Your horse is old. My poncho is new, and it has my name embroidered on the hem," said the *gobernador*, lying through his teeth.

"We'll take the boy and carry the rest ourselves," urged Mac. People were drifting away from the discussion, and I could see that unless we were careful, the boy would leave as well.

"You are all *señoritas* in this village. When my book is published, the village of Pampacucho will be shamed before the world!" I cried in frustration. I could feel the altitude going to my head again.

"Come on, let's get going," John Cowrie said quietly at my elbow, and we set off down through the fields in which the vil-

lagers were hoeing and ploughing, along with all the other villagers up and down the Apurímac valley at that time of year.
Fortunately, the boy was strong, and the valley not too deep;
he carried a good bit of weight on his back and played his flute
in a thin, wailing, mocking way as he strode along ahead of us.

Halfway up the other side of the little valley, we all began to
regret the lack of guides and mules. Still over ten thousand
feet above sea level, the effort of struggling up a long, steep
hill, over false crest after false crest, turned our breathing into
harsh, shallow gasps. Every ten minutes or so, we would pause
for a rest; then the boy would increase the mocking note in his
playing. Before the start of the expedition, I had decided that
Anna must be treated as an ordinary member of the team. I
reasoned that if we accustomed her to special treatment, and
she came to rely on us for the carrying of all her kit, then in
the event of an emergency, she would find it much harder to
cope than if she had been self-reliant all along. Now, on the
long, steady uphill climb to the saddle on the far side of the
small Pampacucho valley, with the boy incapable of carrying
the same load as the mule on the previous day, we were all carrying weight all the time—packs for John Cowrie, Mac, and
myself, and the aluminium camera case for Anna. About halfway up, Anna began to fall behind; she had never done any serious walking in her life, and the uphill work in thin air had
troubled her all the way from Tungasuca. Now, with the added
burden of the camera case, she found it very heavy going, indeed.

A good long pull uphill in thin air provides just the right
head of mental steam for a huge row at the top. When I
gained the saddle, I took off my pack and sat waiting for the
others, and feeling sorry for Anna, who was still some way
below. John Cowrie appeared on the saddle a few seconds later,
having done the last part of the climb with Mac by a different
route, around a little spur. He considered my un-gallant attitude towards Anna's plight to be absolutely disgraceful and
said so in a long string of quite unprintable words that were so
perfectly clear I lay back without reply. I could see his point
very well.

Anna's arrival at the top coincided with that of two Peruvian

horsemen from Arepalpa, which was our next destination;
needless to say, these two characters, who looked exactly like
"baddies" from a horse opera, were intrigued at the bizarre
scene created by the floundering *gringo* expedition. Poor
Anna's sawing breath was further taxed by a stream of ques-
tions from the cowboys, who also told us we had another two
hours walk, along the level at first and then sharply down to
Arepalpa. As we were about to set off again, John Cowrie said
how sorry he was for the outburst on Anna's behalf, and the
incident was closed; he was quite right in that it would have
been much better if Anna had nothing to carry, but this was
impossible if we were to maintain our present rate of progress.
All the way down the valley, we had heard of the impending annual rains and their attendant seas of mud, which could well
bring the expedition to a grinding halt.

For an hour, we moved fast on the level, red, earthen path
that ran around a big spur, forming a corner where the river
Apurímac turns to the west. Red earth, green grass, scrawny
trees, and the hot midday sun all reminded me of days at eight
thousand feet in the White Highlands of Kenya. Speedy
though we were, the two doctors were faster still; they romped
past us, each with his pith helmet and little brown attaché case.
"You'll never get to Paruro today," they called. This did
nothing to improve our spirits. If these two athletes thought it
impossible, then what hope had we with all our gear? Anna
looked close to tears; it wasn't much of a reward for rushing
along, bent under her big red pack.

"I think we'd best take our lunch here," I said rather despairingly. We were passing through a clump of thorn bushes,
which afforded a little shade, and the path dropped steeply
away into what looked like a desert of yellow sand and sun-
cracked rock.

Lunch was our usually light affair of three hard-boiled eggs
and a couple of cold boiled potatoes each. Nobody said much,
but we were all filled with gloomy thoughts of being stuck in
Arepalpa until Monday, with the rains drawing nearer every
day. Anna was disconsolately rubbing more high altitude cream
into her cracked lips, which were even more painful after the
efforts of the morning. "Here comes someone else," called Mac,

through lips that firmly gripped the inevitable thin cigarette. He was wandering through the thorn bushes, trying to trap a few brightly coloured butterflies with his long, white muslin net that always seemed to be getting snarled by the thorns.

It was another few moments before we saw the small, smooth-faced Indian boy in his Roy Rogers hat, as he came riding along the trail on his sturdy, little brown horse. He stopped to have a talk with our young guide, who was still bashing away with his flute, and Anna soon had him interested in carrying some of our kit on his horse to Arepalpa, still an hour below us. The deal was clinched for two shillings and a bottle of Fanta on arrival at the village. As soon as we got to our feet, we realised just how far up we had come from Pillpinto. On the other side of the mighty canyon, we could just make out the thin line of the track leading out of sight towards Paruro. The river itself was too deeply cut into the gorge for us to see it. Anna didn't say anything, but although her pack was now firmly lashed on the small brown horse, it was quite clear that her big Army boots were making her feel like a human hairpin dipped in lead.

At least going down was quicker than climbing up, and we were soon in a dry, stony gully that made the heat reflect in wobbles of distorted air. At one point, I came across the sinister corpse of a deadly tarantula spider where it lay grotesquely in the middle of the path, squashed by some passing horse's hoof. Just above the tiny pueblo of Arepalpa, which is perched high on the valley wall, thousands of feet above the still invisible river, the four of us paused to wait for the boys who were bringing the much slower horses with them.

"Let's try and get them to take us on to Paruro; it's still only one o'clock," urged Mac, his thin fingers busy rolling another fag.

"What do you reckon, Anna?" I grinned.

"Well . . . as long as I keep thinking of the hot bath there must be in Paruro, I think I can make it," she smiled weakly, but behind the big bicycle-wheel glasses, there wasn't a lot of laughter in her eyes.

"There's sure to be a bath in Paruro, but there certainly

won't be down there," John Cowrie said, pointing down at the rash of pink-roofed mud huts just below us.

When the two boys joined us with the sagging horses, we set about coaxing them on by offering them wages triple the normal rate, and they just couldn't resist. I wondered what their parents might think if they knew the boys were away on the far side of the river for the night, in a strange town, but my conscience was easily salved by the yearning to get on before the rains bogged us down.

Once in the tumbledown village, we wandered down the main lane towards the dusty square; on the way through, we poked our heads into several dingy huts and enquired about buying the Fanta orangeade that was so vital a part of our contract with the small boys. "*No hay, señor*" was always the answer. The boys looked unhappy, and we felt desperate, but there seemed to be no Fanta in the village.

On the far side of the square, by a tumbledown stone wall, there was a gathering of Indians having what at first seemed to be a Saturday afternoon jamboree. Everyone seemed to be dressed up and drunk, the women all wore flowers in their hats, and there was plenty of chatter and laughter. "Please, *señorita* and *señores*, join us for a little food—surely it is time for *descanso*," urged a young Indian who was elegantly dressed in black from his Stetson hat to his shining boots. We were keen on the *descanso* (meaning "rest"), but Anna, for one, was not very sure about the plates of stew and wouldn't drink the evil-looking, grey *chicha* beer that was thrust into our hands. Although Anna only picked at her food, the rest of us wolfed down the stew, which contained potatoes, carrots, onions, a sort of mashed pumpkin, and a few lumps of nondescript, tough meat that was yellow with fat.

The man in black, who strongly resembled "the Cisco Kid," told us that he was the foreman of a gang of men up from Paruro to reroof some of the village huts with pink clay tiles. While we sat leaning against the wall eating the stew, this gang of ill-assorted men began roofing the hut on which they were about to start work. They all wore rags; many were drunk on the *chicha* beer; there were old, young, and crippled men, some barefoot and some wearing the typical motor-tyre shoes; but they were a cheerful lot, and there was plenty of joking and much laughter in their work.

After a lengthy stop, we staggered to our feet and set off once more. The boys were cheery because they had two lunches and we had even found some Fanta after all. The narrow path wound crazily down to the river, through various stratas of red, black, green, and grey rock. It was late afternoon when we finally crossed high above the tumbling white Apurímac, over a rickety sixty-year-old suspension bridge. The dusty road wound the ten kilometres down from Paruro to the bridge, but no vehicles ever used it, and we would have to walk every inch of the way, much of it in the dark.

About a quarter of the way up the hill, we came to a little store beside the path. It was a small, whitewashed mud building with a thatched roof, outside of which ran a fast-flowing irrigation channel, about a foot wide and nine inches deep. Close to the store, there was a mill that rumbled in the dusk grinding maize, as four men worked the huge grinding stones by candlelight. While the others sat on an old wooden bench outside the store, I went in to buy two bottles of exorbitantly expensive *cuzcena* beer and a tin of pilchards. All the stores in these remote places are the same: available are tins of tuna or pilchards, a few assorted bottles of cheap wine or brandy, some candles, some crude soap, and stacks of red packets that look as if they contain crisps but really contain soap powder. The whole of this sparse selection is covered in thick dust. In one corner of the inevitably dark and dingy room, which was the store I visited, stood a huge blue drum containing the special alcohol sold to the Indians at around three shillings a litre (and really only 40 per cent alcohol). Often on the outside of these stores there is a solitary notice proclaiming brightly that coca is obtainable within.

After the pilchards, which we couldn't finish, and the beer, which we could, we set off wearily up the winding dirt road behind four Indians who each carried a stack of fifteen-foot green bamboo stems on their shoulders. Darkness came, and we overtook the Indians. The stars came out in a velvet sky without a moon. I smiled happily to myself and wondered whether Chay Blyth was looking at the same stars from his boat *British*

Steel, somewhere in the Atlantic. The pleasant, languid feeling of physical fatigue after a long day added to the achievement of getting further than the two doctors had said was possible.

The boys and the horses were as tired as we were, and it was long after dark when we finally stumbled across a nearly dry riverbed and into the narrow, ill-lit streets of Paruro. The boy with the flute guided us to a grubby little store that also doubled as an inn. We wearily unloaded the horses and hitched them to the doorpost before stepping into the bright pool of light cast from the store's Tilley lamp. After three Fantas each, we began to feel rather better, and paid off the two small boys, who were delighted to have the money in their hands; in addition, we gave old Noddy as a present to the little boy with the flute. The young Indian storekeeper was delighted to see us and with great pride showed us the new bungalow-style bedrooms across the yard at the back of the shop; they had been finished that very day, and the concrete flooring was still just a little wet. There was no bath after all, but a cold water standpipe rose starkly from the centre of the yard; anyway, Anna was far too tired to worry about anything but flopping down on her bed, clothes and all, for the night.

When we returned to the dingy store to wait for the promised meal of fried eggs, onions, tomato salad, and plenty of chips, we found two strangers lounging against the drab wooden counter. Both of these men were light-skinned Peruvians, the larger was perhaps fifty years old and his eighteen-stone bulk was almost completely enveloped in a huge, grey greatcoat, above which leered a pockmarked, Negroid, horror-movie face. It was clear that the storekeeper held the two men in high regard, since he stood stiffly against the shelves adding "*Señor*" to his every reply; it was also noticeable that these men never paid for the numerous bottles of beer they consumed. Although the smaller of the two was so hopelessly drunk that he was unable to hold a logical conversation, his huge companion seemed quite unaffected by the beer. The four of us sat quietly on a wooden bench on one side of the store, mentally urging the storekeeper's wife to hurry up with the meal so we could get to bed. But, inevitably, we were drawn into conversation with the

two strangers, and gradually it dawned on me that this was no
chance meeting.

South America is the land of revolution. During the period of
our expedition, Chile went through severe political upheavals,
and Bolivia, just two hundred miles to the east of Paruro, had
five premiers in only forty-eight hours. The notorious revolutionary Che Guevara had passed through Peru on his way to
his death in Bolivia only a couple of years previously, and the
Apurímac valley had then been the scene of a bitter guerrilla
war. Now, quite suddenly out of the night, down from the
mountains we three young *gringo* men and a girl—all dressed in
varying degrees of military clothing—had wandered into a small
inn in a sleepy little Peruvian town. Was it surprising that the
news soon reached the ears of the police? Two of them, one unfortunately drunk on that Saturday night, called at the inn to
make a few discreet enquiries.

The meal was unusually slow in coming, and while we
waited I slowly became aware that the bigger policeman was
showing an unhealthy interest in Anna. I got up to walk across
the room and get a closer look at a poster charting the history
and growth of the United States, and in a few moments I
heard the big man shuffle across after me.

"You like her, eh?" he asked in Spanish, and with garlicky
breath, thinking I was in fact looking at a 1967 calendar pictur-
ing a naked American girl advertising motor tyres. I smiled in
agreement and stalked back to my seat on the bench. Two
more heavily built men came in and ordered beer. The big policeman seemed to know them and began to make plans for
them to take John Cowrie, Mac, and me "out on the town," as
he called it—with heavy winks towards the nude poster. Both
Anna and himself were left out of the plans, and I visualised all
sorts of terrible situations, mainly featuring three *gringo* men in
a nasty dungeon and Anna "alone" in another.

Luckily for us, the meal arrived at this point, and we were
able to wolf it down and then plead extreme exhaustion before
retiring to bed. Memories of my childhood and the footprints
of famous movie stars in the concrete outside the Granada cinema in Slough were revived as I padded about on the still soft
concrete of my bedroom floor.

Next thing I knew, someone was banging on the door and light was streaming in through the window next to it. It was morning.

"Hang on," I called, leaping naked out of bed and starting to dress as quickly as I could. Before I had even picked up my underpants, a shadow passed in front of the window and blocked some of the light.

"*Buenos días, señor*," rumbled the deep voice of the roly-poly policeman; I felt remarkably stupid standing there by the bed without a stitch on and I wondered if he thought it might be Anna's room. It turned out that he wanted to look at our documents, so I told him to wait a few moments while I got dressed. He didn't leave the window, however. "I will take your passports to the office," he said, when I finally emerged from the bedroom, feeling quite cross.

"I'm afraid not, *señor*. I cannot be parted from my passport," I replied, remembering all sorts of stories I had been told of foreigners rotting in South American gaols. Anna, Mac, and John Cowrie came out one by one and showed their passports to the fat policeman.

"I shall return to the office and a 'specialist' will come here to examine these documents," he announced in a rather chilling manner, before turning sharply and leaving the room.

"Let's get out of here on the first bus. They don't like the military, and I'm a South African as well," said Mac, and everyone nodded in agreement.

By the time the slim, young "specialist" arrived in the yard, we had all washed and had breakfast. Our passports were carefully examined and returned to us; then we grabbed our bags and rushed to the incredibly rickety bus that waited in the town square. The "high walk" phase of our journey was nearly over, and we didn't want it to end in gaol.

7

Into the Unknown

"It's impassable! I've just been to get maps at the Ministry of somewhere or other, and the chief there says there are no maps, few people, but many *bandoleros*, snakes, bears, and jaguars!" John Cowrie burst into the shabby bedroom of the down-at-heel hotel we were staying in, just off the Plaza de Armas in Cuzco. My first reaction was one of surprise at how he could look so excited at such news; then I realised that the gleam in his eye meant that he was pleased that the official *thought* it impassable; we would have some excitement in proving him wrong.

We were just two days in Cuzco, long enough to put our story and film on to the Faucett plane to Nick Ashenhov in Lima, where he would put it on the next plane to London.

Cuzco, fabled Inca city turned tourist trap, lies across the spine of the Andes, 285 miles inland from the Pacific coast of Peru; further still to the east lie the snowy peaks of the Eastern Cordillera. Tourists jet direct from the coast at Lima in twenty minutes, landing (at 11,150 feet) at the modern Cuzco airport. Polished tour arrangements make it possible for hordes of camera-toting Americans to "take in the whole Inca thing" in just two or three days.

The Inca empire began in Cuzco around A.D. 1100. Probably originating around Lake Titicaca, the Incas believed implicitly in the Sun God and his direct descendant, the Inca (emperor), and to this end they extracted "the sweat of the sun and tears of the moon" (gold and silver) from mines up and down the Andes as their empire expanded. The expansion began around

A.D. 1350; it was based on the supposition that war is the natural state of man. But the empire collapsed in A.D. 1532, when the Spanish conquistador Francisco Pizarro landed at Tumbes on the Pacific coast in search of palaces lined and sheathed with gold. Pizarro had with him only a hundred and thirty foot soldiers, forty cavalry, and one small falconet-cannon. The Incas thought the horse and man were one animal with feet of silver (horseshoes), and that if the man fell from the animal, then both were dead; they thought the steel swords wielded by the bearded Spaniards as ineffectual as women's weaving battens and the cannon only a thunderbolt that could only fire twice.

Fortunately for Pizarro, he arrived at precisely the right time and attacked in exactly the right manner. There had been much internal strife within the Inca empire over the question of succession to the late Inca Huayna Capac. Sons fought each other, and Atahvalpa from Ecuador emerged the victor from the bloody slaughter. He was on his way to Cuzco to be proclaimed Inca when Pizarro landed. Surrounded by thousands of warriors to whom he was God, Atahvalpa thought he had little to fear from a mere handful of soldiers, but he had failed to make a proper appreciation of the situation. Advanced though the Incas were in matters of astronomy, architecture, medicine, and social structure, they had no knowledge of the wheel, no written language, and they had not discovered gunpowder or iron. These handicaps were nothing when compared to the main weakness of the empire: the Inca "organised" his people; although they did not want for food and were kept from coca, and although his swift justice prevented crime, by this same "organisation," he also eliminated individualism. Knock out the Inca and the empire would collapse.

Atahvalpa was taking the hot sulphur baths at Cajamarca, a city in the Andes in the northern part of Peru, while he waited for his generals to send word from Cuzco in the southeast that they had wiped out all trace of his late enemy's family, and had prepared the capital for his triumphal entry and proclamation as Inca. His strategy for the Spaniards, it seems—since he believed that no one could get reinforcements from the

sea—was to offer no resistance, draw them in, perhaps to Cajamarca, and then give the signal to wipe them out.

Francisco Pizarro arrived at Cajamarca and sent word to the
Inca to meet him in the plaza. Perhaps in a gesture of "those
about to die," the Inca accepted the invitation and ordered his
accompanying warriors to be unarmed so as not to give offence.

At vespers during the early evening of 16 November 1532,
the Inca, carried in his litter and surrounded by his unarmed
bodyguard, moved into the plaza of Cajamarca. There was an
unintelligible parley between Christian priest and Inca god,
and then the solitary cannon spoke thunder and the Spaniards
butchered the bodyguard. With the Inca captured after an action lasting only half an hour, Francisco Pizarro bargained with
the fifty thousand Inca warriors for the freedom of their god.
As ransom, the subjects brought gold to fill a room seventeen
feet long by twenty-two wide, to a depth of nine feet, and in
addition filled a smaller room with silver. The bargain was in
vain. The Spaniards put the Inca on trial, found him guilty,
and strangled him to death.

By the time we reached Cuzco, the Spaniards had long since
melted down the "sweat and tears" into easily transportable
bars, and used the exquisitely worked stones from the palaces,
temples, and other places to build churches and residences on
the Inca foundations. For us, the tourist oasis in the mountains
provided a means of communication with the outside world before we returned to the river.

I was alarmed by the news that the river valley was thought
to be "impassable" by the local officials, and for two reasons.
First, we needed guides and mules; if there were no villages—
and certainly there was just a blank on our map where we
might expect them—then we could not carry all our kit and
food. Second, if we were seriously delayed, then the rains would
catch us and stop us right in the middle of nowhere, without
much food. We thought about this for one whole day before
making a plan, and it was Mac's practical brain that thought
up its best features. He reasoned that we should cut our kit
down to the minimum and fly the surplus to Lima, where Nick
could get it to the Benedictine mission at Sivia, our next destination down the river. We agreed to set off from Cuzco using

guides and mules until they were no longer available, then abandoning the least necessary items, until we were able to carry all our kit on our four backs. Anna's hacking cough and cracked lips would, we all assured her, vanish when we reached the jungle. She gave us a wan smile but never a word of complaint.

Mac showed genius in his solution of the problem of *"bandoleros,* jaguars, bears, and snakes." We couldn't manage the burden of firearms and ammunition, but Mac had an idea. "These people are always having fiestas," he said earnestly, as only Mac can. "What we need is Chinese firecrackers—they'll be easy to buy here!" And they were, too; the Indian in a store in the Plaza de Armas soon produced a cardboard box from under the counter, and in no time, with the permission of the pistol-packing policeman on duty in the square, we were practising ambushes and imagining all manner of Gideon-like situations.

Armed with two photocopies of a section of almost blank map, a handful of Chinese firecrackers, and twenty-one days supply of packet soup, rice, and sugar, we took our lives in our hands and boarded the ramshackle bus bound for the river again. Seated beside the driver, my knuckles white on the safety bar, I hung on as we slipped and slewed for hours down to the last bridge across the river, still nearly four thousand miles from the sea, then ground despairingly up and along the far side of the huge valley.

The scale of the mountains has to be seen even to be imagined. On the far bank from Cuzco, we looked across to the unforgettable backdrop provided by the cloud-wreathed, snow-capped monarchs of the eastern Cordillera. These mountains realised every dream I have ever had about the solitary majesty of towering mountain peaks: stark rock faces in black relief on vast snowfields, and glaciers fanning down to become iced white streamers plunging through brown rocks far below before finally merging in the depths of the gulf-like valley with the tumbling torrent of the Apurímac itself.

The bus driver, a bland-faced and comfortably built Quechuan Indian, whose forebears had absorbed the Roman Catholic faith from the conquistadors, did nothing to increase the safety of our hazardous journey by his continual demonstration of faith. Whenever we came upon the roadside crosses marking previous fatal crashes, and always on the most sudden and sharpest corners, poised high over the steepest drops, our pilot would let go of the wheel with one hand, shut his eyes, and cross himself, while fervently moving his lips in prayer. The bus, meanwhile, careened on, controlled only by the juggling one arm of a blind man who seemed obsessed with death. Always we just made it, but I wonder how many more trips the poor man made, and I hope he is still rather more than just a simple roadside cross.

At last, after climbing for hours out of the Apurímac valley, we suddenly topped the summit and saw the little provincial town of Abancay, which nestled below us in the valley of the Rio Pachachaca. The milestone showed we had a twenty-five-mile hairpin descent through the quiltwork of fields, which rose up from the valley floor in various shades of green, brown, and yellow, as they reached for the Andean peaks and stretched far further than the eye could see. Occasional clumps of elegantly thin eucalyptus trees cast long shadows in the late afternoon sun. Stalks of sisal-like, giant asparagus shoots twisted thirty feet into the air every four hundred yards. As we neared the bottom of the serpentine white road, Indian children, pigs, cattle, dogs, goats, sheep, horses, mules, donkeys, and chickens scattered before the rumbling white cloud of dust.

Once in the small town itself, we booked into a broken-windowed pension for four shillings each per night, and set about getting information on the route ahead in the Apurímac valley. Some people gave us a widely diverse cross-section of information—with fingers drawn quickly across the throat, or rolling eyeballs, or mutterings about the unknown, the very difficult, and the barely possible. Finally we fastened upon a cultural storekeeper who spoke just a little English and he helped us all he could, although he knew next to nothing of the river. He soothed us with a glass of wine and some biscuits, and rather than labour on about the suicidal nature of our mission, he directed the conversation more towards the greatness of Winston Churchill than the grimness of our future.

"And Lady Clementine, is she still alive?" he cooed.

"Oh, yes," Anna replied shortly.

"Ah, it is good to know," he said with a sigh.

After one more effort, we were directed to the office of the Ministry of Mines, which turned out to be nonexistent in the town. We then found ourselves knocking at a side door of the small Roman Catholic cathedral; but its two Irish and two American priests were too busy arranging a nocturnal floral procession to be able to afford us much time. The result of all this was that we went to bed that night without much more information other than that no one in the town seemed to know much about any point further than five miles outside it, and that the Apurímac was practically unexplored down to the Benedictine mission at Sivia.

Suddenly the whole thing looked rather serious.

At five o'clock next morning, in the predawn pink of a clear Andean day, we started the inevitable deals with prospective truck drivers. After a last desperate breakfast before facing the unknown, a breakfast of steak and eggs, rolls and coffee, all for four shillings sixpence, we settled to go in an ancient Dodge pickup with a narrow-faced Indian who had both a sassy suede jacket and a mean hangover. To me he was a sort of "Sportin' Life" figure from *Porgy and Bess*. The deal was that for the exorbitant price of five pounds, he would take us soaring back up on to the mountain ridge overlooking the Apurímac and then on down a barely discernible dirt track for about fifteen miles to the little pueblo of Huanipaca at ten thousand feet. From there we would go on foot—we hoped.

Everything went well, considering the age of the truck and the condition of the driver, until we set off along the dirt track. Desperate four-point turns on the hairpin bends sent clouds of pebbles arcing out into the abyss as the spinning wheels churned only six inches from the yawning edge. At this point, our cunning driver looked much "less sportin'" and confessed he had never been along the track before. About three miles short of the little village we had to stop. For one thing, the way ahead was hopelessly blocked by a rockfall from above, and for another, the driver had to get out to vomit. As we watched the poor fellow convulsing, head in hands as he retched, John

Cowrie voiced all our thoughts: "D'you think that's hangover or fear?"

We ate our lunch on the grass by the track: it was very like a London common on a good summer day, except that we had incredible scenery in place of people. A few young-looking horses skittered about among the clumps of short bushy trees, and Mac became almost hysterical over the wonderful variety of butterflies and flowers. A couple of mule trains passed us on their way to Abancay. The gaily clad muleteers and the beautiful embroidery on the panniers of maize slung across the animals made a fine sight; they waved cheerily to us as they passed. We were glad they didn't know how nearly the pickup had driven one of the mules in the train, with its protesting owner, almost over the edge. The most we could do to get help with our kit was to persuade one squarely built, barrel-chested Indian to carry two packs, one on top of the other, and between us we managed all the rest of the gear.

It was only about three miles, and the track was fairly level. After a few hundred yards, we came upon the first snake of the trip, a nondescript green fellow about eighteen inches long and crushed very dead across the path. At the rockfall, we heard a tale of woe about a bulldozer stuck on the far side without petrol, while the Indians chiseled away with hand tools to drill holes for blasting. After we'd scrambled through the jumble of boulders, it took us another hour and a half before we finally tottered into the pueblo of Huanipaca; our guide, chomping a big cud of coca with blackened teeth, refused pointblank to stay overnight and come on with us to the salt mine, which was our destination for the morrow.

Once in the village, we were inordinately struck by the comparative affluence of the people, as against the life that was an almost passive plea for existence that we had seen in the *altiplano*. They had a generator for electric light and drew their drinking water from one central point, at which there were signs of a future water filtration plant. After a speedy tour of the school, we were escorted to the equivalent of a village hall: dusty, wooden floor, pale grey walls and high whitewashed ceiling. The long room was completely bare, save for a large wooden table under the big window at the far end, an old Empire sofa, and a Peruvian flag on a long wooden pole propped up in one corner. On the table, which was draped with a plastic cloth commemorating a celebration on Lake Titicaca in 1968, there stood two large, cheap E.P.N.S. cups for football. While we laid out our kit in "bed spaces" on the floor, Anna choosing the narrow sofa, the buxom young schoolmistress fixed us up with food and the hire of the princely total of six horses for the morrow for five shillings each. After thirty-two years I was going to learn to ride.

The setting sun somehow cleared away the cloud from the snow-covered peaks on the other side of the Apurímac valley, and this scene framed, by the open doorway of the village hall, lent a strangely dramatic atmosphere to our situation. It was strange that in Abancay no one seemed to have heard of Huanipaca. We were now on a sort of island of land on the south bank of the Apurímac. Ahead of us the land dipped down to a point at which the Pachachaca River joined the Apurímac; two days hence we must either cross the Pachachaca or the Apurímac. The talk of a rising river and no rafts sent chills down my spine. Right at the far end of the "island," high above the junction of the two rivers, the small Cacicunga (cutthroat) salt mine hung on the side of a sheer cliff: if we got there next day, at least we should know what was what. Over supper in the village hall, the schoolmistress confided to Anna that within a month the fog and rains closed in on Huanipaca and then they called it "*chico Londres*," little London, after the supposedly eternal winter fogs of London.

Next morning, the horses failed to materialise, as usual, and while we awaited developments, an Indian came in with a small brown and white animal resembling a stoat, which he had killed with a catapult made from a strip of Goodyear inner tube. For ninepence, Mac had a catapult made for him, and then in the pale sunlight of early morning, we relived childhood competitions firing pebbles against rocks. "At least we have got some sort of weapon to attack the jaguars with," mused Mac. All this time, we talked of how we should cut our kit down, when we reached the really wild country.

It was well into the morning when we finally left the back of the village and started the two-hour climb up the winding, narrow path. With us we had six mules and a rather surly guide who had clearly been pressed into service. The large mule on which I sat had thick layers of blanket between its back and the heavy leather saddle, a much more comfortable arrangement than Anna's wooden saddle! Unfortunately for my first day on a mule, the cup-like wooden stirrups were too short, and of uneven length for my legs. The path followed the course of a narrow stream up the mountain, and since this was about four feet deep, I frequently had to lift my knees to avoid crushing against the rocky banks; the result of this was that I was left balancing on the animal's back, rather in the manner of a pea on a drum.

The fine drizzle of our early ascent thickened into mist as we neared the summit, and somewhere ahead were the muffled tones of a bell; quite soon a train of eight mules passed us, going down the way we had come. The poor animals looked as mournful as I remembered old Noddy had been, and their eyes rolled under the burden of two slabs of crude, red salt rock; these were slung one on either side of the animals' backs, and together they weighed two hundred twenty pounds.

Passing through a narrow V-shaped cleft on the top of the ridge at around eleven thousand feet, I was struck by the vivid greens and browns of the grass and trees. Hung with mist as they were, they reminded me strongly of my own part of the northwest Highlands of Scotland. I half expected a group of boys and girls from one of our adventure courses to come bursting into sight. Instead, there came shouts, bells, and a crashing of mules through the brush as another train, this time unladen, swept past us on the way to the mine, under the cursing surveillance of a small Indian boy mounted on a sturdy white pony.

Once on the high ridge itself, the mist cleared away, and under a fresh warm sun, we had devastating views of mountains, snowy peaks, rain forest, and the rapidly dwindling Indian holdings.

"You know, this guide doesn't want to go on; he's looking for any excuse to say we won't make it to Cachicunga today," cried Anna, turning in her saddle to shout back at me.

"Well, it's bloody vital we get on before the rains come," I replied grimly.

"The best thing would be not to stop for lunch—just keep on going. Then he won't have an opportunity to say anything," Anna said. It was all right for her; she didn't eat much anyway, but John Cowrie was already mumbling about "starvation," and up ahead Mac was rolling another fag to stave off its pangs. Anna passed the word up the line in English, which the guide couldn't understand, and everyone "bit the bullet"—it was going to be a long hard day.

Winding first down and then up on the sides of steep stream gullies, I had increasing pain in the saddle. I seemed to remember that riding lessons only lasted an hour, but my first lesson was going to be more like six hours. Luckily, Anna could ride, but she was far from practised and nursed a deep feeling of dislike and even fear of horses. No one said anything about hunger or sore backsides. We all knew we must reach Cachicunga that night.

The afternoon wore on, and the end of the "island" came into sight. Ahead and on either side, the mountains either fell sheer down to the river or their slopes were covered with extremely thick-looking, dark green rain forest, into which thundered great waterfalls from the glaciers above. There seemed to be no sign of cultivation, and it was as if the Quechuan Indian preferred not to meddle with the *ceja*, or "eyebrow," of the jungle. Although we were passing through wonderful country, I was filled with a deep sense of foreboding; it was rather as if we were about to plunge into the lion's den.

I had only fallen off my mule on one occasion, while mounting in the early stages of the journey, and it gave us all a lot of pleasure to see our guide sent cartwheeling straight over the head of the vicious black stallion he was riding; all the same, we were glad when he got up out of the dust unhurt and grinning ruefully.

Towards the end of the day, we began to descend slowly through vivid green semijungle, splashed bright with orchids and butterflies; then on through enchanted glades in which a few cattle grazed on lush green grass. Somewhere to our right on the steep valley wall below, a flock of about fifty screaming parakeets exploded bright green against the black of the forest. We were suddenly in a world of green, which provided a complete contrast to the dusty browns of our travels through the *altiplano*.

This patch of rain forest opened onto a grassy plain, across which we wended our way towards the salt mine somewhere ahead. It was fast growing dark, and with the coming of night and our own feelings of exhaustion, the air seemed suddenly much colder than perhaps it really was. Anna had to be lifted off her mule by John Cowrie. She was quite unable to walk for several minutes—after nearly eight hours in the saddle without a break, but after hobbling along for a few minutes, the stiffness began to go and she caught up.

Well after dark, we stumbled down into the tiny "office" of the mine, a solitary grass-roofed hut with slabs of red rock salt piled against the mud walls. The young Peruvian manager made each of us a cup of coffee, and passed around a plate of homemade biscuits. We shook down our sleeping bags on the earthen floor of his bedroom, which was surrounded by piles of evil-smelling, uncured animal skins. "You may not get across— the river may be too high already." The manager's words struck despair in my cold, tired, hungry soul. He neither knew nor cared what happened on the other side, let alone further down the river, and I felt times were going to get hard again.

Working on Field Marshal Lord Slim's principle that "things are seldom as good or as bad as they are first reported," I decided to get an early nights sleep, in the confident hope that all would be better in the morning. Nevertheless, I broke half the handle off my toothbrush in order to save carrying unnecessary weight on the following day.

The next day dawned bright and clear, and the friendly manager provided us with an old guide and two mules for the four-hour descent to the river itself; we were to signal a raftsman or *balsero* on the far side by lighting a brushwood fire on our way down into the gorge. It was Saturday, 31 October, and the manager said the raft never operated from November until March, when the river is in flood. We left behind us at the "office" an assortment of kit from gym shoes to iron pills—in case the manager met any pregnant women, Mac explained.

The two mules were particularly obtuse, wandering in and out of clumps of brushwood, as we descended the exposed and dusty steep spur on the way down to the river; they drove the old guide nearly hysterical with rage. High above us, a huge condor circled lazily, black against the deep blue of the sky: I remembered an incident that occurred while rowing across the Atlantic with Chay Blyth: a dark skua had settled on my bare head—with what I felt sure was the "clutch of doom"; a big storm had followed on that occasion, and I wondered if this great condor was also the herald of trouble.

The temperature rose sharply within the confined walls of the gorge. Below us on the far side of the river, the old guide pointed out the little hut belonging to the raftsman. He set fire to a patch of dry brush and then overlaid it with green leafy branches, to get up a good head of smoke that would surely attract the attention of the *balsero*. Plunging down through a dense forest of small trees, cactus, sisal, vines, and bright orchids all alive with butterflies, Mac was soon darting about quite oblivious of the increasing heat. Anna began to fall behind; she was feeling the heat badly, and her legs were giving her a lot of trouble after the long day on the mule.

By the time we reached the river, it was high noon, and the heat throbbed from the cliffs on either side. No longer were we faced with a playful stream; now fifty yards wide, the flow was a rich brown torrent surging through rising rapids and gliding dark and sinister across pools. Mac got the Millbank bag going; this would filter the mud from the water before sterilising it, after which it could be drunk. None of us had suffered stomach upsets, which was entirely owing to Mac's precautions with water and food. He was firmly of the opinion that travelling without injury for four weeks, we had created a new world record. Anna lay slumped on a rock. It was quite clear she could not continue many more days with this kind of strain. After we ate the remainder of our fresh food for lunch, we washed our clothes and had a swim. It couldn't be long, we thought, before the Indian appeared to ferry us across on the balsa raft we saw tied to a tree on the far bank, well clear of the racing water.

Three hours later, the nice old guide still had produced no raftsman, and there were small smoky fires burning in half a dozen places on our bank. Although he only spoke Quechuan, we thought we could understand what he was trying to say. "He's coming," we thought he said.

"How do you know?" we would reply in Spanish-English-sign language. He looked blank. He wanted to go home so that he could reach the mine before dark. We paid him and gave him a heavy sharpening stone and several other items of kit we decided to abandon there and then. He left with the two mules, and we were alone in the shade of the deep gorge, now that the sun had moved on. "Positive thinking—that's what's needed," I kept muttering weakly.

No raft. We must swim. John Cowrie started to talk of my responsibility as leader to the wives of the male members of the expedition, who had warned us to keep clear of the river, whatever else we did.

Mac and I measured the speed of the current with pieces of wood thrown in at the head of a pool and timed against our expedition watches, which had been kindly supplied by Smith's, back in London. Forty seconds from the tail of the rapids to the rock we would have to reach close to the far bank; twelve seconds passing the rock—not long; thirty-five seconds to the head of the next rapids.

Mac is an Army swimming champion, and I am certainly not, but I reckoned I could make it across at an angle with the current. It needed at least two to bring the raft across. Anna and John Cowrie rigged up safety lines with nylon parachute rigging attached to logs; the lines would be ready to be thrown to us if we needed them. Below, the rapids thundered hungrily, and I had grisly visions of the bloated corpse I had seen pop up from the bottom of the Perak ruin in Malaysia, during a regimental enquiry into an accidental death that had occurred when I was in the Special Air Service.

The tension mounted. Again the chips were down. Mac kept shouting from the rock upstream that he wanted to get it over with. I was keen to get to the other side as safe as I possibly could.

"Hurray! Look!" Anna jumped up and down with undisguised joy. The *balsero* was coming at last. Suddenly everything fell flat. One half of me wanted to have a go at the swim—the other half was delighted we didn't have to chance it.

It was quite clear that the raftsman had only come to bring two others across from his side; a young and heavily pregnant girl and her boyfriend had to reach the mine that night. By a curious method of paddling the twenty-foot narrow raft (that was made of six slim balsa tree trunks), the two men soon had all of us and our gear across on the other bank. On the last of three crossings, I was the raftsman's aide, as the boyfriend and the girl set off up the mountain towards the mine. My job was to paddle furiously, directly across the front of the raft, or *balsas*, as they are called, while the Indian lunged powerfully along the downstream side; while doing this, I suffered a sharp return of the blinding headache I remembered so well from the *soroche* back at Cailloma.

There were no mules or guides waiting for us on the river-bank, and the Indian *balsero* rushed off ahead on the pretext that his cattle were straying. We were left with all our kit, facing a shattering climb up the near-vertical wall of the gorge to the *balsero's* hut, which was in fact only a fraction of the way up. The headache I got on the crossing thumped like a trip hammer. We were soon strung out hundreds of feet apart; one by one, we collapsed on the stubble, when we gained the small sugar cane plantation that the *balsero* worked to supply sugar for his sugar still.

There was no sign of life when we tottered into the shelter, which was no more than a thatch of sugar cane leaves, supported by nine poles. An open wood fire burned slowly in the middle, and a rough wooden table of thin poles stood in one corner; on which there were a few grubby pots and pans. Outside, icy, crystal-clear water tinkled into a little pool from a half section of bamboo stalk; this diverted water from an artificial irrigation channel, itself a tiny diversion from the muffled roar of a torrent of melted glacier high above the forest.

When the Indian *balsero* returned, he was all smiles; with him he had his six-year-old son, who was suffering terribly from whooping cough. While we set to work at the fire to prepare a splendid meal of soup, rice, and stew, excellently supplemented with bananas, onions, and a white root called *yuca* supplied by the *balsero*, Mac got down to the business of dosing the little boy with some of our medicines, principally tetracycline. Somehow or other, we overdid the fire amid the big, round stones in the middle of the shelter, and it was hard to extinguish it when the time came for bed. This problem was not at all eased by the tremendous thunderstorm that flickered around the mountains, sending torrential rain hammering on the thatch.

Our first night in hammocks was an all around pleasure, compared to the hard ground we had been used to. Swinging in my own model of green parachute silk, I was transported back to the jungles of Malaysia, where I had been so impressed with it that I tried to modify it for use on my round-the-world sailing attempt.

When we awoke at five-thirty in the morning, the storm had cleared, and without moving a muscle I was able to see straight across the Apurímac gorge, back the way we had come. From our position on the bottom of a U-bend in the river, we could see cliffs rising to a cone directly opposite; these were framed by the sky and white, cloud-covered peaks all around. The sugar press, which stood just outside the shelter, was surrounded by myriads of gay butterflies that were feeding on dark stains of molasses. Lying there, I felt it would be impossible to improve on the staggering view across the gorge, and the price of which—a rash of tiny spots of blood, resulting from bites of black flies that had struck during the night—seemed cheap indeed. The little Indian *chico* was rather better after a good nights sleep, but he still lapsed occasionally into savage bouts of coughing that resulted in vomiting.

We had all slept well, and Anna once again showed no sign of asking us to slow the pace. The *balsero* produced both a mule and a horse to carry our gear, and even though it was Sunday, we only had to pay a bit extra for them, he told us. For two and a half hours we climbed more or less vertically, and the poor animals were only just able to make it. At the top, we were taken to the *balsero*'s main house, which was composed of three thatched shelters, and here we were served with delicious soup and *yuca* by his wife, who was wearing a bright red cardigan. We were just about all in, and the soup revived us, as we watched the little children playing with chickens and guinea pigs in the main room. Sunlight poured through the vertical slats of the poles that comprised the walls, striping everything within black and white.

We were impressed by the determined face and wiry strength of the *balsero*, who had burnt new fields from the forest and showed great signs of hard work and initiative; this was one man and his little family, striving and succeeding in their efforts to carve a living from the wild.

Although the sun shone hot from the clear sky, it was much cooler than the airless furnace on the floor of the gorge. Our new guide on the three-hour walk, high and level to San Fernando, was the *balsero*'s teenage son. Somehow, we were all feeling fine, and the walk was a great pleasure; perhaps it was because we were surprised that there was a way through the valley forests we had seen ahead of us on the walk from Huanipaca to the salt mine, and even more surprised to find people and mules where the map showed only empty space. John Cowrie was attacked by a swarm of angry bees while trying to photograph an orchid; some of them flew up inside his shirt, which made him run furiously to the nearest one of us, who happened to be Anna. Already shaken by the sight of a coral snake that crossed the path ahead of her, she nevertheless soon helped him beat off the few straggling bees. We crossed an area of bright, shiny, silicon-like rock, and after a drink at a clear mountain stream, John Cowrie and Mac rushed up with the horses and told of a big, black cat with a heavy tail about the size of an Alsatian dog. We later learnt it was an hugaty.

The village of San Fernando hangs high up on the valley wall, unmapped and almost unknown to the outside world; we came in near its football field, to be greeted by warm embraces from all and sundry, as if we had just returned from the moon. An indication of how much lower in altitute the valley was, was the profusion of bananas and the beginning of the valuable coffee belt of the Apurímac valley.

Once again, we were lucky enough to find a young, married schoolteacher, this time with three children, one of whom was sick with bronchial pneumonia, which Mac did his best to cure. The teacher's wife was wearing green slacks, which seemed incongruous in such an outlandish place; we were desperately thirsty, and the two cups of cold lemon tea, produced from a sort of kitchen behind a curtain in their low mud house, were absolutely delicious. Again, we slept on the mud floor of a schoolroom, though Anna preferred a desk. This time, we took a photograph for the teacher to send to Lima to prove to the authorities that the school did in fact exist. We joined his family for a supper of soup with dried mutton in it—very old dried mutton—macaroni, and *yuca*, which absolutely filled us up; this was washed down with several cups of strong home-grown coffee. Dozing in our sleeping bags at eight o'clock, we gazed through the gaping holes in the mud wall, which one day might have windows. Just above the endless peaks on the far side of the valley, the crescent moon lay flat on its back, inspiring us to a long discussion on the scientific reasons for its being flat when seen from Peru, and on end when seen from Britain; this in turn led to the reasons why water going down plug holes in wash basins runs clockwise in one hemisphere and counterclockwise in the other.

After a good breakfast of two fried eggs and floury, home-grown potatoes, we felt we were winning. With two mules for the cargo and the teacher's own small mare to ride, we set out on the glorious walk down the valley to San Martini, seven and a half hours further on. A terrific walk in midmorning fired a desperate row between John Cowrie and myself. All the little petty things came to a head, and he threatened to relieve me of my leadership of the expedition; in return I threatened to smash his teeth in and hurl him however many thousands of feet it was down to the river below. We had coexisted in relative peace since way back in the *altiplano*. The weather was fine and progress good but there was nevertheless always a subtle and exacting pressure: the impending rains, and the worry of reaching impenetrable jungle before the river became navigable. The pressures were bound to have relief, and it was good that the relief took the form of words rather than "sticks and stones." We all acknowledged that we were four individuals, each with widely differing views of life. For myself, I was disappointed that I couldn't make a happier team.

Our arrival at San Martini coincided with fiesta day, and it seemed the entire population was dead drunk; there was some flute and guitar playing, but it was hardly controlled. Sadly, the teacher was away visiting another pueblo, and we fell into the hands of the *teniente gobernador*, who was hopelessly drunk along with all his cronies. They led us to a deserted two-storey mud dwelling, hard by the village square. This place was vaguely reminiscent of a bombed-out house in London: the roof leaked badly, the floor was rotten, and all the windows were broken.

For the first time we saw bats, and as they fluttered around inside the ruin, we jokingly said that we hoped they were not the dreaded *vampiros*, of which we had heard but really didn't believe in. After a rice and pilchards supper, we quickly settled down for the night, not realising how upset Anna had been by the lecherous drunken cronies who had surrounded the *gobernador* at our meeting. "Help me! He's standing here!"—Anna's cry of horror rang out in the pitch dark of the sheltered room. I jerked up into a sitting position, wrapped in my sleeping bag on the floor, and flicked on my torch, fully expecting some dreadful scene where Anna lay on the table in the corner. But it was nothing; she was just having a nightmare about one of the cronies.

The rain was falling steadily when we awoke next morning. This, together with little food and no certainty of mules or guides, only increased our gloom. Luckily, this didn't last, because an educated young fellow from another hut on an adjacent side of the now waterlogged grassy square came across with some fresh bread rolls and a basket of delicious bananas.

The tall, dignified *gobernador*, now completely sober and looking rather young for his high position, arrived at eight o'clock, bringing with him yet another basket of large, fresh bananas. He told us he was doing his best to find mules and guides and then passed the time by telling us all about San Martini, a village once again not on the map.

Primarily, we were warned not to go near the river, which was some two thousand feet below. The village was perched on the outward tip of a long spur that ran down from the mighty peaks of the Quillabamba. The last person who had tried to navigate the Apurímac was Michael Penin; his canoe however, had overturned in 1953, resulting in the death of his companion. Our own experience at the crossing near the salt mine had convinced us all that the "Giant Speaker" was still far from navigable.

Only three years previously, there had been a fierce guerrilla campaign in the valley, and just outside the village an entire family had been wiped out. Although the trouble was now officially over, *fugitivos*, or criminals on the run, sometimes made marauding forays down from their mountain lairs, and the *gobernador* warned us they might waylay us if they believed we carried anything valuable. I didn't really like the way his noble eyes flickered around the room adding up our kit.

Time rolled on, and the rain stopped. The rising sun soon cleared the clouds and revealed the stunning snow-capped majesty of Choquesafra, which means "beard of gold." Legend has it that at the place at which one of the "beards" of snow comes to its lowest point, there lies a rich seam of gold. The glaciers from this mountain rushed down into a powerful tributary for the Apurímac, and made a broad, fertile valley that we should have to cross in order to reach Hatumpampa, our destination for the day. This same valley once had been part of the main Cuzco–Ayacucho highway, and the twin mounds on opposite banks of the Apurímac indicated that there may well have been a bridge directly below San Martini.

Our mules and guide seemed unusually slow to arrive, even by *gobernador* standards, and when midday came and went, I became rather restive—always there was the threat of the rains, and no one ever knew any place further down the river than the next village. It became clear that it was not just a question of mules and a guide; the *gobernador* was more than a little suspicious that we ourselves might be guerrillas, dressed as we were in near-military kit. He was frightened of official reprisals against his village if it transpired that he had aided guerrillas. After all, in 1967, anyone suspected of this crime had been shot out of hand, we were told.

Decisions! Decisions! It was all too much for the *gobernador*. We just sat on the edge of the rapidly drying square amid the usual scrounging mass of pigs, chickens, children, and dogs and chatted with a strangely un-Indian-looking fellow. Pale-skinned, and very powerfully built, he had both a thick black beard and glasses. He had been carrying on, of all things, a long-range cor-

respondence course with the University of Miami, in an effort
to qualify as an obstetrician. He was shortly due to leave on the
five-day mule train journey to reach the end of a track high on
the other side of the snows of the Quillabamba, and then make
his way by truck and bus to Lima for his final examinations.
While we talked, the *gobernador* dealt with a tearful Indian
woman who had come to him for justice in some dark matter
concerning her brutal husband. There was much sobbing and
wringing of hands, and the poor *gobernador* looked as if he had
just about had enough for one day, when a crony arrived with
two pieces of paper, one for him and one for us. Neatly typed
on the absent schoolteacher's typewriter, they proclaimed that
"*Los Expedicionarios de Inglaterra*" had promised that they
were not up to any funny business. When they had been duly
signed by no fewer than seven people, the two mules and a
young guide were produced, and rejoicing, we set off.

For an hour and a half, we zig-zagged down a narrow goat
track towards the side-valley floor, passing through stubbled
fields of one kind or another and little scatters of Indian dwell-
ings. A log bridge took us across the tumbling crystal stream,
and we began the long climb up the other side of the valley
through a delightful woodland where butterflies were so numerous they made clusters on the tiny streambeds we crossed
on our way. The path was clearly defined, and I set off ahead
on my own, feeling some of the old rhythm returning as the big
"Chevvy" engine deep inside me warmed to the task. Emerging into a sudden clearing, I happened upon a gigantic sugar
press among the small trees. Although it was not working, it
must have been powered by two oxen. I waited by the crude
press until at last the desperately slow mules appeared, and we
all went on together. Up ahead, there was the throb of drums,
and I thought of big black cooking pots and how Chinese firecrackers might help me out of them.

Suddenly we realised why the sugar press was not working—it
was "Fiesta Day 2." We were in the middle of the celebra-
tions. Beside the path in a little clearing stood three bamboo
crosses, each adorned with bananas, oranges, lemons, and small
empty brandy bottles. Everyone was paralytically drunk, and
there was much pulling at elbows until we were all sat down on

a bench at one end of a twenty-foot bare earthen square, opposite a six-foot high Roman Catholic shrine. The men rolled
about on benches on another side of the square, with the
women and children, on the opposite side, all dressed up and
seated under a canvas sheet to protect them from the sun or
threatening rain. A three-man band of flute, fiddle, and drum
struck up, and the drink began to flow again—*chicha* maize
beer at first, then the hard stuff: *aguardiente*, a pure cane spirit
which, translated, means firewater. There was not one unhappy
person to be seen. We were given a special bowl of *yuca*, the
others sharing the pile laid out on the poncho in the middle of
the little square. Then came the stew—lumps of fresh mutton
swilling around in what tasted like warm dirty dishwater. However, John Cowrie and Mac were able to eat theirs, Anna's, and
mine.

Soon we had to leave. The guide had already gone on ahead,
fearing we might not reach Hatumpampa by nightfall. We
scurried along to catch up with our kit, not a little fired by
swigs of *aguardiente*. At last we gained the crest of the ridge,
and looking back, we could see the tall eucalyptus trees scattered around the little pueblo of San Martini on the far side of
the valley. Rain clouds looked ominous, and the ridge itself was
a communal cemetery for the Indians, so we set off down into
the next valley of Hatumpampa. There were a few houses,
mostly of cane thatch and poles, but the church and the
school appeared unusually smart; indeed the whole layout
seemed "organised" in a way we had not found before. Sadly
for us, the fiesta continued with joy undiminished, and we were
welcomed by a chain of drunks who pulled at our clothing in
their efforts to impart brotherly love. . . . Things looked none
too good for an early start with mules and guides on the morrow.

Desperately, we made our way towards the school, and then
quite suddenly we came upon a hacienda that had been hidden
from view on our descent by a small hump on the side of the
valley. We were greeted in the failing light by a young man on
a wooden veranda of the smart whitewalled house; for an instant I thought he was Robin Knox-Johnston—slim, young,
bearded, and with the same high enthusiasm and capable air.

Our mules were unloaded and the guide paid off; almost in a
trice, we were seated around a wooden table in a comfortable
room lit by paraffin lamps—a scene reminiscent of my little
croft home in Sutherland. Señor Humberto was the son of one
of four brothers who own the hacienda at Hatumpampa, which
is in fact a sugar cane plantation and distillery occupying practically the whole of the valley leading off the east bank of the
Apurímac. Towering at the head of the valley, the perpetual
snows of Choquesacra send cascades of liquid ice plunging
through the dark green forest to feed the stream on the valley
floor.

Humberto told us he planned to study anthropology at
Cuzco university after his three-year stint as the lonely manager
of the hacienda. When he had instructed several women Indians to prepare supper in the adjacent kitchen, he asked us to
have a drink with him and the local doctor, who travelled the
various villages in the area about once every three months, with
a small Indian attendant. Of course it was *aguardiente* he
offered us, a special brew kept for the manager himself, he told
us: it was the strongest liquor I ever tasted, and when he
brought another bottle 10 per cent weaker, it was still much
stronger than anything I had ever known, and I only managed
a few small sips. Mac and John Cowrie enjoyed theirs but I noticed they didn't take more than the one small glass.

We had a rich stew for our supper, before going off to sleep
on piles of sheepskins on the veranda. Humberto told us that
vampire bats would indeed be encountered further down the
Apurímac. He himself had apparently been bitten four times
in one night on a visit further down the valley. The main snag
with vampire bats is not the fact of waking up in a pool of your
own blood, but that the vampires often carry the incurable disease of rabies, which inevitably leads to a slow and hideously
painful death.

The doctor left the hacienda with his little aide at four-thirty
in the morning in order to reach San Martini before the heat of
the sun could slow him down. We awoke to find ourselves well
and truly in the land of *mañana*—it was Fiesta Day 3. The
mules just never came because, apart from Humberto and the
schoolteacher, the inhabitants of the little valley were all en-

gaged in drinking for the day. The schoolteacher kindly asked us down to see a programme of singing and recitation by the children in honour of the 190th anniversary of the uprising of Tupacamaru II. We were resigned to a day of rest, and took the opportunity to wash our clothes in the clear, cold waters of the river and then dry them on the hot rocks along the bank. Humberto took us around the primitive still that crushed the cane, heated the sugared liquid, fermented it with yeast, and finally distilled it—four times for the fiercest liquor. For our journey next day to Lucmahuayco, he gave us each a large cake of brown molasses called *chanchaça*.

The extraordinary diet for our day of rest consisted of the white floury root called *yuca*, soya milk, a hot ground-nut milk called *maní*, fresh, sweet oranges, tasteless but refreshing sweet lemons, hot bananas, toasted maize, roast duck and orange sauce, home-grown coffee, and chunks of *chanchaças*. Anna felt she must do some cooking for the lonely Humberto, and in the evening she settled down to prepare a duck *à l'orange* in the smoky black cavern of a kitchen with a primitive mud oven. This greatly pleased Humberto, but it upset the pretty Indian girl who ran both the house and Humberto. Although the duck was tough, it rounded off a very pleasant day for us, and during dinner Humberto recounted tales of his five-day journeys up over the seventeen thousand-foot snowy pass, with coffee mule trains, and then horrified Anna with the stories about the huge boa constrictor snakes that are encouraged to live among the sugar cane to catch the rats.

Already at this altitude, the insects were bad, and Anna particularly suffered from what she thought were fleas: gone were the cracked lips and nagging cough, but the rashes caused by the bites were not a better substitute. I suffered from the bites I'd got from the Biting Black-Fly we had encountered back at the *balsero*'s shelter on the night after the crossing of the Apurímac. As soon as the sweat had begun to run down my face and neck on our daily journeys, the bites swelled up into a single, hard, itching lump down both sides of my neck. Mac didn't really suffer much; maybe this was because of the aura of nicotine he always had around him. He felt strongly that the insects would become really dreadful later on, once we reached the navigable part of the river, and to this end he was not keen to use our anti-insect tablets. John Cowrie not only suffered from the bites but also had a long, drawn-out cold, which often caused his head to ache. From the above, it can be seen that we were not entirely a laughing, joking band of happy wanderers.

It was only four o'clock in the morning when Mac shone his torch in my eyes and thrust a hot cup of coffee into my hand in preparation for an early start—whatever else happened, we were always keen to get away early in the morning. Sadly, it was seven o'clock when we finally set off with a horse, mule, and guide. For some reason, neither Humberto nor ourselves came up with any breakfast. I personally felt it had something to do with the affair of the duck of the previous night, for the pretty Indian girl was doing very little smiling as we said goodbye.

Once across the river on the valley floor, we encountered a twelve-mule train bound for the market some six days distant. Their leader was a fine, strapping Indian mounted on a fiery chestnut stallion, and he agreed to take our mail along with his three-quarter-ton of coffee. We had in fact hoped to buy some cheese from this fellow, who was also the assistant manager of the hacienda, but he told us there was none. It looked as if breakfast had completely gone by the board. There was a delay of some half an hour, and Anna and I waited by a lovely stream that came tumbling down an even smaller valley. Two old Indian women were washing clothes in the water. I dug into my only source of food other than the sacred pack reserved for emergencies. By the time Mac and John Cowrie emerged from the trees, with Mac cursing hysterically that the mule train had stolen his butterfly net, I had munched a dozen boiled sweets and a couple of handfuls of toasted maize. I had kept this store in the back pocket of my olive green trousers for a snack along the way. Now there was only the slabs of *chanchaças* for lunch, and I didn't like the sickly stuff at all. Each valley along the Apurímac was getting progressively richer in food, particularly fruit.

Far below us the river wound like a brown and yellow ribbon deep in the stark, rocky gorge. The river looked far from navigable, although the brown colour clearly indicated it was rising with the rains that were already well under way back up in the *altiplano*.

During the ten hour walk high up along the side of the main valley, we saw three snakes, the first of which I nearly touched with my right hand, while moving through a thickly forested area close to where a stream crossed the narrow path. It was nearly three feet long, olive brown on top and paling yellow underneath. I don't know who was the more surprised; certainly the snake reacted first, sliding rapidly into dense green undergrowth while I remained hypnotised. The walk was long, and we were hungry and troubled by heat and the irritating insect bites, but eventually we reached a point from which we could see well down the valley, where the mountains in the distance began to fall back from the river at last. This was the beginning of the *selva* or jungle, and it meant that before too long, the river must become navigable and also that animals and insects would be more abundant—and the going on foot far more difficult. The second snake was another dead coral with red and black bands separated by white. The third appeared suddenly, as we were making the steep descent into the little side valley of Lucmahuayco. We were all exhausted, particularly the horse, which I was dragging along by the head. The path was perhaps eighteen inches wide, and to our left the hillside fell away in a precipice. The small coral snake appeared from under a boulder and slowly slid across the path; luckily for me, the horse was just too tired to do more than stop dead in its tracks—had it reared up, we might have both plunged down the mountainside.

Once the serpent had gone, we coaxed the reluctant horse down the path, into what was really a little jungle village, and the guide led us through a cluster of thatched huts with thin pole walls to one particular dwelling belonging to a friend of Humberto. This friend had not yet returned from his days work up in the fields, which were dotted about on the steep sides of the valley wherever the trees had been burnt. In the soft light of late afternoon, the grey wood smoke drifted slowly across new clearings in the forest, and the stout Quechuan Indian wife bade us sit outside the hut on a number of ponchos laid out for the occasion. A large bag of sweet lemons was produced, and we ate five each, before the owner returned and led us off to an empty mud house, where he gave us two spare rooms on the ground floor.

For two shillings, we bought a big bundle of bananas and nine eggs, after which Anna cooked up a quick supper of soup and scrambled eggs over a fire in the house opposite; not until the next day did we find out that the owners had moved out to let us cook. Dead tired, we were all asleep by nine o'clock, Anna on the table as usual and Mac and John Cowrie on the floor. I went through to a dark inner room in which there was a low wooden bed surrounded by a number of dead chicks. Although the room was filthy dirty, I rigged up the mosquito net and collapsed on the bed.

When I awoke the next morning, the chicks were gone—probably removed by rats. Anna had already made coffee when a very old man appeared, bent under a bundle on his back. From his tattered poncho he unwrapped a couple of lettuces and a dozen green spring onions, more bananas, and a few huge green beans. We paid him handsomely, and he left nodding his pleasure while we settled down to breakfast in style. What looked like eighteen-inch broad beans contained large black pips wrapped in juicy white fluff; it was only this white fluff that was eaten, the remainder being thrown away.

While I was at the village water supply with John Cowrie, we noticed that the water in the mess tin, in which we were going to hard-boil the eggs for lunch, was full of little, black, shrimp-like creatures that moved jerkily about in the otherwise perfectly clear liquid. "Lice—they'll pass straight through you," snorted Mac, when we poked the tin under his nose back in our quarters. We always chlorinated our water near villages, but this seemed unfit even for washing the lettuce.

We got away at nine o'clock for the six-hour journey to Osambre, which the Indians said was a sort of farm belonging to a German. My mind played with ideas of striding into a mud hut declaring, "Mr. Hitler, I presume," but I didn't really expect to find any European out there, more than six days away from the dirt road. Quechuan Indians have the alarming habit of saying whatever they feel the questioner wants to hear, so that they may be left alone in peace and quiet.

With four guides and two horses, we hauled ourselves up the zig-zag path through the dense forest to a point some fifteen hundred feet above the village. There the path seemed to level off, and we found a small Indian dwelling. We all collapsed gratefully in a heap. Out came the oranges and sweet lemons. We quenched our thirst, throwing the peel into the undergrowth over a low wall in a most idle fashion. Five minutes passed. Then, much to our confusion, a grinning head popped up from the far side of the wall. Far from upset, the cheerful Indian dashed off up the hill to his hut and returned bearing a bright yellow can full of the most delicious fruit juice.

After this fifteen-minute break, we set off once more high up along the valley wall. The going became rather tricky when the type of rock changed from a sort of firm, shiny silicon to a crumbling black slate; here the path narrowed to six inches, and we frequently had to wade through black dust and rubble, where the mountainside had come away in avalanches. Far, far below us on our left wound the Apurímac, which seemed just a narrow brown band. We reached a spot at the corner of a rocky shoulder where the track had simply disappeared for some ten feet, and in its place stretched three long poles, each about five inches in diameter. John Cowrie and Mac scrambled across with me—it was more like a dance than anything else—but Anna, the guides, and horses had to make a big scrambling detour far down the crumbling side of the mountain. At other places the horses had to be unloaded lest their loads brush against the projecting rocks and so nudge them over the precipice.

Lunch was lettuce and giant beans under a little clump of bushy trees on the exposed mountainside. We were still some way from Osambre. At first sight, the little square of nine mud huts appeared to be only a short distance away, on the far side of a heavily forested valley, but as it turned out, it took us more than an hour just to wend our way down through the trees to the stream on the valley floor. The path was little used; even the four guides found it hard to follow.

Since Anna was desperately tired, she fell behind with the two horses and three of the guides. John Cowrie, Mac, and I ran down to the stream with the fourth young Indian guide, whose eyes burned bright with the coca he'd been chewing since the start of the day. At the stream, Mac went wild at the sight of the huge blue Morpho butterflies that fluttered about, just above the clear, rushing water. There was a long wait, and we began to think the others had lost their way, but eventually we heard the clatter of horses' hooves on the rocky path above us. By the time they actually appeared, we were keen to be on our way again because the mosquitoes were becoming very troublesome.

Unknown to us as we plodded up through the clean, trackless, jungle hillside, the ever-watchful eyes of the Campa Indians had been on us since the first moment we had rounded the spur high on the other side of the valley. The lookout had sped barefoot and silent through the tall trees to give warning of the extremely unusual approach of strangers: two horses, two soldiers, one ordinary man, a señora, and four guides.

The young guide with us was terrified of the huge dogs the "German" was supposed to have guarding him, but we were too exhausted by the climb to think much about it until we arrived at a huge gate, which was made of more than forty poles: each of these was slotted horizontally through massive vertical wooden posts. "Who's he trying to keep out with these?" gasped John Cowrie. The silence of the jungle was broken only by the mocking hoots of a few monkeys high up in the trees. "Poles, dogs, German. Who is this guy?" I said, quoting from *Butch Cassidy and the Sundance Kid*. By the time we had cleared the way for the lathered horses and the exhausted but still grimly uncomplaining lady member of the British Amazon Expedition 1970–71, they were already waiting to pass through.

"Osambre can't have many visitors," said Mac, voicing the obvious.

. Ten minutes later, we staggered across a small grassy field and crawled over the six horizontal poles which barred the way into the farmyard square formed by the nine mud huts. It was a jungle fortress.

8

𖡼𖡼𖡼𖡼𖡼𖡼

The Garden of Eden

"Welcome to Osambre. I am Señor Berg, and this is my son
Elvin." A smiling, pale-faced man of around sixty-four, dressed
in a light brown denim shirt and trousers, with a blue, peaked,
cloth cap on his grizzled, short, fair hair, ushered us into an
empty room by the gate. We all sat down while Elvin
unloaded armfuls of huge pineapples and a bag of oranges and
sweet lemons onto the rough wooden table at one end of the
windowless room, which was otherwise bare, save for the
benches. We were all in, and just sat there in silence, biting
chunks from the thick slices of dripping pineapple that Elvin
cut up for us on the table. Outside, the farmyard was milling
with life; perhaps fifty yards square, it had a stream running
downhill through the middle and one large soap nut tree standing at the upper end. A multitude of children, chickens, tur-
keys, geese, ducks, sheep, dogs, and pigeons all scuttled about
inside the yard, while outside there were numerous pigs and a
few cattle.

While slaking our thirst with the fruit, we gradually came
around and began to enquire about the history of this strange
Garden of Eden. Señor Berg's father had been a Norwegian
who had somehow come to live in the lofty Quillabamba; there
he had married a Peruvian girl, Señor Berg's mother. During
the First World War, his father had returned to Europe and
was killed. After service in the Peruvian Navy and subsequent
experiences, Señor Berg had moved to Osambre, around 1945.
At that time, the place was just a virgin jungle mountainside,

far from anywhere, but Señor Berg with Norwegian persistence and Peruvian good nature, had brought with him his Peruvian wife, and together they set about building a new world of their own. In the course of the twenty-five years since they had arrived, Señora Berg, now amply built and immensely pleasant, had given birth to five sons and a daughter, all without any form of medical assistance other than that from Señor Berg. Now, in 1970, they were a living Swiss Family Robinson. At forty-five hundred feet above sea level, the little jungle stronghold perches high above the Apurímac, in an idyllic climate, and with far more food and fruit than can be eaten.

Living in a small enclave of almost total self-sufficiency, Señor Berg is a good farmer possessed with remarkable physical and mental energy. Even the wall of our little room bore a small handwritten notice extolling his pride in being a farmer and urging others to strive for greater agricultural efficiency. It took Mac—whose own farming background in South Africa had at least given him know-how—to recognise just what a good farmer Señor Berg really was. Careful planning and sheer hard work have produced fruit in overabundance all the year round, principally oranges, sweet lemons, pineapples, grapefruit, and bananas. Beyond this there is *yuca*, sugar cane, soya, maize, and various fowls, along with pigs and cattle. The jungle itself teemed with deer, pig, and other game, and the river below provided a constant supply of fish, which was easily dried for storing. There was no problem with refuse disposal since the pigs ate everything, and there were no glass, tin, plastics, or paper containers involved. The annual coffee and coca crops provided sufficient income for books, clothes, and fertilizer, which were about the only luxuries. The work force of hundreds of enslaved Indians, exploited by a brutal master, just does not exist; Berg and his five sons, along with a couple of families of coal-black, nomadic Campa Indians from the deep jungle, live and work together in simple harmony. The black children, and the white *chicos* and *chicas*, playing happily together in the stream, bear witness to the word "integration"—a word they have never heard.

We were so absorbed in our talk that we never realised how the time was getting on, and having already overfilled ourselves with fruit, we found places being laid for supper. First, there were huge bowls of chicken soup—not out of a packet, this time; and then mounds of dried Apurímac kedgeree fish, which we just could not finish. Finally, Señor Berg came in smiling from the kitchen, as he did throughout our stay at Osambre, with a fresh set of plates on which he dolloped tablespoonfuls of black, treacly marmalade made from his own oranges and *chanchaças*. Propped weak against the whitewashed mud walls, we had to drink quantities of a fruit drink made from fresh pineapple juice and *chanchaças*; then, in the last stages of gluttony, we were revived a little with cups of strong, home-grown mountain coffee.

Further discussions about the vampire bats ensured that Mac and I tightly enclosed our hammocks with the mosquito nets when we slung them between stout poles by the stream in the yard. These fearsome *vampiros* spend the day asleep in inaccessible caves on the hillside cliff, only emerging at dusk to hunt for food; apparently between twelve to eighteen inches in wingspan, they live principally on fruit, though a good dose of blood is much appreciated. Somehow, it all seemed too much like a Dracula movie to be true, and I kept having to face up to the fact that I was in a remote part of the Andes, not at home in Scotland. The chief victims of the *vampiros* are animals, mainly cattle and horses, which are defenceless in the tropical night. Señor Berg told us that his cattle sometimes were bled to death by ceaseless nightly attacks from the bats. Human beings are not excluded from the *vampiros*' prey. Although it seems that nobody ever wakes up to find one "tapping his jugular," we were absolutely convinced that humans are often bitten. The most plausible reason why the victim fails to wake up when the vampire bites an exposed toe or forehead is that the creature does not actually land on its victim—rather, it hovers silently, just clear of the exposed part of the body. The cooling flow of air from the vampire's wings disguises the swift incision from scalpel-like fangs, and the instant flow of blood is licked up until the sated vampire flies off, leaving the blood to flow freely on the victim. Were it not from the threat of rabies, an occasional bite would cause no more inconvenience than the nuisance of blood-soaked bedding.

Anna decided to forego the comfort of her hammock for the island-like security of the table in our room, with the doors shut fast, and for once John Cowrie had the whole floor to himself that night.

Early next morning, Mac was given a special breakfast of four eggs and a pile of scrumptious fried bananas, to give him strength for the day ahead. We had all agreed to stay the weekend with the Berg family, resting and preparing ourselves for three hard days with Elvin, the twenty-two-year-old second-eldest son, who had kindly offered to guide us down to the first navigable part of the Apurímac at Villa Virgen. This meant two whole days at Osambre, while Señor Berg tried to burst us with food. Mac, however, could not be kept from his butterflies. He had somehow persuaded Elvin (who bore a striking resemblance to Elvis Presley and trained fiercely with huge dumbbells carved in one piece from jungle trees) to take him on a butterfly hunt for the first day of our rest. John Cowrie, Anna, and I knew he was in for a cruel day, but at seven o'clock, Mac set off, clutching his new butterfly net rigged round a bent bamboo frame cut from the jungle. With him went Elvin and a barrel-chested young Campa, who never stopped smiling and who had been brought up with Elvin since he was a baby.

It was a wonderful day of butterflies, and Mac could very easily have believed he was in heaven—but for the incredible pace Elvin and the Campa kept up through the clean ground at the feet of the tall jungle trees. When at last they arrived at the Pampaconas River, Mac was near collapse, but he was in for a bit of a reviver, for the river, though only about thirty yards across, forms one continual, roaring, white rapid on its course from the Quillabamba to the Apurímac. Unheeding the apparently impossible crossing, Elvin and the Campa cut three stout poles from the bank, stripped off their clothes, tied them roughly into a bundle on their shoulders, and went into the thundering water, and were soon chest deep. Mac, unwilling to show fear, though inwardly petrified, gingerly followed into the maelstrom. Somehow, they got across by using the poles as props on their downstream side, but Mac felt sure that if he once lost his footing, then his life would go, too.

On the far bank, the three dressed quickly and set off again at a trot until they reached a clearing, when Elvin prepared a mixture of soybean meal, salt, and calcium in a long, hollowed-out log. They counted twelve huge cows and one vast bull of some kind of European crossbreed. This meant eight were missing, and Elvin found they had been killed by jaguars. These leopard-like, spotted felines, which weigh between two and three hundred pounds when fully grown, are the scourge of livestock in this part of the Apurímac valley. Elvin had himself shot fifteen, and his elder brother, who was out after one at this very time, had killed twenty-two. After dressing the vampire wounds on the cattle with gentian violet, they set about the serious business of catching butterflies, which were so beautiful and so numerous that it was past four o'clock when Mac paused to look at the time. "We'll never get back before dark, Elvin," he said in his curious South African Spanish-cum-sign language.

"We'll run," Elvin suggested. And they did, back to the river, poling desperately across it, and then on and on, until Mac tottered back into Osambre, but Elvin looked as if he were just warming up. The Campa had stayed out in the jungle for a couple of extra days in order to try and find the missing cattle. Dressed in a simple, sack-like garment woven from jungle cotton, he had only one huge edible snail, some four inches across, and a stick of *palmita* to eat, besides what he could find in the jungle itself. *Palmita* is obtained by cutting down a palm tree, chopping a foot or so from the top, and then peeling away the bark and husk until a stick of white core is left, about an inch and a half in diameter.

While Mac went after his beloved butterflies, Anna, John Cowrie, and I went with Señor Berg to visit another Campa family who lived in the jungle, about two miles back along the way we had come from Lucmahuayco on the previous day. Berg looked and acted like a man of forty, rather than sixty-four, and he fairly rushed along a little jungle trail that wound up and down through endless streambeds along the valley wall; every so often, he would stop and wait for Anna, who was feeling pretty rough after the days of hard walking since Huanipaca.

All around us were small plantations of various crops of fruit and vegetables, where Berg had burnt the forest to make a clearing and then broken up the ground for planting. At last we came to a place where the trees were still smoking, as they lay across the black, ash-covered ground. "Campas!" said Berg, pointing down the hillside at two small figures scraping little holes in the burnt earth below us; looking closer, we saw lines of little green soybean plants among the ash.

We went down, through smoke and fine dust, and met what looked like two Stone Age people. Short, slight, and black, they looked up and smiled a shy, frightened, almost child-like welcome to Berg, who held a brief conversation in Campa before we all shook hands. I was unable to tell whether the grownup was a man, or whether the child was a boy, but Berg made it clear by telling us that all the Campas wore the same one-piece, sack-like garment that is spun and woven by the women. Its seams are vertical for a man and horizontal for a woman. With us we had a man and his son.

Padding painlessly through the still-smoking clearing, the barefooted Campa led us to his thatched hut to meet his wife and daughter, who asked us into the simple dwelling for refreshment. "Whatever you do, don't refuse the food they offer, or they will be offended," Berg warned us, and we smiled our thanks for the few bananas and pieces of pineapple they gave us. The Campa Indians are an attractive people with broad, open faces and huge smiles that appear immediately on introduction; they are also extremely simple, and looked ill-equipped to meet the challenging encroachment of the modern world.

While we ate the fruit, all sitting cross-legged on the ground, the sturdy wife, who was all giggles, stopped spinning her wild cotton. Instead she took to chewing up pieces of *yuca*, which she broke off with her fingers, rather than biting from the root itself. After chewing methodically for about thirty seconds, she spat the pulp into an empty gourd and repeated the process. Berg told us she was making beer called *masato*; the saliva in the *yuca* pulp causing it to ferment.

"When you are offered some, be sure not to refuse," he warned us. Sure enough, as soon as we had finished the fruit, around came a gourd full of milky-looking liquid. We all sipped the "beer" and smiled our thanks. Its taste was much the same as the rather bitter *chicha* maize beer we had drunk up on the *altiplano*, but the thought of the saliva took away much of the pleasure.

This little family of husband, wife, two little sons, and a baby daughter lived alone high up in the jungle. They slept around an open fire intended to scare away the jaguars that would attack if driven by hunger; the smoke kept the insects away. All their possessions were hung on the walls or from the ceiling to keep them from the rats. We saw a bow and a set of arrows among the skins and items of clothing. The Campa showed us the various kinds of arrowheads, one by one, for fish, birds, small animals, and an extra large one for humans. Berg smiled, while the Campa fingered the flame-hardened bamboo blade, which was over a foot long. "They always aim at a man's back, and usually the blade sticks out of the chest," added Berg.

Just as we were leaving to return to Osambre for another huge lunch, the Campa woman made up her face with streaks of vermilion dye from a little wooden pot. She dipped her index finger into the vegetable dye and drew wavy horizontal streaks from the sides of her nose across her cheeks.

On the way back, Berg explained a little of his philosophy of life. Although the Campa would sometimes kill if they were wronged, he thought they were the happiest people in the world. He used the Spanish word *tranquilas* to describe the most savage Campas, who lived in deep jungle, well back from the highway of the river, and he thought that sophisticated Europeans were the most "un-tranquil" people in the world.

During the following two days, I thought on the "Tranquil" theory myself. After all, Berg had shown how it is possible to turn from the sophisticated un-Tranquil to the Tranquil. While I appreciated the idyllic life he led, away from the problems of the modern world, I felt he couldn't escape them completely. When the agricultural reforms finally catch up with him, I thought, he has five sons who can each claim ten hectares, and thus more than cover the acre of the farm as it now exists. The problem really lay in the children, all of whom would not wish to live on the farm, and who in fact have been educated in Cuzco. The solitary daughter of eighteen or so appeared deeply unhappy with her lot, and seemed to want a free life in the outside world. There are snags even in the Garden of Eden, and for this experience, just as for any other, a man has to pay.

An unexpected snag at Osambre occurred in 1967, when quite suddenly there was a Communist-inspired uprising that spread from other parts of Peru to the Apurímac valley. The forty Campas who had lived and worked on the farm until then just melted away into the jungle when two hundred soldiers based themselves at Osambre. Although the soldiers were supported by helicopters, they had the greatest difficulty in tracking down the guerrillas who were hiding out in the thickly-forested mountains across the river, for there were no maps. The guerrillas, apparently mostly East Europeans and Americans, failed to gain the support of the Indians, and although equipped with fine modern weapons, they knew little of survival and soon began to starve, in spite of resupply drops at night from "somewhere outside." A number of them were drowned while trying to cross rivers, such as the Pampaconas, and within six months the uprising was quelled. Sadly, a few friendly Campa Indians, who had unknowingly helped the guerrillas, were among those summarily shot for carrying weapons.

Late on Sunday evening, our last day at the farm, the eldest son returned from the jaguar hunt. He had with him a small deer, an hugaty, and a huge pike-like fish he had caught in the Apurímac; but the jaguar had swum away down the river to safety. The family stayed up late that night to prepare the deer meat for our trip with Elvin on the morrow.

Breakfast next morning was fresh steaks of tasty deer meat, three fried eggs each and gallons of pineapple juice. After saying a sad goodbye to all the members of the family in the large kitchen domain ruled by Mrs. Berg, we set off north along the valley with Elvin and two Quechuan guides. By ten o'clock, we were down at the Apurímac, where two waiting Campas ferried us the seventy-five yards across on a balsa raft. John Cowrie was feeling so ill with flu that he took to chewing a wad of coca, like the two Quechuan guides. This seemed only to incense

Mac, because poor John Cowrie seemed to gain no relief from his pain and soon spat the coca out.

After a fifteen-minute break on a sandbar on the west bank, which we spent sucking energy from oranges, sweet lemons, and pineapple, and catching butterflies for Mac, we said good-bye to the two Campa *balseros* and set off up the steep side of the valley. We left them with packets of Mac's cigarettes and his catapult, which was worth more than any money. The going was hard on the way up the mountainside, and at first we had to cut our way through the undergrowth. However, once we reached the cultivation of the village above, the going was easier, if much steeper, and it took us two and a half hours to reach a little pueblo after passing through patches of coca, cocoa, pineapple, maize, bananas, and coffee. John Cowrie saw a tapir among the trees, and at a little shelter, a Quechuan Indian told us that, only a couple of nights previously, he had had to throw a burning brand from his fire to scare off a jaguar.

Lunch was strips of venison and more citrus fruit; the tough meat seemed to pulverise my gums, which for some reason had become quite unbearably tender while we were at Osambre. While we were eating, two old Indians came to me and pointed at their sore eyes. It happened that I had a bottle of eyedrops with me, so I decided to carry out my own "hearts and minds" campaign in the hope of attracting fresh guides to our cause. The bottle was new, and after I had had them lie down side by side, rigidly to attention with fingers outstretched, I set about performing the miracle. For some reason the plastic bottle didn't seem to be working very well, so I squeezed it extra hard; there was a pop, and the whole top came away and shot into the terrified Indian's eye. Clearly used to cauterisation, he never moved a muscle, while I mopped up the damage, pricked the top with a pin, and put a few drops into each of their eyes. The operation was a huge success, for they both smiled their satisfaction. They also gave up making adobe mud bricks to come with us to the little village of Chinchibamba, three hours further in another side valley. After a fine swim in a cold, rushing stream, we arrived at Elvin's friend's hut, only to find his baby sick almost to death. Mac advised treatment for dehydration and gave it some tetracycline, but the dysentery had taken its toll, and none of us held out much hope.

When dusk came to the little jungle clearing and the vampires fluttered round the thatched rooftops, the mother became nearly hysterical, and I thought the baby's last moment had come. Anna began to look distraught herself and implored Mac to "do something"; he in turn looked at his wits' end. As a last desperate measure, he produced an eye dropper and had the mother squeeze warm sugared water into the dying child's mouth. Quite miraculously it began to improve, and soon it was bawling again in a most healthy fashion. Mac had been right about dehydration, but the mother had not followed his initial advice. We all clambered into our hammocks that night feeling that at least it had been worth our while coming to Peru.

Next morning, we got away early. The baby seemed quite normal once more, after Mac's doses of tetracycline, lamotol, and the sugared water. As a reward, the mother gave us each a hard-boiled egg and a cup of hot sweet cocoa from the local trees. A black horse, hired in the village, had a long stream of dried blood leading down from a vampire bite on its right shoulder.

We had a long, hard morning grinding up the jungle-covered hillside, but we were in the land of the True Bug, and Mac was as happy as a sandboy stuffing them into his cyanide "killing bottle." Elvin, in his denim kit, Anna's boots, and a faded pith helmet that was his pride and joy, looked particularly smart. He had the whole trip well organised. For lunch we stopped at a high mountain hut in a jungle clearing for great, juicy, slices of papaya and as many bananas as we could eat. Rodrigo, the guide with the horse, unwrapped a chipped, white enamel washing bowl from his poncho. It was full of cold fried eggs and rice, and we fell on it like a pack of hungry wolves. Since the Indian *campesino* was suffering from some sort of liver complaint and indigestion, Mac gave him a few tablets, hoping they would have the luck of his previous potion.

In the afternoon, we plodded through humid, dense jungle until the thunder and heavy rain on the far side of the valley persuaded Elvin to call it a day at another little hut, high above the rushing Tecsebamba River, a tributary of the Apurímac.

Although our hosts looked pretty sick, it was not through any dietary deficiency, for there was ample food—plenty of papayas and bananas. Leishmaniasis had caused one man's ear to disintegrate, and his nose looked as if it would soon end in the same hideous way. The two children were hopelessly anaemic; their hairlines were encrusted with dried blood from insect bites. The evening meal was mainly fruit, since we had planned to reach Villa Virgen, the first navigable point, on this evening —yet it was still four hours distant.

Next morning, Mac's huge injection of penicillin had the poor Indian with the leishmaniasis limping as if he had had his leg amputated, but at least it would stop his nose from falling off. At last, at around midday, we all sweated through the steaming jungle to emerge on the Apurímac once more, opposite the little village of Villa Virgen. We hauled up the forty-foot dugout canoe onto the ground along the bank. The young Quechuan *balsero* rafted the guides across the smooth, if fast-flowing, river, while we five all swam across at an angle which at least seemed to prove we could swim before starting on the thirty-five hundred miles down the river.

9

The Rapids

Once we had reached the navigable part of the Apurímac, things began to happen, and we were able to cover large distances each day—when we moved at all. In the jungle—remember that there are more than two million square miles of it in the Amazon basin alone—there are only two means of transport: first, by air, light plane-hopping from one tiny cleared airstrip to another; and second, by river, wherever the rivers are navigable. The big seventy-five horsepower outboard motors have revolutionised jungle transport just as surely as the aeroplane has. There are few roads in the jungle, and those few mostly lead nowhere; instead they serve as branches leading out from the few riverside towns to permit localised colonisation in the jungle close to the road. Great areas of the jungle are still unexplored, simply because it would be hopelessly slow and impractical even to move a small distance from the navigable rivers. The main trade highways are, and always have been, the navigable rivers, and the powerful outboard motors have extended the highways by simple virtue of their ability to push a canoe through the rapids that exist on the headwaters of many of the rivers, including the Apurímac.

Of all the villages in the whole Amazon river system, Villa Virgen, a scattered handful of straw huts, has the dubious distinction of being the village at the furthest navigable point from the sea. Only seven years old, it came into existence when some sharp-witted boatman realised that if he braved the desperate rapids with his forty-foot dugout canoe and seventy-five horsepower outboard, he would have the pick of the trade with places like Osambre, which are upstream of the navigable point. The village itself is really only a clearing station for the produce of other villages, and it has a remarkably seedy atmosphere, combining the worst of civilisation and the Indian way of life—honky-tonk gramophone records and disease.

Luckily for us, Elvin knew the cocky young Quechuan Indian who owned the forty-foot canoe we had seen nosed up on the gravel of the bank when we arrived. Señor Berg had often traded through Villa Virgen in the past. After much bargaining, Elvin persuaded Osco, the Indian, to take the five of us and the two Quechuan guides who had come with us all the way from Lucmahuayco to the village of San Francisco. This was on the day after our arrival at Villa Virgen. As this was to be a special trip with no cargo other than ourselves, Osco demanded and got twenty pounds for the hundred-mile trip, which was to be completed in one day: it was an *expreso* trip, as he called it.

For the rest of the day, we lolled about eating pineapple and lemons, or scrubbing, in a none-too-clean tributary, our grubby clothes, which were beginning to rot. Mac and I spent the night in our hammocks and mosquito nets, which were slung between the huge poles of a wooden tower by the river. From this tower, a steel wire rope led across to a similar construction on the far bank. This was used instead of the ferry during the rains, when the raging water made crossing on a balsa raft impossible. The young *balsero* with whom Elvin, Anna, John Cowrie, and the guides stayed told us that the rains were terribly late. I could well imagine what it would have been like in the jungle near Osambre if the rains had been on time.

Next morning John Cowrie was waked at five-thirty, when a chicken walked across his face as he lay on the earthen floor of the *balsero*'s hut. His cry of horror awoke Anna from her perch in the rafters. The day of the "big trip" began. We were all excited at the prospect of covering a hundred miles in a day.

Osco arrived late, his tall, well-proportioned frame dressed in pale grey slacks and a light blue nylon shirt. On his head a blue peaked cloth cap was worn back to front to shield his neck from the sun. The unusually pretty, young wife of the Indian *balsero* had gone to some trouble to make us a fine breakfast, and it seemed a pity to have our departure delayed by a row with Osco, but that's the way it happened. His tawdry younger sisters, dressed in vivid slacks and blouses, far too tight for their porky figures, hoisted crates of empty beer bottles into the canoe. We had agreed on the previous day that he was to carry them at no extra cargo, but now Osco demanded another three pounds. He claimed that the river was dangerously low and therefore the risks in the rapids were greater; also, he had to have a pilot in the bow testing the depth with a pole. Just as there seemed to be no room for further negotiation, Elvin offered his services as the bowman, and Osco rather grumpily accepted. We were off.

Within three minutes, we had reached the first of the rapids: they came as rather a shock so soon after the euphoria and relief of our departure from the friendly waving of the young *balsero* and his family. We rounded a bend and there they were. I glanced up from my seat on the pile of packs in the bottom of the canoe and saw that a lot of arrogance had gone from Osco's handsome brown face. In its place there was concentration, even concern. Quite suddenly, the river seemed a lot wider and the power of the great moving body of water made my stomach sink in an unpleasant fashion. If Osco made a mistake, there was nothing any of us could do. The river went smooth, slick, and fast as it gathered momentum, and then suddenly there was a lot more noise, as Osco gunned the engine into full power. We snaked through rumbling, tumbling white water, dotted here and there with wicked, black, deadly rocks that made a course not unlike the slaloms of Anna's skiing days. It was rather like one of those fairground games in which the player has to keep a pen between the two sides of a weaving road on a revolving drum: Osco had to play with the throttle to avoid hitting the banks of the river, as the canoe rushed around bends and through narrow channels between islands of rock. If the engine failed and we lost steerage, then the canoe would be wrecked. It was as simple as that. All the while, Elvin, crouched in the point of the bow, plunged his stout pole down and ahead of us to test the depth. He was in his element; the sheer excitement of it all filling him with élan. The rest of us sat low, as near to the bottom of the canoe as possible, to help keep balance by getting the centre of gravity as far down as possible. I personally felt that if the canoe did turn over, somehow or other I would survive the battering force of the water and emerge at the other end of the rapids unscathed and able to swim ashore, but I could see from Anna's pale face that she was not convinced. The main danger was hitting one's head on a rock, thus losing consciousness and then drowning: we all had our heavy boots off in case this might happen.

We suffered an odd bump or two, but as the bottom half of the canoe was made out of one huge hollowed-out cedar trunk, it was pretty solid. The plank sides, however, about three feet wide and half an inch thick, and again cut from a single tree, were not so solid. The two Quechuan guides were kept busy bailing out the water that gushed through great splits that were ill-concealed with strips of tin, or gummed on with pitch. Anyway, we got through all right, although the kit was rather wet from splashing and John Cowrie clasped his precious aluminium camera case to him as if it were a newborn baby.

Sitting well back in the canoe, resting pleasantly on the baggage, we all enjoyed the new feeling of speed; even the heat of the sun on the open river was neutralised by the breeze of our fifteen-knot passage. The river itself, although very low for the time of year, was rising; its water, thick and brown, would soon cover the broad white banks of pebbles and the green bushes that had sprung up since the previous rains. There were also banks and islands of solid silt that had been brought down from the mountain valleys. Well protected by hats and clothes from the possibility of sunburn, we relaxed, sucking sweet lemons or mopping the juice of fresh pineapples from our chins with river-wet handkerchiefs, as the impenetrable jungle slipped past. It was hard to grasp the idea that we could make such good speed without having to sweat and grind up and down windy, narrow paths.

Although the rapids occurred on the average at about three-mile intervals, the anxiety was for me always outweighed by the feeling of rest as we sped along. On the previous day, we had all drunk the water from the tributary running into the Apurímac at Villa Virgen when the young *balsero* had brought buckets of it into his little riverside hut to cook with. Elvin had insisted that it was pure, but when we later went up to wash our clothes, I was convinced it was impure; now, next day, I felt drained of energy, and what's more, I felt sure the water was to blame.

Occasionally, when we neared an area of rapids, Osco would pull into the bank, and everyone would have to get out and walk downstream through the huge, grey, water-worn boulders to where the smooth deep water began again. Among the five of us, and with the help of the two ever-cheerful guides, we usually managed to empty the canoe of all the kit, but some-times we felt overcome by lethargy, the result of drinking the foul water. As with most experiences, the sheer repetition of shooting rapids bred a feeling of confidence and then famili-arity. Overhead, the sun burned hotter than we had known it since the day in the gorge below the salt mine, and whenever Osco pulled into the bank, the artificial breeze created by our passage ceased, and sweat welled up, only to trickle down our skins, still sensitive from the insect bites. The weight of the packs only increased our sweating, and gradually we fell into the trap of leaving our kit in the canoe as long as Osco didn't kick up a fuss; I never looked at it from Osco's point of view, which might have been that if he lost his canoe and priceless engine, then it would be no bad thing for the *gringos* to lose their kit as well.

At last we came to a three-hundred yard length of rapids, which looked simple enough on a straight section of the river. At Osco's request, we got out as usual; Anna, Mac, and John Cowrie padded downstream in their sneakers, through sand and boulders, to a position from where they could get good pic-tures of Elvin and Osco bringing the canoe through the creamy white hillocks of rushing water. Above us on either side of the river, the now broad valley was clothed with unbroken dark green jungle as it rose up smoothly to long, straight-backed ridges that were dusted here and there by little mops of fleecy white cloud. I followed the others down to the end of the rapids. Lead-limbed and empty-headed, I wasn't really thinking.

"Look! They're not going to shoot through!" John Cowrie's cry was edged with anxiety. Too late, I snapped into wakefulness. The two guides and Elvin were gradually lowering the canoe downstream, while Osco held it off the rocks with a long pole. Now all our belongings were held only by the rusty links of the cheap light chains that led from the bow to the urgent hands and straining backs of Elvin and the two Indians. It would serve us right if the chain broke and we lost the lot, I thought to myself. Inch by inch, the canoe wobbled and banged along the edge of the foaming water, while the chain was eased or tightened at Osco's command. We were in luck: the chain held, and soon we were on our way, counting our blessings.

For miles there was no sign of man except for an occasional tiny shelter marking, where some lonely Campa Indian had spent a couple of days fishing. These simple lean-to shelters, of six poles thatched with cane leaves, would be carried away on the rising flood waters within just a few weeks. We were looking for a proper Campa settlement, and we heard there was one on higher ground some thirty miles downstream from Villa Virgen. Osco had warned us that the Campas had suffered from the grippe during August, and many of them were thought to have left the village, but this in no way prepared us for the eery atmosphere of the place, when we did eventually scramble up the bank to pay the Campas a visit.

"Nearly all the men have died, I think, and the rest have gone away with their families, leaving only widows and children," Elvin told us, after a brief talk with a sad-faced old-looking woman of·perhaps thirty, who was breast-feeding a painfully thin-looking baby. We were standing awkwardly in a horribly deserted little cluster of thatched huts; the whole place was filled with the fly-blown air of death and, worse still, despair. There was no adult male in sight, just a dozen or so gaunt, desolate women and girls, who sat by a small canoe, absently chewing pink *cassava* and spitting it into the puce-coloured mush that half filled the little boat. But brewing beer wasn't going to help. I don't know which of us was most upset; I suppose it was Anna, who just stood and stared. The Indians stared back, empty and hopeless, not really expecting a miracle; they didn't understand why their men should suddenly have fallen ill and died like so many flies, and why they were left alone trying to cope. I wandered around the deserted huts, still untouched since the death of their owners, and saw the pathetic remains of family life: a few scattered skins for bedding, bows and arrows, and dried river fish hanging from a string. If there had been doors, they would have creaked and swung emptily open on unoiled hinges.

"Mac, surely we can do something for this poor little boy," pleaded Anna, looking almost tearfully at a naked three year old, whose matchstick arms and legs stuck out grotesquely from a great balloon stomach.

"Anna, it's no use. You know we aren't carrying anything for worms. It's no use giving him some aspirins and hoping it will all get better, because it won't." Mac was bitter with frustration, but he was right; it would be wrong to pretend we could do something when we couldn't. If only we'd had some worm pills. There was nothing for us to do except go away and leave them to their plight. We felt pretty rotten.

"The next rapid's a bad one," said Elvin, as we shuffled dejectedly back to the canoe. "Osco is going to let the other fellow take it through for him, and he says you should walk around." We had taken on another pilot, a Quechuan Indian, just a few miles upstream of the Campa village. He had come on the trip on the spur of the moment, having sent his companion back to his tiny jungle holding (called a *chacra*) to tell his wife he wouldn't be back for a couple of days. Life in the sun seemed to be run on a delightfully casual basis, or so we had thought until we saw the Campa settlement, but no amount of casualness could make up for the lack of a doctor.

Feeling rough, I persuaded Osco to let me ride down the rapids in the canoe. "Eight people were drowned here already this year," said Osco, but I felt too ill to walk. The rapids were in a sharp bend in the river, and in fact it was more like a cataract—the whole river fell down a short, steep hillside into a whirlpool. We waited while Anna and John Cowrie got into position on a promontory on the opposite side. The thunder of the teeming water seemed to grow ominously louder while we waited.

"If we go over, stretch out like a surfboard; it'll help against being sucked down," advised Mac, who had also managed to persuade Osco to let him come in the canoe. I'll be all right, I thought, with the same stupidity that had risked all our kit on the end of the chain earlier in the day.

Then we were away, with the engine roaring above the thunder of the water. There was a strong, muddy smell in the foam-filled air, and everything seemed quite straightforward, as long as the engine kept going. I looked across at the fleeting bank, rather as one looks at the roadside from a fast-moving car. Ahead and below us on the bank, I could see Anna; it felt odd to be looking down on someone from a canoe only inches above the surface. Up in the bow, Elvin was kneeling with his pole, but like a tight-rope walker keeping his balance, while our pilot aimed the bow at Anna to cut between the point of the bank and a great bulging plume of water that concealed a murderous rock. The engine coughed. I thought of the foam drowning the sucking carburettors, and felt the muscles in my arms tightening the grip I had on both sides of the canoe.

Here we go, I thought, with visions of surfboards in the Cornish rollers of my childhood. We're going to hit Anna, I thought again, as the forty-foot dart speared towards the rocky promontory. Then, just as all seemed lost, the coughing stopped, the engine surged into full power, and we shot through the gap into the whirlpool below. Long and shallow, the canoe crossed the edge of the pool without difficulty, and soon everyone was talking exultantly of the "fantastic" photographs they had taken and we were on our way again.

After more hours of the drumming engine, rapids, whirlpools, and long, smooth reaches of river, we finally pulled in alongside several other canoes on the squalid waterfront of San Francisco. The little shantytown is actually on a dirt road that winds up into the Andes to Ayacucho, which has an airfield and road connections with the outside world. This Catfish Row of a place is at the end of a tentacle stretching far down into the jungle. There is only one other such "road end" in the jungle, and that is at Pucallpa, some six hundred miles further downstream. We walked around the little stalls that served as shops and bought such rare delicacies as real bread rolls and crude chocolate before persuading Osco to take us down the river a further half-hour to Sivia.

It was late afternoon, and we all were exhausted by the dramas of the day, combined with the hot sun and the noisy motor. Quite suddenly, we rounded a left-hand bend in the river, which was now all of two hundred yards wide, and there, perched on the bank, was a small, modern, timbered chalet. It was almost like coming to a sailing club boathouse on the Thames at Staines—I felt that I should shut my eyes in case it was not real.

"You must be the Amazon expedition. Hang on a second—I've just got to brief this chap." The slim, dark-haired young man, immaculately clad in crisp white shirt and grey slacks, was as matter of fact as if we had just stepped off a bus somewhere in London. He turned back to the Indian on the porch of the chalet, continuing his conversation, and we knew that we were dealing with a proper Englishman again.

"Have a vermouth." Mrs. Elsa Douglas-Duffraine smiled as we sat awkwardly in comfortable armchairs in a corner of the dining room. Only half an hour had passed since we had waved a sad goodbye to Elvin, who, with Osco and the guide, had returned to San Francisco for the night in readiness for an early morning start on the slow journey back to Villa Virgen and then Osambre. We owed Elvin a great deal, and as a small token of our esteem, we made him a present of one of the expedition's watches.

Now the river seemed far behind. We were in a piece of England. Only half a mile up a track from the riverside chalet, now shrouded by jungle trees, we were at the Benedictine mission of Granja Sivia, where four monks, temporarily looked after by Elsa, were carrying out the recommendations of Vatican II and actively helping the jungle colonists to improve their standard of living.

After two years of discussion among the twenty-four monks at Worth Abbey in Sussex, the abbot, who is also president of all the Benedictine houses in the United Kingdom, decided to start a separate house at Sivia in Peru. First, Father Bede Hill, then thirty-seven years old and an ex-farmer, was sent out to test conditions in 1967.

The Peruvian government showed considerable enthusiasm for the idea of free agricultural advice and offered Granja Sivia as the site for putting this advice to the best use. The government reasoned that the problem of encroaching city slums was becoming daily more acute, and that if the subsistence-level peasants could be persuaded to leave the slums and colonise the jungle, then everyone would benefit. The area around San Francisco, on the eyebrow of the jungle, was selected as a suitable place for colonisation, because over the past thirty years, thousands of poor peasants had come down from the mountains and gradually settled in the jungle nearby on the west bank of the Apurímac. In 1958, the government moved five hundred twenty-five families into the jungle on the east bank of the river. Across from San Francisco, a road was built, and the colonists built sixty one-hundred-thirty-acre *chacras* close to the road, which was in turn supplied by farms from San Francisco. As with many schemes that include the regrouping of population, this one ran out of money, and unlike the spontaneous colonists on the west bank, the folk on the east expected a great deal to be done for them by the government that had imported them in the first place. All was not well when the Benedictine house was founded on the thousand-acre site of an already defunct Agricultural Educational Unit.

After only one year of real operation, the four monks had begun to get things moving. Although only using fifteen acres in 1970, they planned to use a hundred in the end and colonise the other nine hundred acres. They had already employed seventeen people at a good wage—in fact double the normal daily rate of five shillings. Their main achievement has been the formation of a co-operative for the colonist-owners. While previously the Quechuan Indian colonists had been at the mercy of unscrupulous merchants for the sale of their perishable crops, the co-operative offered a firm price, and the empty trucks returning from Ayacucho brought stores with them, thus reducing transport costs. We were all four impressed by this practical effort to improve not only the spiritual welfare but also the physical lot of the Indians.

We stayed a total of five nights at the mission and slept most of the time we were there. Anna suffered badly from an upset stomach as well as general fatigue; we hardly saw her at all. Father Michael Smith, fifty-four, a mild-mannered but wiry little man whose modesty belied his Oxford classics degree and the record of quite remarkable lone journeys he had made in the jungle to minister to distant villages, told me that Julian Latham was keen to travel downriver to Atalaya by balsa raft. Julian, thirty-five, was an ex-farmer from Rhodesia and a South African rugby trialist whose sports experiences had left him with a crushed left ear. Unruly black hair and a ready grin combined with a straightforward, open character and quiet sense of humour to make him a more than welcome addition to the team. He had worked at the mission for fourteen months and felt the time had come for him to move on to something new.

On the day after our arrival, I crossed the river with some Indians to visit the co-operative and collect bananas from an Indian further on in the jungle. We also called on one or two Campas who Julian had heard might make good *balseros* for our raft journey, two hundred fifty miles downstream to the little town of Atalaya. There was no question of a canoe—canoes simply can't travel between San Francisco and Atalaya. By lunch time, we had signed a contract with a young Quechuan who agreed to build a ten-log balsa raft, twenty-four feet in length, with a cabin to shield us from the sun. We were to set sail at five o'clock in the morning on Tuesday, 17 November. Even with a full boost of coca, the fellow would be hard put to build the raft in four days. When he showed us the *chacra*, where the balsa trees were already cut and dried, and the beach half a mile from it, where the balsa would be built, Julian thought he could do it. We called him Polly, which was short for Policarpo.

On Monday afternoon, still feeling weak from mysterious stomach upsets that I firmly believe were caused by the foul Villa Virgen water, we all trooped down to help with the final details on the balsa raft. Of course, it was far from finished, but somehow the logs had been peeled and lashed with bark from young balsa trees, the shelter of ten poles erected and ready for the groundsheet roof, and the rough plank platform nailed to the main logs. Julian found another Quechuan Indian, called Dimas, an older, more experienced fisherman, who wanted to make the whole trip to Atalaya, whereas Polly only wanted to go to Cutivirene, two days downstream. We signed him on as well, hoping they knew how to negotiate the rapids as well as they said they did.

At four o'clock on Tuesday morning, Julian flashed a torch in my face; it was time to get up and get on. We were surprised to find Elsa already up and breakfast made. We all felt the monks were lucky to have her there to organise the running of the household for them. In the dim light of early morning, we slid the raft on the launching logs down the bank into the river. Our packs were lashed down to boards, and after a few hurried goodbyes to Fathers Bede Hill, Michael Smith, and Edward Crouzet, we were away towards the first of the rapids, which were only a few minutes downstream.

The river was running fast. All we had to do was paddle the raft into the right approach path for the rapids, and then keep the front end pointing forward. Simple, we thought—no walking—all we had to do was sit there. Our kit was lashed in two lines across the balsa, one just forward of the middle and the other across the back end of the plank platform, with our packs lashed upright against the rear corner poles of the shelter. Anna sat on the forward line of kit and Mac, John Cowrie, and I sat in the gap between the two lines. Up in the front, with his cap back to front, Polly stood on the left of the platform, thin, bright-eyed and silent, chewing a wad of coca; Julian stood in the middle, head and shoulders above the other two, a carbon copy of Clark Gable; and Dimas, looking slim and shrewd, stood on the right: all three worked hard with big light balsa paddles.

With three stalwarts on the front, we had nothing to fear, as the roar of the first rapids grew louder at our approach. We were a silent matchbox being sucked towards a waterfall. I looked around me at the others. They were tense, with knuckles white as they held onto the sides of the packs. "It sounds like the grinding of broken bones," said Mac, and he should know. The water was shallow now, and under the balsa, we could all hear the current rolling millions of small pebbles along the bottom towards the distant ocean.

Suddenly, we seemed to accelerate in a smooth patch at the very start of the rapids proper, and then we were away into the tumbling, roaring water which had that same "river-watery" smell that drifts downstream on the breeze from the Thames weir. "*Chocko! Chocko!*" cried Dimas. We all looked at him in surprise. Then—BANG!—the left-hand side rose up on a rock, and the river reached hungry arms across the other side of the platform, splashing angrily up and over our packs. It was only a bump; then we were free, whirling round and round, out of control. There were a few more bumps, but always the water retreated in a few seconds, leaving behind only a brown and white lacing of foam on the planks and gear.

"I think we must have two men paddling on the back of the balsa to help us keep her straight when we go through rapids in future," Julian said, grinning hugely at our anxious faces when we reached the smooth water at last.

"It's a good thing we lashed down the packs; we'd have lost the lot," mused Mac.

After that, the day warmed up, and we got into routines for emergencies. With rapids every ten or twenty minutes, we were soon convinced that neither Polly nor Dimas knew every one of them; we just hoped they knew where the really bad ones were. The sun was shielded by cloud for most of the day, and we thought how heavily it would be raining back at "*chico Londres*" near Abancay, as we sat having a lunch of raw cabbage and tomatoes from the monks' garden at Sivia. The new clothes we had picked up there smelt fresh, and we felt quite civilised. It was so much quieter and more natural than the vibrating roar of the outboard that had so exhausted us in Osco's canoe. Life on the river seemed quite peaceful on the steady level reaches, where the mantle of the jungle was broken only occasionally by the Indian *chacras* that stood like little islands in a green tide. After just a few hours, we passed the northern limit of colonisation on the east bank; then all was virgin country, the land of the Campa whose boundaries had been pushed back by the Quechuan newcomer.

There were estimated to be only about seven thousand Campas left in the jungle, barely a quarter of the twenty-eight thousand, which is supposed to have been their maximum; a smiling, friendly people, they seem to have retreated from, rather than advanced towards, the inevitability of civilisation. There may have been many on the banks who saw us, though I doubt it; we certainly saw none of them—just a few deserted straw shelters by the water's edge, marking places where they had spent a few days fishing.

Once, at the tail of some rapids, we swung across the sheltered mouth of a narrow backwater and surprised a sinister alligator, or *caiman*, as it lay on a mud bank, and many times we came so close to the bank that beautiful, snowy white birds like small herons lurched into flight, flapping crossly away to a new fishing spot. We caught glimpses of other beautiful birds among the trees fluttering from branch to branch at our approach. Cries of *"Chocko! Chocko!"* became the accepted alarm for the two resting men to leap to their paddles on the stern. We became quite good at steering the balsa raft, and if it spun, we perfected a way of making one complete revolution in only a few seconds before stopping it dead when the front pointed the right way again.

But even constant practise didn't rule out the occasional disaster. Late in the afternoon, we were drawn into a fast flow, where the current raced around the outside of a bend above some rapids. We were pinned close against the bank, which was bad since the water, running deep and fast, was undermining a crumbling wall of silt. If we bumped against it, we might set off a small avalanche that could sink the balsa. All of this seemed fairly unlikely, as the silt was splashing down in quite small lumps, but ahead a broken tree trunk was sticking six feet out from the bank. As the silt was washed away, the trunk, perhaps a foot in diameter and five feet above water, would stick out further and further until it would topple into the flood.

We were perhaps a hundred yards above this projection when all hands sprang to work at the cry of *"Chocko! Chocko!"* We had to get a good ten feet clear of the bank to miss it, and we all thought it could be done. It just couldn't. From where I stood on the right forward side of the platform, everything seemed to happen very suddenly: we began to spin left, and the stern of the balsa moved in nearer to the bank; I realised we were moving much faster than I had thought. We were going to crash. I lunged at the tree as it flashed past, and the light paddle snapped like a matchstick. Then the tree caught the middle and back poles of the shelter. The balsa lurched heavily to the left, nearly throwing the three of us on the front of the platform into the river. There was a nasty tearing sound, and then we were spinning free into the rapids.

Everyone seemed to keep cool as we bumped through, fighting to regain control. Once again we'd had a lucky escape, especially since some of the kit, including Mac's camera, was hanging from the superstructure. The shelter now had a weird geometrical pattern, but at least we had not lost anything.

During the afternoon we passed the Mantaro River, where it flowed in from the west; there the Apurímac became the Ene.

It was fast growing dark when Dimas suggested we should stop for the night so that he could shoot a monkey for the next day's meat. In the trees close to the bank there was the fearsome roar of the particular kind of monkey he thought most suitable and easily shot. We moved the balsa into a quiet stretch of water and against a long bank of silt; then Dimas and Polly scuttled into the trees with Julian's shotgun. Immediately the dancing swarms of Biting Black-fly fell on us, leaving little signatures of blood on every inch of skin. Darkness came and, thank goodness, the flies disappeared as the air cooled. After an hour, our two intrepid hunters returned empty-handed, but Dimas took his gill net upstream, where he and Polly managed to catch nine heavy-scaled, silvery fish, each around one and a half pounds in weight. We all agreed they would be welcome for breakfast.

Next morning we found large paw marks in the dusty silt. We awoke at five o'clock and stowed away our sleeping bags, which now served only as mattresses; then, rolling up our mosquito nets, we found evidence that the frustrated marauders had jammed their long snouts into the mesh in desperate attempts to reach our blood. The platform slept four easily enough, but Mac had elected to sleep on the bank; next time he said, he wanted an island—something had waked him during the night by sniffing hungrily at him under his groundsheet shelter!

We drifted down the river, which was steadily growing in size and power. The mud-sucking fish Dimas caught the night before were eaten with relish by some and distaste by others, who were not yet hungry enough to appreciate them, myself included. We were now deep in Campa country, and twice we saw long, narrow dugout canoes being poled against the fierce current by crews of six men, each clad only in the dark brown sack-like garment they call a *cushma*; on both occasions, we were in the middle of the river and they close into the bank. In one of the canoes we saw a brightly coloured macaw in a small cage made of twigs and vine; perhaps they were going to push the canoe all the way up to San Francisco to sell it; at least they had the time.

At one o'clock, we arrived at Cutivirene, a little Campa village that also served as a Franciscan mission. Unlike the Benedictines, the Franciscan monks did not necessarily live in a community or house, but were to be found working on their own or in pairs. The Franciscan dream at Cutivirene was to form a huge reserve for the embattled Campa Indians who were in danger of gradually being pushed out of existence in their natural environment. Once the reserve was established, the monks hoped to help the naïve Campas achieve an easier integration with the inevitable encroachment of civilisation than would otherwise be the case.

We hitched the balsa raft to the steep, muddy bank amid a welter of naked black children who were splashing away their lunchtime after school. We met the young American Father Mario, alone in his thatched hut. It was a different setting from our first meeting in the restaurant at Lima airport on the first morning after our arrival in Peru. Now he looked a slim, boyish figure in his early thirties, and was dressed in shirt and slacks. His bright blue eyes burned with enthusiasm as he told us of his adventures since he flew back to the jungle mission. For a start, he had hired a canoe at San Francisco and bought stores for the coming months of isolation; then, after dropping our film at the Benedictine mission, he had set off downstream. Shortly after the start, his boatman misjudged a rapid, and the canoe was swamped in a whirlpool. They both narrowly escaped with their lives and lost all the precious stores. Eventually, they had made it down to the mission, but life had not held many luxuries in the past couple of months. Father Mariano, the elder American monk, was away drumming up support for the expansion of mission activities, and Bill, as Father Mario preferred to be called, tried to persuade Julian to stay on at Cutivirene and help with the agricultural side of their work. Julian, however, said he was determined to see the balsa trip through, and we four all heaved a sigh of relief.

We stayed the night at Cutivirene. In the course of a visit to the Campas themselves, we agreed to take a crippled ten-year-old boy called Patricio with us down the hundred and fifty miles to Atalaya, where he could at least get hospital treatment. The little boy was lame in his right leg; the trouble had something to do with his thigh. Mac discarded the idea of morphine to relax the muscle in favour of proper treatment from a doctor. Once it was decided that Patricio would come, we then persuaded his father Christopho to accompany him on the journey.

The river had risen suddenly during the night, and when we set off at two o'clock in the afternoon, we were assured of swift progress on the turbulent brown water, which we now shared with huge trees and islands of weed drifting in the flood. We waved goodbye to Polly and the solitary figure of Bill, who was now alone again with his plans and dreams for the innocent children that scampered about the bank at his feet.

We made a much faster passage now and found the river tearing through a country of narrow, black gorges with sheer cliffs rising a thousand feet or so straight up from the water's edge. How does Dimas know there is no waterfall? I wondered to myself, but we weathered the rapids and spent the night, at Mac's request, on an island. Anna prepared a splendid hot drink of peanut paste and sugar mixed with water, and we fell asleep on the small island, safe in the knowledge there were no jaguars to eat Mac. All the same, Christopho with his son and Dimas, kept a little fire burning all night.

During the night, the river fell by more than a foot, and we woke at five o'clock to find the balsa high and dry on a mud bank. But it didn't take the seven of us long to slide it off, and we were soon away downstream in the pink of early dawn. Around us the jungle came alive, and the noise from the banks gradually increased to a vibrating crescendo, as if the rising sun was bringing it all to a boil. The gorge of the previous day grew deeper and narrower; banks of fine grey silt, brought down by last years rains, overlaid the natural red mud along the sides of deep quiet pools and below mighty cliffs of yellow and black rock. Sometimes the pools were not so still, and the balsa would spin around and around, dancing to the sucking tune of the whirlpool as it sought in vain to drag us under. In places, the rock had been twisted into crazy shapes as it cooled long long ago, while in other parts, wind and sun had formed their own almost manmade patterns of symmetrical holes and regular square blocks, rather like the Thames embankment in London.

Gorgeous butterflies of all shapes and sizes wobbled across the narrow river, always managing to evade the frantic flapping of Mac's makeshift net. Mac, who had suffered perhaps the least from the minor ailments of colds, stomach upsets, and insect rashes, was now in the throes of an almost manic belief in his own wisdom. Any questioning of facts as seen through his own eyes set these same eyes bulging, as if to start from his face, as he shouted down his questioner with rather bigoted but usually correct arguments. Tolerance had somehow temporarily evaporated, and Julian, with his relaxed approach, tended to send poor Mac into almost violent rages over incredibly minor details, such as lighting a fire at night.

In the middle of the afternoon, we came to the point at which the way north was by a huge tree-covered ridge running west to east in front of us. Here we saw the river Pirene, which flows under the southern face of the ridge until it meets the Ene; then both rivers turn sharply to the east and become the Tambo.

The new river was narrow, fast, and deep, and above all, treacherous. The sheer weight of water now caused Dimas to increase his cries of "¡muy peligroso!" (very dangerous) whenever we heard the thunder of rapids ahead of us. We were all much more vigilant, and after a number of close scrapes, we arrived at a clearing in the jungle on the left bank of the river, near the face of the great ridge to the north. A great white plume of a waterfall cascaded down many thousands of feet over yellow cliffs to emerge clear and cold at our feet. The little plantation, which apparently belonged to "El Commandante," who lived at Puerto Ocopa a few hours upstream on the Pirene, seemed the ideal spot for us to spend the night.

10

The Raft Wreck

The morning of Saturday, 22 November 1970, dawned clear and sunny. It was going to be hot. We finished our breakfast of tea and porridge and munched several juicy, golden papayas, as we drifted down the river to the wafting strains of Chopin that tinkled from Anna's small tape recorder. Confident she could buy fresh batteries in Atalaya, Anna laid on the canned music, and we all lolled back safe in the knowledge that there were only a couple of days to go. The hotter the sun, the more lethargic we became, clouds of inquisitive grey doves circled the balsa, lending the day an aura of peace, while on either side the green hills seemed to be smiling on us. Dimas and Julian were content to manage the raft through a series of quite ordinary rapids and whirlpools; in any case, there were only two paddles left unbroken. Anna studied advanced Spanish, while Patricio, the little crippled Campa boy, sat patiently beside her; Christopho nursed a badly poisoned left hand, for which Mac had dosed him with tetracycline tablets; he wasn't in any sort of shape to do more than just sit next to his son and keep quiet. John Cowrie, Mac, and I sat at the back of the platform, leaning against our packs and trying to keep out of the hot sun.

After six hours of this, we were all half asleep. Anna was thinking of making lunch, while overhead the sun beat down from a clear blue sky; Julian was grateful for his big straw hat as he ploughed away with his favourite paddle. Dimas was sitting on an upturned box thinking of *descans* ("rest"). John Cowrie was deep in his Spanish–English dictionary, while Mac sleepily thumbed through sheafs of butterfly envelopes, and I was reading a condensed book about the KGB in a tatty old number of *Reader's Digest* that Julian had brought with him to make Mac's butterfly envelopes. The river seemed quite straightforward to all of us.

"Sounds like quite a waterfall ahead," remarked Anna quietly, as she switched off the tape recorder and reached for a saucepan. Looking up from the *Digest*, I could just make out a few cream-coloured waves on the outside of a bend about a quarter of a mile ahead. "Can we have a couple of oars at the back to help get us into the middle?" asked Julian calmly.

"Sure," I replied, struggling to forget the KGB and get some action from lazy limbs.

John Cowrie and I paddled away at the stern with the remains of two broken paddles. "O.K. I reckon that'll do," called Julian from the front, wiping the sweat from his forehead with the sleeve of his shirt.

"Yes. We're clear," I replied, already halfway back to New York and the KGB. John Cowrie and I settled down again by our packs. As we drifted on, the roar seemed well to our left.

"Come on! Get stuck in!" Julian suddenly shouted at Dimas. I looked up again to see an ugly bulge ahead. It was a big rock, half hidden by the racing water. The roar, however, came from another rock nearer to the bank, but it was the empty drum that made the most noise. Though less sound came from the rock ahead of us, it was infinitely more dangerous. We had been deceived by the noise.

"O.K.—*'Sta bien.*" Julian stopped paddling; we would clear it all right.

But I could see another even worse rock dead ahead. "No! We're going to hit it!" I shouted in alarm.

"No. We're O.K.," replied Julian, still looking at the wrong rock.

"Look out! We'll hit it slap in the middle!" I cried. The crash was inevitable.

CRASH! CRUNCH! The front of the balsa raft rose high into the air at an appalling angle; then the back was swung swiftly around to the right by the tearing current. The right-hand side of the balsa then stuck firm on the rock, while the left dipped down below the surface. From now on, the air was filled with the steady roar of the water rushing over and around the balsa.

From my place in the back right-hand corner, all I could see was a wall of creamy brown water sweeping almost gleefully down towards me from the front. Anna let out an awful cry of horror as she was swept over the side, but Mac just caught her by the left ankle, and inch by inch he pulled her back on board. "Save the kit! Save the kit!" he shouted, as soon as Anna was able to hold on for herself; everything not lashed down with our packs on the platform was fast disappearing over the back of the raft between Mac and me. Shovelling away with both hands, we managed to save a few things, among them John Cowrie's emergency belt, but I saw precious items such as Anna's aluminium camera case, with its cargo worth seven hundred pounds, floating away downstream through the whirlpools beyond our rock.

For some reason, I was still convinced that the balsa would come off the rock and float on as before. This was wishful thinking. I hung on to the main structure and tried to take stock: the most important thing was to keep everyone together and make no more mistakes. The chips were down; a mistake would mean death. The balsa was at an angle of some thirty-five degrees to the surface, pointing across the river with the whole left side pinned below the surging brown water. We were about thirty yards from the bank, where tall trees reached right to the water's edge, and the current rushed through the gap like an express train. The far bank was two to three hundred yards away. With the lethargy wiped from our eyes by a very rude shock, we now saw the colossal power of this huge expanse of tearing water for what it really was.

I looked at my watch. Twelve-fifteen—six hours until nightfall. If the balsa didn't break up, a Campa canoe might come and rescue us from our tiny island; otherwise we were in for a pretty rough night. It was miraculous that not one of the eight of us had been lost in the wreck. But now, there was barely room enough for us all to sit down. Everyone looked rather pale in spite of the suntans. My main concern was for Patricio, the little Campa boy; clearly he wouldn't swim far with his bad leg, and he looked really frightened.

I felt the same sense of peaceful relaxation that I remembered from similar situations in the past. No longer was there anxiety about what *might* happen; now something *had* happened, and we were faced with the practical problem of how to get out of it. First of all, we tried a variety of balancing combinations at either end of the balsa to see whether we could get her free again; but nothing worked, and Julian was worried that the movement might cause the already frayed vine lashings to snap, making the balsa break up. I was also anxious that no one should overtire himself, in the event that we had to swim if it did break up. I forced myself to eat a banana that had survived the flood and sat down to talk it over with the others. This was not helped by the roar of the water—even a shout barely carried half the length of the balsa. The sun was beating down, and there was no shelter because the whole superstructure had been carried away in the first rush of water. Worse still, Anna, John Cowrie, and Mac had their packs lashed to the side of the platform now buried in water. John Cowrie had been quick enough to save his still cameras, but the ITN movie camera was buried somewhere below the surface.

Patience seemed the best course of action. We waited an hour, everyone trying to put a brave face on it, with their sleeves rolled down and collars up to ward off the fierce sun. Nothing happened. The water roared hungrily along the balsa, and there was no sign of rescuers up or down the river.

Mac—swimming champion Mac—was keen to swim to the bank and go searching for help. It was only thirty-five yards across but at least sixty the way he would have to go down and across, through surging up-currents and sucking whirlpools. It was an ugly decision. I thought he could do it, but all the same, it was horribly dangerous. Quite simply, Mac would be risking his life for us. If he died, the responsibility was irrevocably mine. On the one hand, it meant a greatly improved chance for Patricio and Anna, whom I gave little chance of survival if the balsa broke up suddenly in the night; and on the other, Mac might drown just before a canoe turned up on its own.

If Mac did reach the bank, Julian thought he could throw

him a pair of basketball boots, at its nearest point; with these and the trunks he would swim in, Mac would go down the river for two hours. If he was unlucky and found no one, he would then return, reaching the bank opposite us by nightfall. I hardly dared to think what sort of night he would spend, clad only in trunks and with no mosquito net.

"O.K., Mac, give it a go if you're really keen," I said at last.

"I'll go all right," he grinned, clambering down onto a shelf of rock below the balsa. We agreed that it would be unfair to photograph the attempt, in the event that it failed. It all seemed so cold-blooded.

"Good luck, Mac," called four desperately sincere voices.

"Here goes!" He hit the water hard and fast, in the clean shallow dive of a class swimmer. My heart was in my mouth, and I had to brace myself to watch. Mac used a powerful breast stroke that enabled him to keep his head up, thus judging the water and distance. Either he does it or he doesn't, I thought, steeling myself for the worst, in my usual pessimistic fashion. If he gets a cramp or misses the bank and gets swept beyond the point, I considered, then that's it.

There were two large eddies, one clockwise, one counterclockwise; as he neared the boundary between them, Mac checked himself and pointed his body between the separate currents, then broke into a desperate strength-sapping crawl. Huddled on the raft, the rest of us realised he had gambled his reserves of energy in one great effort against the might of the river.

"Keep it going, Mac!" croaked Julian.

"He can't hear!" I shouted, over the thunder of the water.

"God, it's stopped him!" Julian cried. Mac was not making any ground at all. He was just held there, thrashing against the current. This he couldn't keep up for more than a few seconds, but then he made a subtle change of course. Suddenly, he shot forward and through—and into the bank!

"Well done! Well done, Mac!" we all shouted, but he couldn't hear. With his head dropped between his shoulders, he made one last heave and hauled himself up onto a rocky ledge at the water's edge. For a few moments, he just knelt there gasping for breath, while the racing water clutched hungrily at his trailing toes. Then, feeling refreshed, he turned his head, grinned, and shouted something none of us could hear, before crawling slowly up the smooth face of a boulder that led about ten feet up to the edge of the trees. Once at the top, he walked gingerly along with unaccustomed bare feet until he was directly opposite the raft. There, he lowered himself to the water's edge again to catch the basketball boots.

Up on the highest point of the balsa, Julian was winding up, like a baseball pitcher, but the boots looked too light to make the distance. "I hope he doesn't throw himself in," I heard Anna say at my elbow.

With a tremendous effort, Julian hurled the white boots in a high curve towards Mac. Up and up they flew, turning slowly in the air; then they fell sharply and splashed right into the middle of a curling whirlpool, some dozen feet short of the bank. "Maybe they'll float," I shouted, thinking the boots would drift into the point of the little bay that Mac reached. But they vanished down the whirlpool and we didn't see them again.

Mac shrugged and turned to crawl back up the boulder before disappearing into the jungle. "His feet will get dreadfully cut," winced Anna.

"I hope he keeps out of the sun," I replied, and we all sat and waited, trying to cover up every inch of bare skin.

Christopho, the Campa father, had added nothing to the party since we left Cutivireni. With his hideously swollen hand, he would have been in hospital in any European country: but this wasn't a European country, as we were only too well aware, and the poor man just sat and endured with an impassive stoicism, as if pain was simply an accepted part of life. Now, sitting with his crippled and frightened son, he began to show the animal cunning of the jungle Indian. Suddenly, the square, primitive, coal-black face came alive, his ears, eyes, and nose reacting to things in a way our dulled, European senses never could. After about an hour of peering downstream, he said one word: "Campa." Dimas also looked, and then pointed excitedly, shouting "Campa! Campa!"

Sure enough, there were three primitive dugout canoes, being poled upstream along the far bank, about a mile or so down the river. "Campa! Campa!" we all shouted with delight and relief.

Mac had done it: making his way through the trees, he had found a clear stretch of bank on which he could make good time without lacerating his feet too badly. He had decided to chance the sun on his bare back, and after a couple of miles, he saw a Campa hut on the far side, at a place where the river flowed fast, but deep and silent. After some shouting and waving of his arms, a Campa and his wife had come across in a canoe to see what the strange *gringo* could be up to; then they all three crossed back again, paddling upstream in company with two other larger canoes that were travelling up the river at the same time.

When the three canoes were opposite us, the one Mac was in came across and moored just downstream of us in a sheltered bay, while the Campa came up to have a look at the situation. The other two canoes kept poling upstream until they were out of sight; at that, we began to wonder just how highly the Campas valued human life. After a minute or two, the Campa clearly decided he would need bigger canoes, so he signalled Mac back into the little canoe and they pushed off downstream, moving at a great speed on the boiling river. Halfway down to his village, the Campa met another canoe poling about the bank, and this barrel-chested, almost gorilla-like Campa, together with a wiry young friend, immediately offered to come and help.

Once at the village, Mac's new-found friend dropped off his wife and found the bigger canoe he was looking for; then they both set off to find the owner to see whether they could borrow it. Instead of walking straight up to the thatched hut, the Campa first skirted around the edge of the little clearing, and then he attracted the inhabitants with a strange half-whispered "whoop." Straightaway, another man and a young boy were enlisted to help, and the four returned to the wreck in a big canoe.

By the time Mac arrived, we had been working with the "gorilla" man and his friend for about half an hour; the two men handled their tiny dugout with a skill and nonchalance that was a pleasure to watch. From a point on the bank about thirty yards upstream of us, they shot their little canoe down and across eddies and whirls on each of five separate occasions, arriving within inches of the same place on the rock each time. The wiry fellow in the bow threw the jungle creeper they used as a mooring rope, and it was caught by hands eager to pull them into the relative shelter below the balsa. First, they took the crippled Campa boy and Anna ashore; then Christopho, with some of the kit; then three more trips with the remainder of the kit and John Cowrie.

When Mac arrived with the other canoe, the job was done, and we were left with the problem of trying to float the balsa off the rock. The four Campas joined Dimas, Julian, and myself on the balsa, and we tried again to lever it free. For the Campas, this was all a game. One minute, they would be up to their necks in the river, with a huge collar of creamy brown water piled high above their glistening black hair and flashing white grins, as they strained to lift the sunken leading edge of the balsa; the next minute, they'd be jumping up and down at the very top end of the logs, trying to jerk the balsa free. When one of them slipped, barely grabbing the trailing rope as the racing current whirled him away, the others dissolved in laughter and whistles.

It was all no use. The weight of water held the balsa against the rock just as surely as if it were welded there. The next plan was to cut the balsa into two equal halves and float it off that way; we had lost the machetes and two big knives in the wreck, but I had my small featherweight skinning knife. I could almost hear Frank Sinatra singing about the "ant and the rubber tree plant," as one of the Campas seized the tiny, blunt blade and proceeded to attack one of the two stout hardwood crosspoles to which the main balsa logs were bound. It was the flicking dexterity with which he wielded the blade in a double chopping action, faster than the eye could follow, that made me realise he was really serious about the improbable task. Indeed, he was halfway through the pole when another Campa told us, through Dimas (for they couldn't speak Spanish) that he would get us down to Atalaya in a day by dugout canoe. Support for this plan was much reinforced when he said it would again be *mucho peligroso* in the next ten ·

miles, before the river finally wound out of the mountains and into the smooth waters of the jungle itself.

Julian and I talked the idea over. A dugout was at least quick and sure, and the lashings on the bottom of the balsa were bound to be pretty well worn-out in any case. We agreed, and the grinning axeman handed me back the little curved skinning knife. The balsa was abandoned, we were taken to the bank to collect the others and our belongings, and I found my boots a crawling chocolate-coloured mass of ants where they lay on top of the bank. Soon we were racing downstream in the dugouts to the Campa village.

Since Julian, Dimas, and I had been on the wreck five hours in the broiling sun, this time the cool pink *mansato* drink was very welcome, even if it had been prechewed by the good ladies of the village. We were put for the night into a big empty hut that was built on stilts. After rewarding our rescuers, we tried to hang our remaining kit out to dry. But there, in the dark, we had little hope. Although we had lost a lot of stuff and felt wet and miserable, we tried to console ourselves with the thought that it could have been much worse; our names could easily have been added to the hundreds of others drowned in the river each year.

It was a pretty hungry little party that followed the Campa guide through the dark jungle to another hut for supper. When we arrived, we were motioned to a rough table and a couple of benches by a smiling and heavily pregnant Campa woman. We ate the plate of *yuca* as if we'd never seen food before; this pleased the hostess, who then produced a large dish of boiled fish, each one six to nine inches in length. There was no choice: we just had to eat them, heads, tails, innards, and all. The woman watched us eat every mouthful; all this didn't taste too bad, really, but I suppose I was just hungry. After the meal, we made our own way back to our hut. Mac made a cup of tea over the little log fire outside, but prospects for sleep were not good because everything we had was soaking wet; but in the end, we all dropped off to sleep on the dirty floor, covered with wet sleeping bags and groundsheets.

It had been an eventful day.

It wasn't a good night. John Cowrie and Mac were unable to

sleep much because whichever way they turned, they were troubled by sunburn. The rest of us also kept tossing and turning in our wet clothing, and I think we were all awake when the first flush of the new day filtered through the trees into the little clearing. For breakfast, our hostess produced more *yuca* and a boiled chicken, but we were more than ready when the "gorilla" man came grinning into the hut to tell us that two big canoes were ready to take us to Atalaya. Laughing villagers helped us lash our still-sodden packs to their bamboo frames, which were especially prepared to minimise further soaking as the long, grey, hollowed-out tree trunks dove through the remaining rapids.

The early sun and clear sky promised yet another scorching day. The river ran wide and fast as if anxious to be rid of the encircling mantle of hills, so that it could slide its way across the thousands of miles of flat, featureless jungle in its search for the sea. John Cowrie, Mac, Christopho, and the Campa child Patricio went in one canoe with one of the Campas who had helped with the rescue; he was assisted with the paddling by Dimas and a young Campa boy. Anna, Julian, and I travelled with the "gorilla" man and another Campa boy. The grinding noise of the pebbles rolling along under the surface as we crossed the shallows sounded all the more ominous after the wreck of the previous day; this, combined with the fact that we were seated much lower on the water now than we had been on the raft, made the shooting of rapids rather a nerve-wracking experience. But the power and deft paddle strokes of the "gorilla" man soon had us completely confident in his ability.

After about three hours, we crossed the last of the rapids. Now, the river, emerging from the mountains of the "eyebrow of the jungle," rolled wide into a new, beautiful land of contrasting colours. Banks of bright, white shingle changed to vivid green grass, then into the bottle-green of the jungle itself, and this had a background of dim, blue-green wooded hills, standing far distant from the river. The silent passage of the two dugout canoes was broken only by the lapping of the water and the rhythmic strokes of the Campas, who plied their diamond-shaped paddles with a seemingly inexhaustible muscular power. As we moved swiftly downstream under blue skies and a hot sun, I was filled with a wonderful, calm sense of peace with the world. Swallows swooped high in the clear air above us, while hawks hovered above the banks; in the shallows, the snow-white herons waded carefully in search of fish. On and on we swept, pausing only for a few minutes to gather juicy pineapples, papayas, and bananas from friendly Campas along the way.

It was nearly dark when we reached the little town of Atalaya, and deep purple cumulus clouds, piling high in the red of a glorious tropical sunset, gave warning of an approaching storm. We could see from the variety of small riverboats moored along the bank that our journey through the unknown had come to an end. From this point to the sea, we would only be ordinary travellers on a well-worn highway. We thanked and paid the Campas, who suddenly seemed shy and out of place in the garish lights of "civilisation"—a scattering of mud-walled buildings topped with corrugated iron roofs; the village was itself just a little island in the jungle, connected only by the river to the bigger places downstream.

For us, it was now only a question of booking our berths on a series of riverboats, meeting Marie Christine, and saying goodbye to Julian in Iquitos, then we would have to wait patiently to make the various connections that at last would bring us to Belem, on the other side of Brazil.

We looked into a *pensión*, arranged for Patricio to be taken to the hospital with his father, had a meal at a little bar, and then booked our passage down to Picallpa for the following day aboard a little riverboat.

We had all gone to bed when the rains finally came, sending long tongues of water along the concrete corridor and under our bedroom doors, while the greatest electrical storm I had ever seen lit up the town with a weird bluish light, as in a scene from *Gone With the Wind*.

I was so glad we weren't still stuck in the wreck.

11

〰〰〰〰〰

Three Men and a Girl—
How It Really Was

"They won't have just a simple triangle; it'll be a trapezium!" I had shrieked at John Cowrie, when he phoned me proposing we should take Anna on the expedition.

Since much of this chapter will be of a somewhat critical nature (because it's written by a rather pessimistic person) it would be best to deal first with the successful achievement of our aim: to complete a journey along the course of the Amazon from its furthest source to the sea. I will then deal with human foibles, as seen in the light of this success.

As it turned out, the expedition was quite simply a race against time. The rains, which luckily only caught up with us on the night we reached Atalaya, would have made the river too dangerous for us to travel, either by canoe or raft, and we could not have made any real progress through the impenetrable jungle on either bank. Had the rains overtaken us, we should have been delayed for at least two months, and this would have meant abandoning the expedition in the face of pressing commitments at home.

There are two reasons why we won the race against time. First, the rains themselves were late in coming to the Apurímac valley in the last quarter of 1970. Second, we won because our planning and preparation had been, broadly, correct, and when it came down to it, the four individuals involved were able to keep on going, practically without respite, for seven long, hard weeks. The kit, although necessarily light, stood up to the rough going with no serious breakdown, which meant we never had to fall back on our emergency belts. Medical security, provided in the person of Mac, immeasurably decreased the stress to which I was prepared to submit the four members of the expedition; at all times, Mac was ready and able to deal effectively with injury or disease.

All four individuals possessed sufficient self-reliance to cope, without ever causing delay, with a series of problems. First, the speed of preparation in the U.K. called for a high degree of independence and flexibility; then, in Peru, four strangers had to become a team and straightaway endure the forty-eight-hour marathon from Lima to Cailloma. The struggle to reach the source and the penalty of altitude sickness were followed immediately by the rigours of long treks at high altitude—all this under the subtle pressures of a race against the oncoming rains.

After the couple days in Cuzco, we set off into the unknown part of the Apurímac valley, threatened by numerous obstacles in addition to the rains: *bandoleros*, wild animals, snakes, savage Indians, heat, and insects—but all these failed to delay the urgent progress of the four individuals. Once at the navigable part of the river, we had to stifle our fears of the "Great Speaker," and each rapid was met head-on and dealt with on its merits; after my lapse of vigilance that caused the raft wreck, the measures taken to rectify the situation were carried out with unfailing calm.

After Atalaya, there followed six weeks of frustration and delay, as we battled with the classical *mañana* temperament of the riverboatmen. We went from Atalaya to Pucallpa on a stumpy little tug-barge that had no batteries to start its Diesel engine. From Pucallpa we travelled aboard an ancient, double-decker riverboat—something from a bygone age—to Iquitos. On this trip, we learnt how to distinguish tortoise from turtle stew; we only got the feet, travelling steerage, and tortoise claws are easily distinguishable from turtle webs even when cooked. At Iquitos, the Indian Latham obeyed his conscience and returned, via Lima and San Francisco, to help Father Mario improve the Franciscan mission at Cutivirene, and

Marie Christine, my wife, flew out to join us on the remaining two and a half thousand miles to the sea.

After seemingly endless delays at Iquitos, we hired a straw-thatched motor canoe to take us out of Peru to Leticia in Colombia. There we spent Christmas among a group of American hippies who had come to the river in search of the cheap cocaine and the marijuana that is reputed to be grown on some of the islands. They were mostly university graduates who had been given too much for too little, and I spent many hours listening to their plans for revolution and a new culture. One poor fellow's life—apparently he was a graduate of Roosevelt University in Chicago—revolved around the production and sale of pornography in Chicago in order to amass funds for his drug-sampling tours of Mexico and Central and South America; he accompanied us on the boat from Tabatinga, Brazil, via Manaus to Belem. While I had more than a little sympathy for his grievances, I emerged at the end with a feeling of relief that I didn't smoke or drink, much less scuttle ashore every time the boat stopped to seek out the kind of death he was searching for. A few hours with Chay and myself in a hurricane on the North Atlantic might have given him a few new ideas.

At Belem, our journey came to an end, and with the end came the inevitable feeling of anticlimax: we had done it, start to finish, and no one had been swallowed by a giant boa constrictor or struck down by a poison dart from a silent blowpipe. The very fact that we had escaped the ever-present dangers of disease and drowning made the journey seem rather commonplace in modern terms, but there were times along the way when the four individuals concerned had thought it far from commonplace.

It was in the secondary aim of trying to make a team out of four individuals that I think I failed. To begin with, it is worth considering what would make four separate people, each around thirty years old, think of undertaking an expedition that in London, before we started, showed all the signs of being a rather desperate one. Why, weren't we all settled down to steady jobs and big mortgages? Each one of us had achieved, to some degree, a form of extreme individuality, or even a reputation as a loner, and it wasn't a question of being out of work. The three married men each appeared to have healthy, working marriages with partners who did everything they could to assist with the smooth execution of the expedition. I think that the primary quest for each of us was for adventure, and that noun is defined in the Oxford Dictionary as "risk, danger, enterprise; unexpected incident; commercial speculation; hazardous activity." There was something of all this in each one of us. Whatever the motives, the expedition was a positive action, and we would all gain from the experience.

In addition to straightforward adventure, each one of us had a subtly different angle of approach. Anna was keen, above all, to contact the unknown and take photographs, while Mac was absorbed with the quite incredible variety of the insects and with his responsibilities as a medic. John Cowrie was utterly dedicated to proving himself as a photographer, and left everything beyond that to me, just as we had agreed before leaving London. Beyond establishing a good photographic record of the expedition, I had absolutely no interest in camera mechanics and never took one picture on the whole journey; my own interest was the successful achievement of the task and a close study of the human side, in an effort to make a team of four individuals. These differing interests were to play a considerable part in our relations as the journey progressed. Anna, for example, told me at the end that she had come to Peru quite certain that it was impossible for four people to live at such close quarters without upset, simply because it is not possible to change adult behaviour in such a way.

Quite a number of normal human faults came to the surface under the combined pressures of altitude, speed, and having up to eight people live on a ten-by-twenty-four-foot balsa raft. I will go into these in some detail so that other people engaging on similar enterprises may know what to expect and how we tried to deal with the various problems.

We found that we were all rather short-tempered at high altitude. Our outbursts could be quite savage and unexpected; it was as if the mind, subconsciously under pressure, exploded without warning. The result of this was, sometimes, quite illogical thought, and in my own case it meant poor judgement. An example was the ragged start from Tungasuca, when the expedition was spread out, in two parts, for over a mile of countryside; another was my subsequent outbursts of temper at Cochapata, where we bought Noddy the horse, and the following morning at Surimana.

Intolerance was a feature of the party throughout the whole journey. I have read somewhere that in a normal discussion, 75 per cent of a person's brain is occupied with thinking of what to say next and only 25 per cent is actively listening to what the speaker is saying. Three months of this imbalance is rather wearing.

In retrospect, I feel that my hard line towards Anna was unnecessary. It was my concern that she should not come to rely too heavily upon our gallantry because in an emergency she could easily find herself alone; therefore the more she practised self-reliance, the better chance she would stand if the worst came to the worst—and until we reached Atalaya, I had every reason to believe that it might. My policy towards Anna was also coloured by the reasoning that if she had chosen to come on even terms, then even terms she would get. The result was that my attitude enraged John Cowrie and Mac at different times; witness the magnificent thrust: "You not only look like an ox but also think like one." One happy product of this policy was that Anna became more and more withdrawn from the three men. This aloofness, which had doubtless been well practised on London "wolves," certainly annihilated any possibility of marital tangles for the three married men.

A problem resulting from having only one person who spoke fluent Spanish (Anna) was that she was often so tired at the end of the day, that if we entered a new village full of curiosity, she was unable to interpret our enquiries to the *gobernador*. Sometimes the result was that negotiations for mules and guides had to be carried out between the *gobernador* and Anna, rather than directly with the Indians, and we came to the conclusion that the Quechuan Indians don't have a high regard for women in any business sense.

It is probably fair to say that none of us had the maturity to grasp fully the effect that the altitude and confined relationships were having upon our tolerance and judgement; a little more open discussion on this subject would have helped, but usually we were too tired in the evenings to do anything except eat and get to sleep. This particular aspect of the expedition was nevertheless one of the most interesting parts of it.

Mac, far from being the mild-mannered fellow we all thought him to be, turned out to have perhaps the most aggressive attitude in argument of any person I have ever met; in spite of the fact that he was nearly always right, this aggression was something to be endured rather than admired. As always, when in a situation of prolonged fatigue, each of us was engaged in a personal battle with the worst points of his own nature. It is so hard at the end of a long day to volunteer to cook a meal, or in the half light of early morning to help with the breakfast or tidy a place up before leaving; but these disciplines mark the thin difference between an efficient team and an untidy rabble heading for disaster.

Before leaving Lima, I decided to make a rule that there should be no swearing. It would have been easy for three ex-soldiers to resort to barrack-room language; yet not only would this have been unfair to Anna, it would also have led to a lowering of our general morale and probably have stored up trouble for the future. I wish I had also ruled out talking behind other people's backs, for it is a thing which, once started, is difficult to stamp out—and if each of us had thought hard beforehand, we never would have said what little *was* said.

There is little to be said for splitting up on any leg of a journey, because once split up, it is never easy to come together again. Whenever possible, on the other hand, it pays to avoid confined spaces, for if people are to spend a long time together, they appreciate what little privacy they can get, such as sleeping in separate rooms if at all possible. While it is not possible to force adults, in this kind of situation, into any one uniform pattern, it is fair to ask them not to adopt extremes of behaviour; few things are more infuriating than to have your clean sleeping bag walked on by an undiscerning person in muddy boots. At the same time, overneatness has little to recommend it in a group situation where others are of not such finicky tastes. Long-distance sailing alone tends to produce a state of mind that demands that everything should be so well looked after that it lasts forever.

Over a period of weeks, it does pay to rest occasionally. A policy of "bashing on, regardless" even if pursued as a result of something like the rains, can easily result in "more haste, less speed". The two days we spent at Osambre with the Berg family set us up very well for our jungle-bashing on the way to Villa Virgen, and without this break we might well have lost our momentum. Equally, it is important to maintain personal standards of dress and hygiene, and knowing where the first aid kit is packed could save your life. Other things to avoid are harbouring grudges when they can easily be discussed and healed if dealt with quickly; talking about food if there is none; and asking "How much further? How much longer?" when everyone is tired. In a foreign country, there is much to be said for speaking the language, which has the advantage that the members of the team are not totally dependent on conversation within their own limited circle.

Mac made several points of a more or less medical nature that are worth noting. The flight from London by jet, followed by the car journey to Cailloma produced subtle upsets of physical rhythm as well as fatigue. Violent disagreements usually took place at the top of a climb. The reasons for this were possibly the effect of altitude, physical tiredness, and the sheer boredom of the grinding uphill walk itself—all this preying on the nerves and building up to an explosion. Many of our petty problems, Mac said, were caused by the natural competitive tendency of four competitive individuals. Mac also felt that in a situation of stress such as the "high walk," the persons involved had all day to ponder minor ailments, such as colds or insect bites, and this led to distrust of his medical advice. Also, in the event of wrongly diagnosed serious illness in the wilderness, the consequences are likely to be severe. His explanation for his unusually aggressive attitude towards us at times was that he missed his family, as most married men will.

Finally, I would add that in any undertaking of this kind, a sense of humour provides a wonderful way of taking the steam out of an explosive situation.

Appendix 1

Clothing and Equipment

This expedition set out from the near arctic conditions of the Andes, at fifteen thousand feet, and descended into equatorial jungle.

In order to preserve mobility, our clothing and equipment had to be of a light order. What follows is a list, with recommendations and other comments, of the equipment the three men of the expedition carried. Anna carried a variation of the same, with additional items for her own use.

In some cases, items were duplicated and sent to points along the river, for collection as we passed those points.

CLOTHING

HATS

Some form of sun hat is vital at high altitude; all the Indians wear them. I wore a floppy cloth hat because straw hats are badly affected by rain.

CLOTHES

1 *Shirts*—Strong, washable, yet lightweight. The army tropical green shirt is ideal.
2 *Pullover*—Should be heavy wool because when needed, it must be good and warm. Most important to keep it dry in the rucksack; a heavy, wet pullover weighs a great deal. The army heavy duty type is fine.

3 *Duvet Jacket*—Vital at high altitude, light and very warm; it must be kept dry.

4 *Cagoule*—Light, easily packed, and irreplaceable. Trousers are also useful.

5 *Underpants*—Cottons are best.

6 *Handkerchiefs*—Wash daily; also useful worn around the neck to prevent sunburn.

7 *Trousers*—Long, light trousers that protect against insects and dry fast. Army olive greens or denims.

8 *Swimming trunks*—Can be used in insect-free areas or on raft. Avoid nude bathing; usually offends natives.

9 *Puttees*—A little-known item that seems to have disappeared with the Empire. A four-inch band of woollen cloth a yard long, with four feet of tape attached to one end. The puttee is carefully wound around the ankle, over the boot and the bottom of the trouser leg; then the tape is also wound tight to keep it in position. It is necessary that puttees are wound well up and over the ankle. The result is firm support for the ankle, and a way of stopping water, dirt, and insects from getting into the boot from the top. It also gives a feeling of security if there are snakes around. Puttees are worn by British parachute forces in preference to gaiters.

10 *Gloves*—Necessary at high altitude; the leather skiing type are better than woollen gloves which can get wet.

11 *Insect Hoods*—We were fortunate in not experiencing insects at their "smoking" worst. A hood of muslin, with a thin transparent plastic visor, can be a godsend.

12 *Money Belt*—A useful way of carrying emergency currency and of handling a load of notes of small denominations.

FOOTWEAR

1 *Boots*—We used army lightweight combat boots. Light and waterproof, they are good for use with puttees. There are really no suitable boots made in the Andes or Amazon basin. Make sure the boots you buy have good rubber soles, and wear innersoles against the possibility of nails.

2 *Basketball boots* (sneakers)—Useful in the evenings, on a

raft, or anytime ordinary boots would be too heavy. Also useful for emergency swimming. Not advised for walking because the sole could be pierced by a nail or the side cut, and they don't last long.

3　*Socks*—Short, yet of fairly thick wool; the best are army grey Angora wool; should be changed daily. For care of feet: first grease feet with Cocholine; put on woollen socks, then a pair of the thinnest black evening socks to prevent wear on the woollen ones. Feet should be supple, not hard; if feet get wet, the grease prevents the water from affecting the skin.

EQUIPMENT
(Keep it perfectly clean.)

1　*Lodestar Rucksack*—A framed high-pack of very light construction. With seams double-stitched and the screws in the frame secured with masking tape, this equipment was most suitable. Care must always be taken with light equipment to ensure that it is properly handled. The zippers were poor and heavy gauge polythene bags had to be used inside to ensure waterproofing.

2　*Tents*—We took the Mountain Equipment lightweight tent but didn't often use it since we managed to reach some sort of habitation each night.

3　*Sleeping Bags*—We used the Erve Eskimo de Luxe and found it most suitable as long as it doesn't get wet.

4　*Sleeping Bag Inners*—These are homemade from parachute silk and are used when sleeping in a hammock in a sleeping bag. They need to be washed regularly.

5　*Hammocks*—Lightweight and easily packed—these are the most important considerations. In South America, we found a small nylon net hammock that hung between stainless steel rings at either end, weighing a total of about 6 ounces and folding into a space the size of a fist.

6　*Mosquito Net*—Vital in the jungle, but really rather bulky.

7　*Groundsheet*—Must be light and able to be used as a roof over a hammock to protect from rain.

8 *Maps*—Hard to obtain in South America. Should be covered with clear fablon, neatly folded, and always carried on one's person, never in the pack, in case of separation from one's pack.

9 *Silva Compass*—Lightweight, it can be hung by a string around the wrist and this avoids the tiresome business of fishing around in a pocket or pouch when exhausted and in need of it most. Remember the compass is right and the directional "bump" or "instinct" is always wrong.

10 *Notebook and Biro*—Essential. Use biro, not pencil or pen, and double-space all writing.

11 *Whistle*—Work out a code of blasts with the rest of the expedition. Useful when lost.

12 *Torch* (flashlight)—A small pencil-torch is useful, but bring enough batteries. Always turn the batteries upside down during the day, so that the torch will not accidentally be switched on inside a pack.

13 *Candles*—Always useful in emergencies.

14 *Waterproof Matches*—Very hard to get. Carry lighters and flints as an extra precaution. Ordinary matches must be kept dry.

15 *Waterproof Watches*—Vital. Our Smith's Astral watches were excellent. It's handy to know how to navigate, using a watch as a compass.

16 *Boot Polish and Brush*—Keeping boots clean improves morale and maintains the boots themselves. If short of polish, Cocholine can be used in an emergency.

17 *Knife*—Any strong, light sheath knife.

18 *Toilet Articles*—Cut down the weight here. Soap, soapbox, toothbrush and paste, razor and blades. Use a napkin for a towel and wash it often.

19 *Sewing Equipment*—Needles, safety pins, nail scissors, darning wool, nylon thread (cotton rots in the jungle).

20 *Fishing Tackle*—100 metres of plaited terylene 25-pound breaking strain; 50 metres of 10-pound breaking strain, monofilament nylon; and a selection of single-eyed hooks.

21 *Knife, Fork, and Spoon*—Only the spoon is necessary.

22 *Mess Tins*—For cooking and eating. We carried only one

mess tin each. We also had a "billy can" for tea and a small saucepan.

23 *Water Bottle and Mug*—Use an army plastic bottle and mug, hung on an emergency belt in a pouch. Carry water purifying tablets, also in the pouch.

24 *Parachute Rigging Line*—100 feet, light and useful for all sorts of lashings, even as a rope, if necessary.

25 *Machete*—Light model essential in the jungle.

26 *Life Jacket and Safety Helmet*—Useful when going down rapids, but we couldn't take because of the weight problem.

27 *Emergency Ration Pack*—Since we were in an area in which abundant water was available, we took one pouch full of high-value foods, for the most part dehydrated, e.g., meat bars, oatmeal blocks, fudge, and biscuits.

28 *Marking Tape*—4-inch wide. Get the black adhesive tape used in the motor industry; it comes in rolls. Useful for all kinds of jobs in the wild.

29 *Can Opener*—The 1½-inch Morefed Baby can opener is the best in the world for this kind of job.

30 *Cooker*—We used Optimus petrol cookers, which we found very good, but paraffin cookers would have been better since paraffin is more easily obtainable along the Amazon.

31 *High Altitude Suncream*—Vital at high altitude. Sunburn can soon incapacitate an entire team.

32 *Curry Powder*—One tin goes a long way and helps disguise many nasty tastes. We should have bought it in London before leaving; it is very hard to find in Peru.

33 *Petrol Bottle*—A small plastic water bottle is needed to carry fuel for a cooker. Whatever else you do, mark this bottle well—fuel tastes bad, even when you are very thirsty.

34 *Water Filters*—The Millbank bag removes silt; a sterilising solution or pills remove any chance of disease. Perhaps the most important medical item of all.

35 *Chinese Firecrackers*—Keep them dry; much lighter than firearms.

36 *Daily Medical Requirements*—Paludrine (anti-malaria), salt tablets, vitamin tablets, mycote cream for athlete's

foot (we found it better than the powder), water sterilising tablets (or a solution from powder), and insect repellent.

EMERGENCY BELT KIT

A strong, one-piece belt with a simple, quick-release device.

Four strong canvas pouches, preferably slid into the belt rather than hung from it. Army ammunition pouches are suitable, two on either side of the belt; don't fill them too heavily. Either wear the belt or have it at hand at all times, so that in an emergency, if separated from the expedition and your pack, you can live off your belt for at least a week. Your map and compass should be in your pocket. Arrange as follows:

1 *Forward left*—medical kit.
2 *Rear left*—water bottle (full) and mug.
3 *Forward right*—emergency rations.
4 *Rear right*—spare compass, fishing tackle, flint lighter, insect repellent, paludrine, salt tablets, knife, string, and any other items thought necessary.

Appendix 2

Medical Cover

Medical cover is a question of personal choice. For our part, we were restricted by the need for light equipment. The choice of drugs, dressings, and prophylactics for the British Amazon Expedition 1970–71 were discussed extensively with Colonel Macfarlaine, Professor of Military Medicine, and Colonel Adam, Professor of Applied Physiology and author of *A Traveller's Guide to Health*, both of the Royal Army Medical College, Millbank, London.

The medical cover was assembled with three considerations:

(a) The treatment of the common diseases likely to be encountered;

(b) Geographical and weather conditions;

(c) Humane considerations—the treatment of Indians who do not have access to modern medicine.

Our choice of drugs was more than adequate, and I can only blame myself for the major setback of *soroche*, the high altitude sickness that drastically reduced our capability at Cailloma in the early part of the expedition.

We were able to help many of the Indians, but to our regret, we did not take anti-helminthics (used in the treatment of worm infections), which were essential. It was bitterly disappointing to have to turn away pathetic young children suffering from worms and the accompanying problems of anaemia and malnutrition. When Indians were treated with any degree of success, the news spread fast, and to his embarrassment, Mac was always referred to as "Doctor"; he had to turn away many nontreatable and imaginary ailments, while at the same time trying to avoid causing offence. Perhaps a supply of inert chalk tablets would have proved useful; although unethical, they would have done no harm.

The emphasis was always on prophylactic precaution rather than curative medicine. We worked to British Army principles, and while it was not always possible to stick 100 per cent to these principles in all circumstances, their effectiveness saved us from most of the illnesses that often hinder and embarrass expeditions: we were able to avoid almost entirely the gastric disorders so common in South America, particularly traveller's diarrhea. Perhaps the average reader has little interest in the medical cover of an expedition. If the medical cover is inadequate however, it is likely that an expedition will fail. We were very lucky to have Mac to look after us.

MEDICAL KITS

Before assembling these kits, it was essential to study the hazards we were likely to encounter on a route that would not only expose us to diseases but also to a number of contrasting geographical and weather conditions ranging from extremely cold, windy weather in the high Andes to tropical heat and humidity in the jungles of Peru and Brazil.

DRUGS AND PROPHYLACTICS

Since we were to be on the water and exposed to the danger of rapids, the packaging of drugs was considered to be of prime importance. The drugs were broken down into individual doses, then hermetically sealed in polythene packets with written instructions, in case the team was inadvertently split up. This method proved effective, and in the balsa raft wreck, when the drugs were submerged in rushing water for more than three hours, we lost only 10 per cent by water spoilage. This loss was directly caused by rupturing packets; although these had been well sealed in London, the expansion of the air inside them as we ascended to sixteen thousand feet burst the seals in a few cases.

1 CONTENTS OF MAIN MEDICAL KITS CARRIED IN RUCKSACKS.

a. *Tetracycline* (doses of 18 capsules)—dysentery and infection.

b. *Penicillin* (tablets and liquid)—the liquid for injection. For treatment of localised infections, a single dose lasts three to four days.

c. *Piriton* (12 tablets)—allergic reaction and insect bites.

d. *Lamotol* (16 tablets)—diarrhea.

e. *Morphine* (12 Syrettes and labels to attach to the patient)—treatment of shock caused by injury.

f. *Paracetamol* (15 tablets)—similar to aspirin; can be used with safety at high altitude.

g. *Flagyl* (20 tablets)—mouth infections and amoebic dysentery.

h. *Chloroquin* (10 tablet doses)—malaria.

i. *Paludrine* (9 packs totalling 1,500 tablets)—one tablet daily to prevent malaria.

j. *Senna* (10 packs, each of 6 tablets)—constipation.

k. Four bottles of *eardrops*.

l. *Salt tablets* in quantity.

2 CONTENTS OF MEDICAL KIT CARRIED BY EACH INDIVIDUAL IN EMERGENCY BELT KIT.

a. *Paludrine* (70 tablets, one to be taken daily)—malaria prevention.

b. *Senna* (6 tablets)—constipation.

c. *Chloroquin* (one course of 10 tablets)—malaria.

d. *Tetracycline* (one course of 18 capsules)—broad spectra antibiotic.

e. *Lamotol* (16 tablets)—diarrhea.

f. *Salt* (20 tablets)—to compensate for salt lost in perspiration.

g. *Paracetamol* (15 tablets)—used at high altitude in place of aspirin.

h. *Piriton* (12 tablets)—allergic infection and insect bites.

i. *Morphine* (3 Syrettes and labels)—shock caused by injury.

j. One *triangular bandage*.

k. Three *sterile dressings.*
l. A selection of *assorted plasters.*

3 PREVENTATIVE MEASURES.

a. *Insect-Borne Diseases* (malaria, viruses, leishmaniasis, onoherceriasis):

(1) *Paludrine*—To avoid confusion and to ensure we all did remember to take it, this was taken daily as a group. Such a method was easy enough in the routine of travelling in the wild, but harder to enforce in towns.

(2) *Mosquito Nets*—These were vital; any night without them below 8,000 feet resulted in severe biting.

(3) *Insect Repellents*—We were not convinced of their effectiveness. Both mosquitoes and Biting Black-fly seemed to bite even after heavy application of repellents.

(4) *Clothing*—We were lucky that the weather never made it necessary to wear protective hoods; but the wearing of puttees and long sleeves was necessary.

b. *Ingestion Diseases* (diarrhea, dysentery, typhoid, parasites):

(1) *Waterborne Diseases*—Water purification was our main problem. At high altitude, we did use mountain streams in wild country, but in the jungle the water was badly contaminated and we always sterilised.

(a) *Millbank Bags*—These were essential. We took one five-gallon and three one-gallon bags. The water of the Amazon and its headwaters is heavily contaminated and laden with silt and colloids. The bags would only function very slowly, owing to the heavy contamination; the one-gallon bags were therefore almost useless for the volume of water we required. The five-gallon bag wore out rapidly; in the later part of the expedition it was barely 90 per cent effective. Ideally, we should have taken four of the five-gallon bags and used two of these for refiltering only.

(b) *Water Sterilisation*—We used water sterilising powder to give a chlorine concentration of 2.3 parts per million, but we did not "detaste," that is, remove the taste of the chlorine. When Mac raised the level to 3.3 parts per million, we all complained, but gradually this level became tolerable; he used that high concentration and a minimum of 30 minutes sterilisation to destroy parasites.

(c) *Boiling of Water*—Each evening and whenever possible at other times, we boiled the water instead of using chlorine; this ensured that tea and coffee would taste normal.

(d) *Shistosomiasis*—Fortunately, Mac found no trace of this on our journey.

Food and Refreshments

We avoided sausages, which are reputed to be badly sterilised in parts of South America; also, lettuce and other foods on which human compost was supposed to have been used. Sometimes we ate at the invitation of our hosts. As long as the food had been cooked, we might have been troubled by other worries, but not disease. The Sierra Mac found surprisingly free of parasites. Cool drinks were taken straight from the bottle; glasses supplied by our hosts were little used.

Mac never felt that we went so short of food that we were drawing on our body reserves to any marked degree. The *cassava* root, known locally as *yuca*, was often our main source of bulk; we all found it difficult to get used to. At no time were we forced to live entirely on our "iron" ration of packet soup, rice, sugar and salt, nor did we have to touch our emergency belt ration.

CONCLUSIONS ON DISEASES

Thanks to Mac, our preventive measures and drugs were adequate. For a party of four people spending four months in primitive conditions, we suffered little, and we could have reduced even this if I had been more sensible about the difficulties of altitude.

Cases Suffered:

a. *Traveller's Diarrhea*—2 cases. These responded to treatment of lamotol in under three days; as both these cases occurred while we were resting, they caused no delay.

b. *Tropical Fever* (a mosquito-borne virus)—1 case. John Cowrie did not respond to penicillin or chloroquin; he saw a doctor in Iquitos and was admitted to the military hospital for a few days, but the fever cleared up; they were unable to give a firm diagnosis.

c. *Bronchial Pneumonia*—1 case. John Cowrie suffered a slight case as a complication of *soroche*, but it cleared up within a couple of days.

d. *Soroche* (*altitude sickness*)—3 cases. Contrary to Mac's suggestions, quoted from Colonel Adam's *Traveller's Guide to Health*, I listened to local people who had no knowledge of *soroche*, and on their advice took no preventive measures. We went up from sea level to 15,000 feet in less than a day and, except for Anna, were able to do a good days work. But on the next day, the entire expedition was brought to a halt. At the same time, John Cowrie contracted a mild bronchial pneumonia; Mac was glad to let the mine doctor treat the case, because of the added complication of *soroche*. Anna and I were suffering badly; Mac says we suffered the following symptoms:

(1) vomiting and nausea
(2) cyanosis of lips and fingernails
(3) difficult breathing—rapid, heavy inflations
(4) marked depression and inability to reason clearly
(5) insomnia and lethargy

It was interesting that John Cowrie and Mac, two heavy smokers, suffered little more than breathlessness, while Anna and myself, both nonsmokers, felt as if the world was ending; it is possible that my heavier body weight and Anna's lower hemoglobin (blood thickness) had something to do with this. Much of Mac's time was spent trying, in vain, to get Anna and me to eat and in telling stories of the Zulus and the South African bush to raise our morale.

The symptoms of *soroche* rapidly disappeared as we descended to an altitude of about 10,000 feet. Unfortunately, it was untreatable—other than by oxygen, which we did not have, so we had to go down. Since this seemed a moral defeat, I delayed it as long as possible.

Another interesting feature of high altitude was that friction between members of the expedition usually occurred after long climbs; this may have been caused by a number of factors:

1 *soroche*
2 physical exhaustion
3 mental boredom with the slow, sustained physical effort

Had we been aware of this the small number of rows could have been avoided.

Few of our medicines were used on ourselves; most of our supply was expended on the Indians. Mac discouraged the use of piriton during the day because of its side effect, drowsiness, which itself could have caused accidents.

Mac was disappointed that the piriton tablets tended to disintegrate; he said he would in future try and find a substitute. Also the tetracycline capsules were badly affected by heat and stuck together; their strength, 250 milligrams, was too great for the treatment of babies, and breaking a capsule open is not very easy.

DRESSINGS AND EQUIPMENT FOR FIRST AID

It is almost unbelievable that we suffered no minor injuries, such as cut fingers or sprained ankles; this reflects the care with which each individual approached and carried out his tasks.

   a. Dressings Taken on the Expedition—Fingerstalls, Band-Aids, assorted dressings, triangular bandages, and a shell dressing each.

This combination would have enabled us to deal with both small and serious injuries, but the only use we put them to was in patching mosquito nets (with Band-Aids) and using triangular bandages as sweat rags. Missionaries and Indians alike benefited from our supplies.

   b. Equipment Carried on the Expedition—Thermometers, scalpel, forceps, scissors, tracheotomy tube, butterfly clips, and catgut stitching.

c. Dentistry—Clove oil and zinc oxide were taken but not used.

SNAKE BITE TREATMENT

After numerous enquiries Mac decided against taking anti-venom serum, for several reasons:

a. The serum is in itself dangerous and could produce serious sickness, even death, through anaphylactic shock; it is therefore extremely unwise to use it as a first aid treatment; it also would have required the inclusion of adrenalin in our medical packs.

b. Specific serum often has to be used, and this requires the capture and identification of the snake; this is unwise, since it may lead to another bite and is usually impossible in the wild.

c. Only about 25 per cent of bites from poisonous snakes are dangerous; thus first aid will suffice in most cases. The chances of being bitten were slight because snakes choose to avoid humans whenever possible.

d. First aid for a snake bite casualty—As in all things, prevention is better than cure, and trying to kill or otherwise interfere with snakes is unnecessarily dangerous. Firewood should be kicked before it is picked up, and while moving through the jungle, the head man should keep his eyes open; he should also be changed frequently with other members of the group.

(1) Wear boots, puttees, and long trousers as protection.

(2) Wash any wound with soapy water to remove the venom splashed on the skin near the bite.

(3) Do not apply a tourniquet or suction, and do not slash the wound.

(4) Calm the victim down and reassure him, while at the same time keeping him inert to prevent an increase of circulation that would carry the venom to the heart.

(5) After a bite, the wound may well become septic; then antibiotics become essential.

VAMPIRE BITE

These were very common in the foothills of the Andes; their marks could often be seen on horses, cattle, and even humans. While a small loss of blood would not be serious, the possible resulting case of rabies could prove fatal. The use of mosquito nets gave us absolute protection against the bats, as long as we didn't touch the sides.

DOGS AND FLEAS

We always seemed to suffer from fleas whenever we were in contact with dogs. The fleas caused much irritation; otherwise there were no ill effects.